Advanced Information and Knowledge Processing

Editor-in-chief
Lakhmi C. Jain
Adelaide
South Australia
Australia

Xindong Wu
University of Vermont Dept. Computer Science
Burlington
Vermont
USA

Information systems and intelligent knowledge processing are playing an increasing role in business, science and technology. Recently, advanced information systems have evolved to facilitate the co-evolution of human and information networks within communities. These advanced information systems use various paradigms including artificial intelligence, knowledge management, and neural science as well as conventional information processing paradigms. The aim of this series is to publish books on new designs and applications of advanced information and knowledge processing paradigms in areas including but not limited to aviation, business, security, education, engineering, health, management, and science. Books in the series should have a strong focus on information processing - preferably combined with, or extended by, new results from adjacent sciences. Proposals for research monographs, reference books, coherently integrated multi-author edited books, and handbooks will be considered for the series and each proposal will be reviewed by the Series Editors, with additional reviews from the editorial board and independent reviewers where appropriate. Titles published within the Advanced Information and Knowledge Processing series are included in Thomson Reuters' Book Citation Index.

More information about this series at http://www.springer.com/series/4738

Tom Addis

Natural and Artificial Reasoning

An Exploration of Modelling Human Thinking

Tom Addis
University of Portsmouth School of Computing
Portsmouth
United Kingdom

ISSN 1610-3947
ISBN 978-3-319-38493-1   ISBN 978-3-319-11286-2 (eBook)
DOI 10.1007/978-3-319-11286-2
Springer Cham Heidelberg New York Dordrecht London

Printed on acid-free paper

Springer is part of Springer Science+Business Media (www.springer.com)

Preface

*When all come to the Great Game he must go alone—
alone, and at peril of his head*
Rudyard Kipling (Kim, 1901)

Originally this book was going to be written as a joint effort between the late Professor David Gooding and myself. David Gooding was a Science Historian in Department of Psychology at the University of Bath and one of the world leaders in his field. Alas, David died from leukemia before we could start writing. Nevertheless, we did sketch out a possible book outline from which this one was eventually derived. I thank his wife, Sandy Gooding, for allowing me to use some of his unpublished material that relates to our work together.

David and I first met in Dubrovnik, Yugoslavia, during the summer of 1989 at the Philosophy of Science Conference (Inter-University Centre). Originally, what got us talking was his work on the '*Visualization of the Research Process*' and my wife Jan's and my work on the '*Visualization of Computation*' (see '**Drawing Programs**' published by Springer 2010). We spent all our time at the conference walking round the castle wall (you could then), talking through our ideas on visualization.

The discussion led to funded joint research from the MRC and the SERC in 1991. This then allowed David, Jan, Simon Grey (an expert systems engineer from the University of Bath) and myself to form a small research team to implement a computer program that would model the discovery process. This was to be a model that was founded on evidence drawn from the historical records of past scientists. Our main model was Michael Faraday FRS (22nd September 1792 to 25th August 1867) and we were particularly interested in his investigations into electro-magnetic forces. David at that time had already reproduced and used much of Faraday's original equipment.

The model of research we developed was founded on the records that showed the thinking processes and behavior of scientists actively researching. These records were historical documents, such as original laboratory notes and diaries. Our observations were thus drawn from history and our work on developing a computer model was supported by such observations.

This book describes our work and explains the design of the computer model. The actual 'belief system' can be downloaded from my website, www.clarity-support. co.uk, and played with. I am not including such code within the book other than to explain the principles by which it was developed.

The term 'belief' here relates to the belief a scientist has in a theory. The process of modeling is equivalent to a scientific theory and so our model should produce results that can be tested against history. The modeling of the way a typical scientist believes in a set of theories is based upon their experimental results, and also talking to other scientists. This 'belief' leads the scientists, along with their experimental results and discussions with other scientists, to new beliefs and further experiments. All of these interactions have been simulated, run and compared with historical records.

In a very minor sense this book is also my memoirs: it is a summary of my professional work and my 'take' on the computer modeling of people. The use of the word 'I' (or 'we'), normally avoided in scientific writing, was intended to maintain the use of active rather than passive sentences, to keep the sentences shorter for easy reading and to spell out that certain elements of the book also have a personal origin.

Also the term 'Wisdom' is used in a very technical sense. In particular it was prefixed by 'Machine' to make clear it is not being used in the normal human sense. The term 'Wisdom' here means that the machine intelligence program is modified by itself in response to its experience (the learning process).

The examples of intelligence given early in the book include the natural theory of evolution (Charles Darwin FRS, 1871). This is included to show how evolution falls within the framework of an intelligent system; it is just an example of a mechanism that has all the properties of intelligent behavior as defined here. No suggestion is made that such a system may be 'conscious'. It is there simply to show that evolution describes a 'problem solving' process.

The schematic programming language Clarity is referenced (see Drawing Programs) because that was the language in which these systems were implemented. Any other functional language, such as ML, FPL, Miranda or LISP, could do the same job. The source code of Clarity is written in C++ and is available to download free from my website.

The other reason for using Clarity diagrams is that they are also a flow chart (a schematic) showing how a program works. These schematics are converted into a functional language similar to any functional language (actually a variation of ML). Because the schematic is converted automatically into a running and tested functional program, I am therefore absolutely certain that the description is both correct and sufficient. This is a guarantee of accuracy and completion.

Since programming languages are transient and ephemeral, adding a specific language would limit the time in which such representation could be fully understood. As I am not writing a software specification, I do not need to refer to any particular computer language. It has always been the case that software developers will mostly use the language with which they are familiar and it was not in my remit to suggest a different one. My aim is to explore some philosophical questions and to write about the ideas behind systems that behave intelligently. This book investigates the limitations of computer models and asks the question, *"Why do we still not have a working model of people that is recognizably human?"*

I would like to thank my colleagues of the Artificial Intelligence Reading Group in the Department of Information Science at Reading University for their patience in going through some of the early investigations with me. They helped ensure that these ideas are at least coherent. I would also like to thank Drs. David Anderson, David Rotheram and Greg Leonard as well as Dr. David Salt for his detailed statistical analysis of the correlations between the musical extract raw score discussed in Chap. 13. Dr. David Billinge did most of the experimental work described in Chap. 13 and also provided the in-depth understanding of classical music. The results of his research into music were both surprising and enlightening.

In particular, I am very grateful to Professor Max Bramer of Portsmouth University, who has given me good advice on how to present these ideas. Further, the hard work and professional expertise as a technical writer of Meredith Tanner, my daughter in-law, has greatly improved the intelligibility of my presentation.

My gratitude is particularly given to my good friend and colleague, the late Prof David Gooding (University of Bath), for directing me to the ideas of metaphor and for his work with me on the belief system. Most of all I would like to thank my wife, my love and my colleague Jan Addis for her support, the construction of the Clarity programs that illustrate the ideas and for never complaining while I indulge myself in these pursuits.

Any errors in this book are mine.

Contents

Chapter 1
Insight and Reason

If a lion could talk, we could not understand him

L. Wittgenstein,
Philosophical Investigations IIxi.

1.1 Introduction

One way of understanding a natural process or mechanism is to build a working model and then see if the model has some of the behavior or features of the observed phenomenon. In this book I will describe an attempt at understand the nature of people through computer modeling. It is hoped that this understanding will lead to the possibility of increasing our abilities through artificial mechanisms.

This endeavor to construct artificial people is not new. The earliest recorded effort was in about 270 BC by a Greek engineer named Ctesibus who made musical organs and water clocks with movable figures[1]. Ctesibus discovered that the problem of constructing a machine that even approximates a complete working human body is not easy, since it requires engineering involving sensors combined with a complex control system that is still beyond our ability to emulate completely. However, practical machines have been made that copy some aspects of the body. One example is the power shovel shown in Fig. 1.1.

As with the power shovel as a representative of a limb, I intend to emulate only certain useful aspects of human thinking, and the result will not always be recognizably human. We may note that with the advent of the modern computer it is easier to model just human intelligence—the problem solving aspect of human thought processes—than a complete person's intellect. After all, intelligence might be considered a significant feature of being human. A test for intelligence would only require a simple means of communication, such as a computer screen and keyboard, in order to display its usefulness. I have chosen this basic approach since communication via speech recognition and synthesis is difficult and still limited to a specified context. Further, the mode of communication is not really my main concern here (see Addis 1972). Nevertheless we should not ignore this essential mode of human interaction, for it might also be a significant part of the human thought processes.

---

[1] http://inventors.about.com/od/roboticsrobots/a/RoboTimeline.htm.

© Springer International Publishing Switzerland 2014
T. Addis, *Natural and Artificial Reasoning,* Advanced Information
and Knowledge Processing, DOI 10.1007/978-3-319-11286-2_1

Fig. 1.1 Power shovel
reflecting jointed limbs

I will take a strictly pragmatic stance in this chapter by asking the question "What features must be present that make behavior intelligent?" I will demonstrate that the often-quoted Turing Test, where machine intelligence is compared with a person, can be shown to be insufficient to support any useful discussion. Even intelligence measures such as IQ tests only suggest problem-solving specializations and little else.

There is an alternative view, backed by experimental evidence, of practical intelligence by Jaques et al. (1978) which shows that intelligence in children develops in stages and is not continuous as originally supposed. This calls into question the validity of the IQ test, which assumes a smooth uninterrupted growth with age. However, Jaques' Discontinuity Theory does identify the notion of 'insight' in problem solving. I will go on to show that information theory, developed by engineers to quantify communication systems, can also provide a means of measuring the practical consequence of 'insight' as well as providing an argument for the need of 'purpose' in intelligent behavior.

Another powerful tool to help us understand human problem-solving is found in the work of Charles Saunders Peirce (Peirce 1958, 1966a, b see Tursman 1987), in which he introduces the three types of inference: Induction, Deduction, and Abduction. These types support a range of specialization for different aspects of reasoning. I will suggest that each of these aspects can be improved through experience, leading to the notion of 'wisdom' and a practical measure of intelligence in both machines and people. In Chap. 3 a simple kind of intelligence is constructed as a computer program, illustrating that intelligent machines, as they are currently conceived, are unlikely to function outside of their human context. The reason for this will be explored in later chapters.

The problem with the pursuit of programming machines to behave intelligently is that in practice, as soon as it is done the program no longer seems to be intelligent because we know it is only a defined and understandable procedure. It usually is assumed that any understandable procedure cannot truly reflect human intelligence. This view of retaining the mystery of human thinking is partially explained by the fact that the results of all attempts to construct machine intelligence have been so disappointing that the 2013 British Computer Society Machine Intelligence competition was cancelled due to insufficient suitable entries[2]. One noteworthy reason for this inability to create an intelligent engine is that there has never been a clear and objective definition of intelligence independent of personal opinions. Such a definition, if it can be formed, is that it can also be used to judge its existence in non-human systems. The purpose of this and the next chapter is to see if such a definition is possible.

1.2 Testing for Intelligence

It has always been assumed that people would recognize intelligence when they came across it (see *The Imitation Game* below). This may be true. But to ensure that we can do this unambiguously and independently of the human context we also need to examine what is meant by intelligence, initially without reference to machines or even people, and later to consider if an implementation is possible. If such an implementation is not possible then we ought to ask, "why?"

Before we begin, there are certain tools of thought or methods of approach that we must know and adopt. We need these tools to help us overcome our natural prejudice in accepting a specification of intelligence and to achieve an unambiguous description of it. This is driven by our wish to implement and recognize intelligent behavior that will exist outside the human form. The main tool is 'Pragmatism' as proposed by Charles Saunders Peirce, which is now described.

1.2.1 The Imitation Game

In a lecture series given by William James (James 1906) at the Lowell Institute in Boston he relates in Lecture II (p. 27) the following story (James 1842–1910).

> ... being with a camping party in the mountains, I returned from a solitary ramble to find everyone engaged in a ferocious metaphysical dispute. The *corpus* of the dispute was a squirrel—a live squirrel supposed to be clinging to one side of a tree-trunk; while over against the trees opposite side a human being was imagined to stand. This human witness tries to get sight of the squirrel by moving rapidly round the tree, but no matter how fast he goes, the squirrel moves as fast in the opposite direction and always keeps the tree between himself and the man, so that never a glimpse of him is caught. The resultant metaphysical problem is this: *Does the man go round the squirrel or not?*

The issue here was really what do you *want* 'to go round' to mean in practical terms. If you want 'to go round' to mean successive compass positions until you return to your starting point then you do go round the squirrel. If you want it to mean that you are first in front of him then to the side etc. then in this case you don't go round him.

---

[2] http://www.bcs-sgai.org/micomp/.

This leads us to the important principle of investigation that will be our touchstone for the acceptance or rejection of an idea. The principle is encapsulated in the philosophy of C.S. Peirce (1839–1914)—Pragmatism; but is better expressed by his friend and colleague William James.

> The pragmatic method... is to try to interpret each notion by tracing its respective practical consequences..... Whenever a dispute is serious, we ought to be able to show some practical difference that must follow from one side or the other's being right.

The issue I wish to explore is that of intelligence. The practical consequence of this exploration should be a clear enough understanding of intelligence to recognize its existence in any alien environment, and in particular as it may be exhibited by artificial devices. This can then lead us to the question, "Can we create an intelligent machine?"

Alan Turing, in 1950, addresses this question in a more general way. He felt that the acceptance of a thinking machine was a question of crossing an intellectual boundary. To ease the way he modified the parlor game (called the imitation game) thus[3]:

> "It (*the imitation game*) is played with three people, a man (A), a woman (B), and an interrogator (C) who may be of either sex. The interrogator stays in a room apart from the other two. The object of the game for the interrogator is to determine which of the other two is the man and which is the woman. He knows them by labels X and Y and at the end of the game he says either "X is A or Y is B" or "X is B and Y is A". The interrogator is allowed to put questions to A and B thus:
> C: "Will X please tells me the length of his/her hair?"
> Now suppose X is actually A, then A must answer. It is A's objective in the game to try and cause C to make the wrong identification .... The objective of the game for the third player (B) is to help the interrogator.
> .... An intermediary can repeat the question and answers.
> .... We now ask the question, "What will happen when a machine takes the part of A in this game?"

Turing goes on to say is:

> .... These questions replace our original "Can machines think?"

I interpreted this as:

> The original question of gender is now replaced by, "Which one is the machine? If we cannot tell then we may assume that the machine can think.

The assumption here is that a person displays the thinking process and this process represents our standard for thinking. The game is intended to introduce us to the idea that a machine might think; it breaks through a psychological barrier that assumes thinking is the prerogative if mankind. What is *not* described is how we might distinguish this thinking process from any other kind of activity? The real problem, unstated by Turing, is, "What should be our game plan? What questions should we ask?"

---

[3] Note that '....' refers to missing text.

The implication is that *if* we cannot devise a test that will distinguish between a thinking person and a machine that imitates thinking then for all *practical* purposes the machine can be said to think.

Rather than deal with the general notion of thinking, let us limit ourselves to considering an important by-product of thinking: the display of intelligence.

Intelligence has practical consequences that can be observed and tested, for example, through the ability to solve problems. So we will change the imitation game so that the objective is to determine the question, "Is the machine intelligent?"

If we can identify the practical effects of intelligence we are then in a position to test if X or Y displays these effects or not. But if we can identify features of intelligence where the answer will be "X is intelligent," or "Y is intelligent," then we no longer need to distinguish between them, since the answers are not exclusive anymore (i.e. machine and not machine). We have already crossed the intellectual boundary that rejects out of hand that anything other than a human can be intelligent.

The only reason for such a comparison between man and machine is to act as a standard so that we might calibrate an answer to the enquires: "Is this intelligence like that displayed by a person?" or "How much intelligence is shown?" or "What are the limitations of (this) particular intelligence?"

We now no longer need play the game; we only need tests for intelligence; tests that depend upon well-identified features. Further, we no longer have to show that machines are of equal intelligence or have the same breadth of intelligence as a person. We merely have to find a distinction in observable behavior that separates intelligent behavior from non-intelligent behavior. We don't even need to detect every kind of intelligent behavior, only to recognize a form of intelligent behavior. In this case we might expect to provide some scheme that will give a measure, a grade or a limitation to the observed intelligence.

Of course, once given such tests, the scheme can be applied to a collection of any interacting objects other than a recognized machine.

So what are the practical effects of intelligence?

Rather than pursue the unusable definitions of intelligence that take the tortuous route to avoid the notions of animal behavior and unconscious actions but include some unobservable aspect of people, let us ask the pragmatic question, "What do we want intelligence to achieve?"

Let us consider one possible answer through the measurement of intelligence as carried out by psychologists on people where this decision has already been made and agreed upon. This consideration may provide a possible game plan.

1.3 Intelligence Tests

We should note that according to one of the early intelligent tests leading advocates (Eysenck 1962, 1966a, b) intelligence testing:

- has no firm scientific basis.
- is, however, successful in its application.

Fig. 1.2 What figure fits into
vacant square?

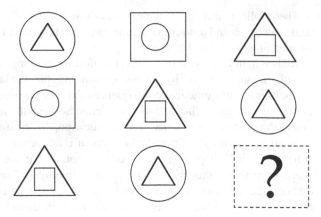

The functions initially considered to represent intelligence were Judgment, Comprehension and Reasoning.

Intelligence should be measured by means of tests that clearly involve these abilities and functions (Binet 1904). Much later creativity was added to this list (Guilford 1967).

We can make the reasonable assumption that as a person grows through childhood to become an adult their mental abilities will also grow. We can grade a range of increasingly difficult tests according to the average age of the children and adults that can solve a sub-range of the tests. In this way, an individual child or adult is assign a Mental Age that is measured from the problems he or she can solve.

The tests must involve problem solving that requires both observation and insight. These are built of questions such as:

Q1 (Fig. 1.2).

Q2.
Find the missing letter.

F J N R _

Q3.
Insert the missing number.

8 12 10 16 12 _

It is characteristic of these tests that people who do them report that the answers come clearly either at once or after reviewing plausible insights. The tests presume a single 'correct' answer, and only a limited time is allowed to find it.

It was noted that, *generally*, those children who have a Mental Age of twelve when they are six would *tend* to have a Mental Age of sixteen when they are eight. Hence the ratio of Mental Age over Chronological Age tends *on average* to be a constant. This is not too surprising since such a result is inherent in the original definition. What this also shows is that the growth of intelligence tends to follow a stable pattern, as do other physical attributes.

Fig. 1.3 Some functions of Thurstone's model of intelligence

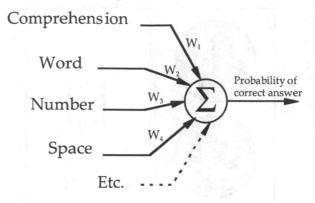

We can thus have a measure associated with an individual; the Intelligence Quotient (IQ):

$$IQ = \frac{Mental\,Age}{Chronological\,Age} * 100$$

I do not wish to examine the actual measurement of intelligence. What I do wish to draw from this is the nature of the tests and what is involved in doing them.

Models of intelligence have been derived through statistical analysis of IQ tests showing a range of specialized dimensions of intelligence such as Verbal Comprehension, Word Fluency, Number, Space, etc. (Thurstone 1938). More complex models have been suggested through the statistical technique of factor analysis, where it is assumed that a measurement is a consequence of several independent influences (Guilford 1967). Both these ideas propose independent mechanisms that combine in a simple additive manner to support the intelligent process. Further, the latter proposal suggests that the mechanisms are mostly different from the initial proposed functions of Judgment, Comprehension, Reasoning and Creativity (Fig. 1.3).

The notion that intelligence is a combination of skills that come to bear on a problem in an additive fashion may be considered too simplistic. Certainly such an analysis is open to a very wide range of proposed alternative mechanisms but this model does suggest that *the components of the intelligence are discrete specializations*. This observation will help us construct a potential working model of intelligence in that it will reduce the range of activities to be included. This will greatly simplify our task.

1.4 Discontinuity Theory

The work of Elliott Jaques and colleagues proposed that intelligence does not conform to the smooth growth usually assumed but moves in distinct plateau. The plateau is related to people's ability to abstract concepts. This view is still consistent with

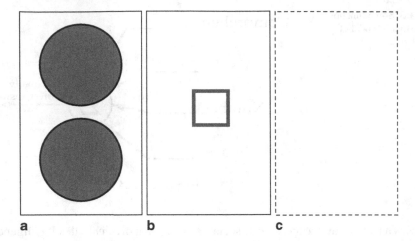

Fig. 1.4 Two display cards for the test concepts '*red circles*' and '*blue squares*'

initial definition of IQ, which does not take into account the shape of a developing intelligence with age or experience.

In order to capture a realistic character of intelligence in their tests, the problems to be solved in these tests are practical activities. The subjects are asked to repeatedly solve a set of similar tasks, such as sorting cards, as one might do for a paid job. In particular, there is the problem of sorting cards into three groups. Each card has a pattern (similar to Q1 above) involving five dimensions (color, shape, size, number, and content) (Fig. 1.4). Two cards are displayed for two of the three piles as a descriptor of what should be placed in that position. The subject is told if the choice is correct during the sorting.

The point of these kinds of tests is to provide an opportunity for subjects to discover from experience the underlying concept that governs a correct sorting. The dimensions such as number, color, shape, size and position are numerous enough to include in their structure many alternative concepts that can show partial success. The results of the number of successes for subjects show a multi-concept distribution as seen in Fig. 1.5.

Each peak indicates a concept that provides some correct scores. Some people may spot the resolving concept straight away and others will perceive a range of different concepts ordered in terms of complexity. The first choice may not be effective so the next elaboration is used that will move towards a better solution. This process continues until an optimum is found.

Again the results are not too surprising, since they confirm the observation that solutions to problems come in stages of realization. Since a concept is either perceived or not perceived, then at least one or more discontinuity is clearly an aspect of intelligent behavior. Initially the subject will consider a simple concept that can be used to reduce mistakes, and as the subject gains experience a more refined theory that will result in fewer errors will be perceived.

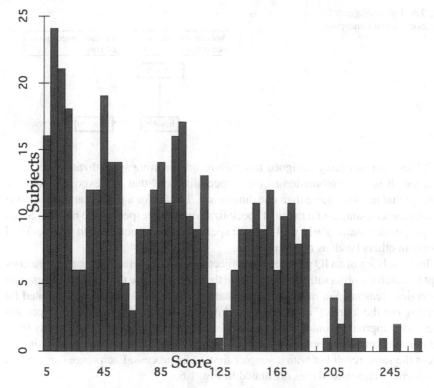

Fig. 1.5 Histogram of scores for card sorting. (Isaac and Connor 1978)

It is suggested from this and other experimental results that a necessary mechanism to be engaged in problem solving and *intelligent activity is the ability to abstract and evoke concepts; ibid the notion of insight*. However, such insights are then used through the process of reason to generate an answer or to instigate an action. These two mechanisms are also needed to model intelligence.

The person doing the test can see these two mechanisms of abstraction and concept generation at work in the IQ tests, since to solve them first requires the creative act of insight. This involves perceiving what concept might be at work given the information so far observed and then using this concept to infer an answer. The concept, in this example, is usually constructed from one of more dimensions such as size, color, position, number, meaning, etc. These dimensions may also be related to the different specializations as suggested by Thurstone's Model of Intelligence (Fig. 1.3).

To construct concepts, a set of specialist mechanisms for generating or remembering possible dimensions is required. These specializations can be exposed through the use of Factor Analysis (a formal mathematical technique) from the way different people perform over a range of diverse IQ tests. What Factor Analysis does is re-express the set of observations from repeated tests as a set of independent simple generators. These generators create values for each observed result by combining their outputs additively. We will not cover the details of this process here.

Fig. 1.6 The intelligence
process: the first conception

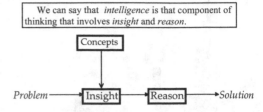

IQ tests are normally designed to measure one or more specializations in combination. It is the combination of these specializations that can expose a possible concept that involves more than one dimension. The IQ for a particular individual is an average assessment of a range of specializations with respect to the normal. Some people perform particularly well in some specializations (such as with pictures) and poorly in others (such as number series).

In the solving of an IQ problem the subject must firstly selectively generate a concept to match the observations (insight) and then secondly use this concept to generate a solution (reason). We might consider that the first process could be emulated by filtering out the 'correct' concept from a large collection of potential concepts. An alternative approach would be to guide a concept generation process selectively from the observations. In our model we take the former approach, since externally it produces the same result but with a simpler first-stage process. Each stage can then be considered independently, as illustrated in Fig. 1.6.

In summary:

> We can say that *intelligence* is that component of thinking that involves *insight* and *reason*.

It is clear that insight, which draws from a source of concepts, must occur first in order for reason to be applied; reason requires a model, hypothesis or proposition to work on.

References

Addis TR (1972) Human behavior in an interactive environment using a simple spoken word recognizer. Int J Man–Mach Stud 4:255–284

Binet A (1904) The measure of merit: talents, intelligence, and inequality in the French and American Republics, 1750–1940 by John Carson (2007). Princeton University Press, Princeton

Eysenck HJ (1962) Know your own IQ. Pelican Original, London

Eysenck HJ (1966a) Check your own IQ. Penguin Books, London

Eysenck HJ (1966b). Know your own IQ. Penguin Books, London

Guilford JP (1967) The nature of human intelligence. McGraw-Hill, New York

James W (1906) What Pragmatism means. In: James W (ed) Pragmatism and the meaning of truth. Harvard University Press, Cambridge, 1975

Jaques E, Gibson RO, Isaac DJ (1978) Levels of abstraction in logic and human action. Heinemann, London

Peirce CS (1958) Science and philosophy: collected papers of Charles S. Peirce, vol 7. Harvard University Press, Cambridge

Peirce CS (1966a) How to make our ideas clear. In: Wiener PP (ed) Charles Peirce: selected writings. Dover, New York

Peirce CS (1966b) The fixation of belief. In: Weiner PP (ed) Charles S. Peirce: selected writings. Dover, New York, pp 92–260

Thurstone LL (1938) Primary mental abilities. Psychometric monographs, no. 1. University of Chicago Press, Chicago

Tursman R (1987) Peirce's theory of scientific discovery: a system of logic conceived as semiotic. Indiana University Press, Bloomington

Chapter 2
Information and Intelligence

2.1 Introduction

The key to understanding intelligence is 'information', since it is information that
is the raw material used to gain insight. So we need to appreciate 'information' in a
very precise way. The next section will explore a formal definition of 'information'
to see if this will help us. It may also give us a different perception of intelligence.

2.2 Information

One of the important consequences of insight is the formation of a hypothesis that has
been triggered by a puzzle, as I have illustrated in Chap. 1. In general, hypotheses
are propositions that express constraints, laws or rules about the world. From a
pragmatic point of view we can say, *hypotheses are useful if they make the world "a
less surprising place"* (after Peirce 1958, 1966).

It so happens that independently to Peirce, a measure of surprise had already been
derived from communication theory (Shannon and Weaver first printed in the Bell
System Technical Journal in 1948 and published in book form in 1964). The problem
they were trying to resolve was getting some kind of measurement in communication
engineering. This measure should provide a precise assessment and comparison of
any non-perfect communication systems. They needed a way of asking, "How good is
this communication system?" In particular, they wanted a measure for such systems
so that their performance and limitations could be predicted; a measure similar to that
of horsepower for engines, where the limits of speed and acceleration can be defined.
The model of communication or paradigm they had in mind was the transmission
of Morse code. A schematic diagram of the components of a their idea of a typical
communication system is shown in Fig. 2.1.

Thus if someone transmits a message that consists of string of digits (or letters)
such as:

© Springer International Publishing Switzerland 2014
T. Addis, *Natural and Artificial Reasoning,* Advanced Information
and Knowledge Processing, DOI 10.1007/978-3-319-11286-2_2

Fig. 2.1 Communication
system (Simplified from
Shannon Fig. 2.1 1948)

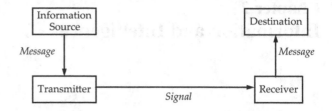

314159265358979323846...

where the digits will be converted into a signal by a transmitter, passed down the
channel of communication (e.g. a telephone cable), and en route may be changed
by the effects of noise (not shown in diagram). The receiver then converts the noisy
signal back into digits. From the destination's point of view we should note that:

> The significant aspect (of this communication system) is that the actual final message is
> *selected from a defined set* of possible messages. (Shannon 1948, 1964).

If we take the simplest notion of a message at the receiver by considering that each
digit is a message, then our expectation of a message (i.e. a digit) before it arrives
is given by the choice of 1 in 10. So, if each digit were equally possible then the
probability that we could guess at the destination point what the next digit would be
is 0.1. When a message arrives our uncertainty will reduce to zero because there is
now no need to guess (probability is 1). The larger the choice the greater is the initial
uncertainty.

We can therefore propose a measure of 'uncertainty' that is inversely propor-
tional to probability: it increases as the probability of choosing correctly decreases.
However, this inverse probability measure should also reflect our own perception of
uncertainty.

It has been shown that a person's sensitivity to sensations such as hearing or
touch is 'logarithmic'. This natural detection system allows us to cope with very
loud sounds or firm pressures and yet still remain sensitive to very low sounds or
gentle touches (say).

From these observations of choice and the logarithmic scale of sensation, it would
be reasonable to define the 'unit' of uncertainty as 0.5, because uncertainty is highest
when the probability of either choice is the same. That is when there is zero bias in
the choice.

To reflect both the unit of choice and human sensitivity, we can create a function
by using the logarithm measure to the base 2 of the inverse probability of a message.
The inverse of the probability is used because as the probability of a message rises,
the less information it provides. The advantage of this is since a probability is always
less than 1 the inverse will always be greater than 1. When a log is taken it will
always provide a positive number: (Fig. 2.2)

$$\text{Uncertainity} = \log_2 \frac{1}{\text{probability}}$$

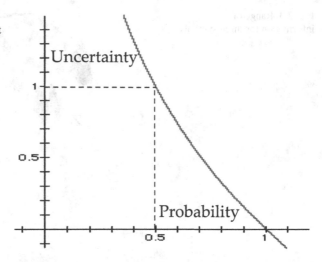

Fig. 2.2 A possible measure of uncertainty where the Unit is probability $= 0.5$

or

$$\textbf{Uncertainty} = -\textbf{log}_2(\textbf{Probability})$$

On the other hand, if the digits were not equally probable such as in the string:

2222221222222242222232

then we would have a good chance of guessing that the next digit would be 2. In the extreme case, if the digit was always 2 and the system was noise-free, our chance of guessing correctly is certain and no further information is obtainable; that is, the information provided by each message is zero.

- *So we can say by extension that there is more information in a string of symbols where the probability of each symbol is the same than there is in a string of symbols where the probability of the symbols is **not** the same.*

If we imagine the message is coded so that the significant characteristic of the number (the symbol) is whether it is even, odd or prime then our choice is reduced to only three symbols. In this case we would have a better chance of guessing the next symbol (even, odd or prime) than for guessing one of the ten numbers.

- *So there is more information (uncertainty) in a string of symbols where the choice of symbols is higher.*

Finally, the measure of information should have additive properties with a consistent interpretation. So if there was a 1/2 chance that the number is odd and then a 1/3 chance that the odd number is prime (say), the probabilities should combine such that there is 1/6 chance of guessing it to be prime at the start.

- *Thus if the choice to be made is broken down into two or more choices such that the final outcome has the same uncertainty, then the information should be the same.*

Fig. 2.3 Range of
information for three symbols

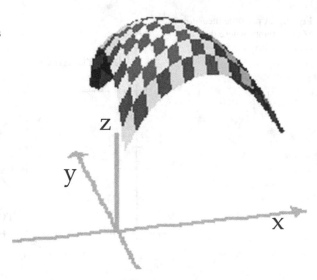

The only known function that satisfies these requirements is one based upon the expected (similar to average) logarithm of the inverse probability (p_i) of each symbol (**i**) thus:

$$\text{Information of an event} = -\sum p_i \log_2 p_i$$

We can now define the unit of information, which has been called a 'bit', where the two choices are equally likely thus:

$$1 = -(0.5\log_2(0.5) + 0.5\log_2(0.5))$$

This information measure of a system is called *entropy*, and its behaviour for three choices can be illustrated in Fig. 2.3. In this graph, z represents the information value (in bits) as the probabilities of two (x, y) of the three symbols (w, x, y) are changed. The probability of the third symbol w is determined from the other two probabilities because:

$$w + x + y = 1$$

The information measure (entropy) falls to zero when the probabilities are 0 or 1, and rises to a maximum for equal probabilities. The maximum in the zx or zy plane is less than the maximum for a plane that includes all three dimensions zxy. The equation for this surface is:

$$z = -\log_2^{-1}[(x\log_2 x) + (y\log_2 y) + ((1 - (x + y))\log_2(1 - (x + y))]$$

- *So we can say that the greater the entropy, the larger the uncertainty.*

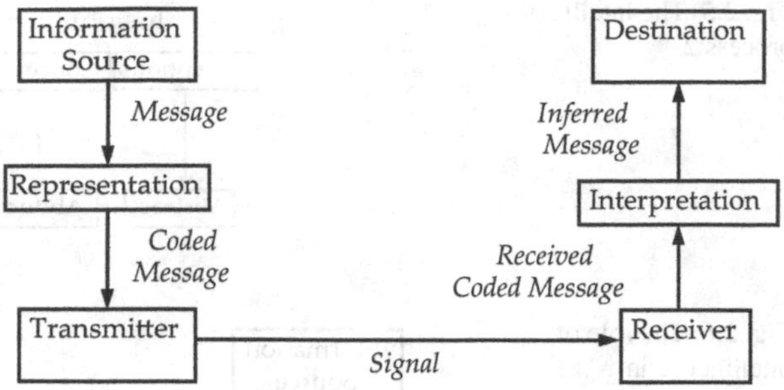

Fig. 2.4 The role of hypothesis in communication

2.3 Insight

So far I have suggested that the message is represented by some characteristic of the transmitted symbols, and this is considered to be a single event. Because of the additive properties of information, the entropy of a sequence of (say) N symbols *that are independent* is the sum of the entropy for each of the symbols.

It could be the case that the sequence of symbols is significant (as in Morse Code) and that each message is identified by a different sequence. If we at the destination 'know' the key of this code, the sequences can be interpreted and the information measure relates to the number of encodable messages (see Fig. 2.4). This will usually be less than the sum of the entropy for the individual and independent symbols.

However, if the key is not 'known', the information is perceived to be that of the uncertainty of the independent symbols rather than the potential messages. This greater entropy we will call *Perceived Entropy*.

- *We can thus say that the perceived entropy is either higher than or equal to the actual entropy of a system.*

In the original sequence of digits above, the probability of any digit occurring is about 0.1, but the insight that this sequence is the value of *p* means that the sequence of numbers can be calculated from an equation such as:

$$\frac{\pi}{4} = 1 - \frac{1}{3} + \frac{1}{5} - \frac{1}{7} + \frac{1}{9} - \frac{1}{11} + \frac{1}{13} - \frac{1}{15} + \dots$$

- *In this case the perceived entropy falls from that of approaching infinity to zero in a single moment, and it is this insight that characterises the intelligence process.*

Insight can now be seen to involve at least two processes (see Fig. 2.5). The first process is the identification of the symbol (Wittgenstein L 1921). Since the symbol is to be abstracted from the signal we will call this process *abstraction*. The symbol is not always the obvious sign such as a digit, but may be a feature of the sign such as the notions of even, odd and prime. Abstraction may be considered formed through the *perception* of significant features. In this case a perception is a concept that involves bringing together the features into a single unit. That is the identification of the elements observed that carry the important information.

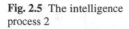

Fig. 2.5 The intelligence
process 2

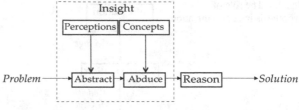

Fig. 2.6 The role of
intelligence in
communication

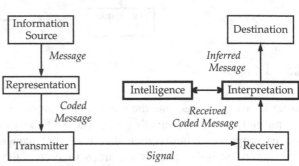

The second process is the proposal or generation of a model (an equation in the above case for π). The model must be guessed from the signal, and thus the process of guessing will be called *abduction*. Note that the abductive process does not guarantee a completely successful model. Strictly speaking both these processes are abduction, and to distinguish between them, the second process may be called *retroduction* (after Peirce).

We can now see that intelligence changes the interpreter (the model) so as to minimise the entropy of the communication system (see Fig. 2.6). *We need 'purpose' in order to avoid the trivial solution of minimising of entropy by switching off the signal altogether.* We must assume that the correct identification of the message is important. The problem is that the intelligence process does not know either what the range of messages might be or what part of the signal carries the messages.

2.3.1   The Distinction Between Information and Knowledge

As an aside, it has puzzled some people that noise turns out to have high information because of its unpredictability. We can now see a distinction between *information* and *knowledge* by asking the question of a signal, *"This is information about what?"* Only those events that provide material evidence towards the act of insight and lead towards the reduction of entropy can be called knowledge. Events that are uncertain have varying degrees of information, but *events that are uncertain and contain the seeds of certainty (an insight is possible) represent knowledge.*

2.4   Induction

The process of generating a model and then proving it is useful (i.e. can be used to make predictions) underlies the well known mathematical process of proof by *induction*. For example, if we examine the sum:

$$1 + 3 + 5 + \ldots$$

of the successive odd numbers then we *may* notice that:

$$1 = 1^2$$

$$1 + 3 = 2^2$$

$$1 + 3 + 5 = 3^2$$

$$1 + 3 + 5 + 7 = 4^2$$

and so on. We can *abduce* (infer) the model that *for every natural number n, the sum of the first n odd numbers is n^2*. This is certainly true for all the first n odd numbers from 1 to 4 we have observed so far, and we could continue in this vein until we find an exception. For many scientific endeavours this may be the best we can do but for mathematics this is not considered good enough. Since we have access to the underlying foundations of mathematics the possibility of a sound proof is available.

Such a mathematical proof by induction follows the style: if we provide a general form that shows this model to be true for any number n, then we are entitled to suppose that it is true for any number less than n. We are also allowed to suppose that we already know that the sum of the first $n - 1$ odd numbers is $(n - 1)^2$. The sum of the first n odd numbers is obtained by adding the nth odd number, which is $(2n - 1)$. So:

$$\text{Sum of the first } n \text{ odd numbers} = (n - 1)^2 + (2n - 1)$$

$$= (n^2 - 2n + 1) + (2n - 1)$$

$$= n^2 - 2n + 1 + 2n - 1$$

$$= n^2$$

It should be noticed that:

1. First a proposition (i.e. hypothesis or model) must be proposed (insight). The proposition comes from a set of *concepts* in which each proposition can be used to generate a potential series through deduction. Usually the series here involve sums rather than multiplication. Multiplication series are much more difficult to prove.
2. Then the proposition is tested against observation (reason); a process of *validation*.

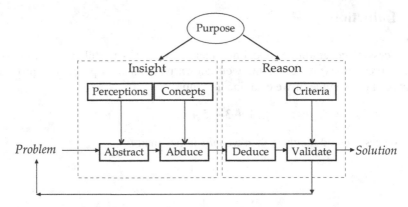

Fig. 2.7 The intelligence process 3

Using a proposition to infer a consequence is the process of *deduction,* and the *deductive* process generates consequences (results). In this case, the sum of odd numbers proposition, we tried out several examples of the series and within these limits the proposition works. However, mathematics does not consider this form of validation sufficient; it has a more exacting *criteria.* This is because, unlike empirical science, mathematics can often produce a general proof that will show a proposition to be true for all possible cases. For such proofs an accepted protocol is laid down. We can now extend our model of intelligence by expanding the process of reason as in Fig. 2.7.

We indicate here, with the feedback loop, that validation can fail and the process will cycle until a solution (of some sort) is found. The decision to finish a cycle depends upon a *validation criterion.* Such a criterion will be different depending on the kind of problem to be solved.

Mathematical induction will thus explore formally every natural number. This can be done through a proof, but if a proof cannot be determined, a search is often performed to find an exception through simple enumeration. Even this latter approach may be too extensive to be practical.

Exactly what *criteria* are invoked to satisfy the validation is left unstated. If a formal proof is not possible (as is the case with empirical science) at what stage do you stop enumerating and testing; when do you just accept the hypothesis? A verse written by a school friend in my wife's autograph book expresses the problem nicely.

> With what confusion thinking's fraught,
> I often think I'll think no more.
> For when I spend much time in thought,
> I un-think things I thought before.
> Anon

The pursuit of better interpretations of uncertain events characterises intelligence. We have shown that insight is the key that unlocks these interpretations from the events. The question now is, "What are the mechanisms of insight?"

Fig. 2.8 A diagrammatic
equivalent of syllogism

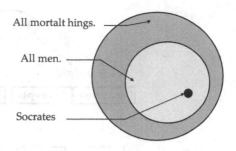

All mortalt hings.

All men.

Socrates

2.5   Deduction

Clearly deduction is one of the processes required, since once a proposition is proposed it is needed to create a result from given 'facts'. The normal *deductive* process
can be illustrated by the syllogism:

1. **All** (men), **are** (mortal)
2. (Socrates) **is a** (man)
3. **Therefore** (Socrates) **is** (mortal)

The deduction process is a formal procedure that is clearly mechanical, since it does
not involve the meaning of the words or symbols (given in brackets) when framed in
this structure. The first sentence (the 'proposition') links two phrases together such
that the first phrase 1 is said to 'contain' the second phrase 2 as a 'fact'. The first
phrase states that a general class of object (men) a share a property (mortal). The
second sentence gives an example of the general class (men) as an example of the
general class of objects. It therefore follows that this particular example (Socrates)
will have this property (mortal); after all, it has just been stated (also see Fig. 2.8).

Deduction contains no uncertainties and therefore does not provide any information. During deduction a marker called the Truth-value tracks the tracing of the
certainties. The general form of this deduction is:

1. **All** (A) **are** (B).
2. (X) **is an** (A).
3. **Therefore** (X) **is a** (B).

We can replace the three phrases in brackets by any other statements of facts that we
like. If the first two sentences are True after this replacement then the third sentence
will also be True since deduction preserves the marker True.

Deduction is a single step in a set of steps that will lead to conclusions that are
guaranteed to be True. Consider the following conundrum:

   a. Brothers and sisters have I none
   b. but this man's father
   c. is my father's son
      Who is he?

We can choose the following route of syllogisms:

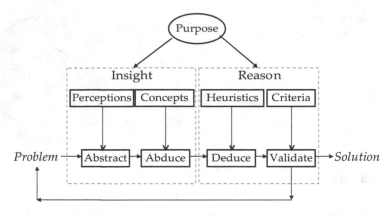

Fig. 2.9 The intelligence process 4

Chose hypothesis(the general case):
All (male who has no brothers and sisters) **are** (the *only* son of a father)
Then given (from line a):
(I) **is a** (male who has no brothers or sisters)
1. Therefore:
(I) **is** (the *only* son of a father)
We infer (from lines b. and c.):
(This man's father) **is** (the son of a father)
And using 1:
(This man's father) **is** (I)
Therefore using a known relationship:
(this man) **is** (my son)

What is not described by this formal layout is why we might choose this particular set of facts to make these particular steps as against the infinity of other possibilities. We never considered the line of daughters, or the many other human relationships that might have been chosen. There is nothing in the rules of deduction that offers guidance to a useful conclusion.

To solve a problem using deduction requires direction; deduction needs problem-solving knowledge that limits the choices amongst the known facts and possible hypotheses. Such problem solving knowledge provides a compass from which to steer our course through a labyrinth of possible steps. This guiding knowledge is known as a *heuristic*, and we should include it in our intelligent process (see Fig. 2.9).

We can now extend the model of the intelligent process to include:

- *perceptions* that identify the combination of features for a useful abstraction,
- *concepts* which are a set of generalisations that can be fitted to abstractions,
- *heuristics* which select the route through to a solution,
- *criteria* which provide the basis on which to accept viable hypothesis.
- *Purpose* that governs all the above.

2.6   Lookup or Generate?

In Plato's Meno (c.427 to c.327 BC), there is a description of Socrates illustrating to Meno his belief that all knowledge is somehow already within us all. He takes a slave boy who has been brought up in Meno's household and proceeds to question him in such a way that the boy 'discovers' for himself the relationship between the area and the sides of a rectangle. Socrates comments:

> You see, Meno, that I teach him none of these things which he (*the boy*) asserts; I only ask him questions. And now this boy imagines that he knows of what length the lines are which contain a space of eight square feet.

Meno was not convinced at this point but after a further set of intensive questions from Socrates to the boy Meno agreed with Socrates' final statement:

> If the truth of things therefore is always in the soul, the soul should be immortal. So that whatever you happen now not to know, that is not to remember, you ought to undertake with confidence to seek within yourself, and recall it to your mind.

The reason Socrates presumed that we have within us all knowledge is because it is not easy to detect the difference between mechanisms that 'look up the correct responses' from mechanisms that 'generate a correct response'. I would go further and state that in principle it is *impossible to tell the difference*. However, in practice any finite mechanism will have limitations that make storage of predefined knowledge very unlikely. From a modern point of view, where a finite brain bound us, we do not have access to the virtual storage of an infinite soul.

   On the other hand, an infinite amount of a certain kind of knowledge can be 'stored' within a generator. For example the two times tables can be extended indefinitely through the mechanism of multiplication. This suggests that the generators, or at least the components of the generators, must be predefined. In this sense the notion of 'recall' as a substitute for intelligent behaviour being born within us from the beginning is correct. The specialisations of comprehension, word, number and space associated with intelligence (Thurston) is supported from this analysis. The underlying intelligence mechanisms of abstraction and abduction are only workable if there is some predefined set of generators that invoke perceptions and concepts.

   One of my research students, Mohamad Zakaria (1994), created a model, based upon the above view of intelligence. This model is limited to a world of numerical series. The abstraction of the basic features of the numbers was fixed to be the number value. The range of concepts involved different kinds of curve fitting and series. The criterion for success was based upon a notion of simplicity, and each hypothesis generator was associated with its own notion of what that means. The first hypothesis to satisfy its criteria for success was offered as a solution.

   Thus, if you take the series:

18 10 6 4 _

   The first successful hypothesis might be:

$$y = 18 - \frac{32x}{3} + 3x^2 - \frac{x^3}{3}$$

Answer = 2

An alternative hypothesis could also be:

$$s_i = 1/2s_{i-1} + 1$$

$$10 = 18/2 + 1$$

$$6 = 10/2 + 1$$

$$4 = 6/2 + 1$$

$$? = 4/2 + 1$$

Answer = 3

where s_i is the ith value in the series.

A more human answer would be:

$$s_i = s_{i-1} - 1/2 (s_{i-2} - s_{i-1})$$

$$6 = 10 - (18 - 10)/2$$

$$4 = 6 - (10 - 6)/2$$

$$? = 4 - (6 - 4)/2$$

Answer = 3

However, it is the second and third hypotheses that give the correct answer from the human testing of IQ. It is the last hypothesis, which is human because it uses all the given data within its structure; the same criteria for cryptic clues in crossword puzzles. Yet the first answer is not wrong given the problem.

To get the right answer in the right way indicates that the selection of a hypothesis generator is important, and must depend upon some abstract features of the series; abstract features such as rising, falling or fluctuating of the numbers in the series.

Mohammed Zakaria tried four different learning strategies, where the program modified its selection of a hypothesis to fit with a human choice (see Chaps. 11 and 12 for more detail). He compared the results of the strategies with a control (no learning and no bias). Sometimes the hypothesis chosen would give the right answer, but for the wrong (inhuman) reason. The answers were counted as correct in these cases (see Fig. 2.10). A human quotient (HQ) was introduced that was defined as:

$$HQ = \frac{\text{Number of correct Answers with Human Hypotesis}}{\text{Number of correct Answers}} * 100$$

Notice that in general the number of 'correct' answers increases with the HQ.

What we have here is an illustration of *learning* that improves the *acceptability* of the range of potentially correct solutions. It is an acceptability that goes beyond the criteria of validation since it involves all possible styles of solution; it is an illustration of *machine wisdom*.

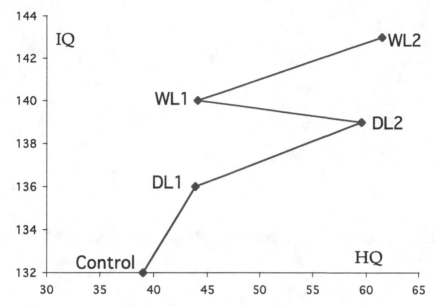

Fig. 2.10 Learning human intelligence

So in this chapter we have shown the operational components of intelligence and the role of learning from experience. In the next chapter, I will be exploring the possibility of creating a very simple and primitive intelligence using these components in the form of a computer program.

References

Peirce CS (1958) Science and philosophy: collected papers of Charles S. Peirce, vol 7. Harvard University Press, Cambridge

Peirce CS (1966) The fixation of belief. In: Weiner PP (ed) Charles Peirce: selected writings. Dover, New York, pp 92–260

Shannon CE, Weaver W (1964) The mathematical theory of communication. University of Illinois Press, Urbana, (first published 1948)

Wittgenstein L (1921) Tractatus logico-philosophicus (English edition 1961). Routledge and Kegan Paul, London

Zakaria MS (1994) A framework for machine intelligence based on the pragmatic approach. A Doctor of Philosophy Thesis submitted to the Faculty of Science, Reading University UK

Fig. 2.11 ... ...

... this ... ... upon the ... ... and
the ... ... from ... ... will ... ... the ...
... ... to ... ...
in the ... of ... ...

References

... ...
... ...
... ...
... ...
... ...
... ...
... ...
... ...
... ...
... ...

Chapter 3
Identifying Intelligence

> *It is not good enough to have a good mind. The main thing is to use it well*
>
> Descartes,
> Discourse on Method (1637)

3.1 Introduction

Formally identifying intelligence would seem like a gross simplification of what has always seemed a complex and slightly mysterious process. What we have done is created a starting point for our investigation by proposing a concrete description we can then try to use. We will expect that this initial description to be inadequate in explaining many aspects of our experience of intelligence, but it will give us a starting point to grow something better as in the following story. The 'concrete description' is the 'stone' in the soup.

3.1.1 Stone Soup: A Folk Story

Once upon a time, somewhere in Eastern Europe, there was a great famine. People jealously hoarded whatever food they could find, hiding it even from their friends and neighbours. One day a peddler drove his wagon into a village, sold a few of his wares, and began asking questions as if he planned to stay for the night.

"There's not a bite to eat in the whole province," he was told. "Better keep moving on."

"Oh, I have everything I need," he said.

In fact, I was thinking of making some stone soup to share with all of you.

He pulled an iron cauldron from his wagon, filled it with water, and built a fire under it. Then, with great ceremony, he drew an ordinary-looking stone from a velvet bag and dropped it into the water.

By now, hearing the rumour of food, most of the villagers had come to the square or watched from their windows. As the peddler sniffed the 'broth' and licked his lips in anticipation, hunger began to overcome their scepticism.

© Springer International Publishing Switzerland 2014
T. Addis, *Natural and Artificial Reasoning,* Advanced Information
and Knowledge Processing, DOI 10.1007/978-3-319-11286-2_3

"Ahh" the peddler said to himself loudly.

I do like a tasty stone soup. Of course, stone soup with cabbage—that's hard to beat.

Soon a villager approached hesitantly, holding a cabbage he'd retrieved from its hiding place, and added it to the pot. "Capital!" cried the peddler.

You know, I once had stone soup with cabbage and a bit of salt beef as well, and it was fit for a king.

The village butcher managed to find some salt beef... and so it went on until there was indeed a delicious meal for all (after the stone was removed).

The villagers tried to buy the stone from the peddler but he would have none of it. After all, how would he feed himself on his travels? So off he went and the villagers still talk about the wonderful stone soup as being one of the best meals ever.

As for the stone, soup intelligence needs more than just insight and reason (the stone). It also needs, for example, a purpose. So far the intelligence process as described has been passive. Signals arrive and these are eventually turned into messages. What is required of intelligence at this stage is to infer a pattern in the sequence of messages so that future messages become less.

3.2 Uncertainty

Uncertainty can also be described. It is sometimes known as 'surprise', or 'information' and is measured in terms of the average probability of a finite set of messages. If you can always infer a new message from a string of given messages then such a message is not surprising, and will contain zero information. If there are many messages that conform to no conceivable pattern then the information will depend upon the probability of guessing correctly. The average probability of guessing correctly is related to a measure of information obtained from a message (see Shannon and Weaver 1964). More will be said of this later.

For now we can say that if you have a hypothesis or rule that allows you to make a more accurate guess at what the next message in a sequence of messages will be then we can say that the 'information' is reduced, i.e., it is not so surprising. There are situations where insight (a hypothesis or rule) comes through the process of experimentation (a validating action) rather than just passive observation of a sequence of messages. This requires a further stage in the intelligence process in that an *action* is needed based upon the current observations.

3.3 Selecting an Action

As we have seen, the IQ test does not usually require an action other than a choice or generation of the next message expected in the sequence of messages (information source) in order to show that a pattern has been recognised. In general, an action is

Fig. 3.1 Intelligence
stimulating action

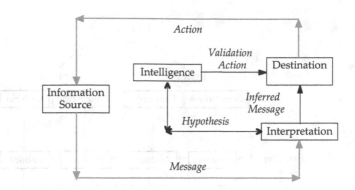

often the consequence of a process involving intelligence in normal daily situations; after all, that seems to be the main purpose of intelligence. The overall sequence is shown in the reproduced diagram from Chap. 1 in Fig. 3.1. The detailed intelligence process of insight and reason is also reproduced in Fig. 3.2.

The diagram Fig. 3.2 shows a feedback loop as the final result of insight followed by reason. Johnson-Laird and Wason (1977) explored the nature of this feedback loop in human problem solving, where an action is required based upon a given insight.

In one of their tests:

"... you are presented with four cards showing, respectively:
'A' 'D' '4' '7'
and you know from previous experience that every card, of which these are a subset, has a letter on one side and a number on the other side. You are then given this rule about the four cards in front of you: "*If a card has a vowel on one side, then it has an even number on the other side.*"

So here the insight normally required by intelligence is already given.

Next you are told: "*Your task is to say which of the cards you need to turn over in order to find out whether the rule is true or false.*"

Here the investigation is to see if you can determine the correct action to test the validity of a given hypothesis.

The most frequent answers to test this concept are 'A and 4' and 'only A' (Wason and Johnson-Laird 1968). Both these answers are logically wrong. *The correct formal answer is 'A and 7'.* This is because the rule can be expressed as:

Vowel **implies** Even

This means that given a Vowel there will *always* be an Even number on the reverse side but given an Even number there may or may not be a Vowel. This is because 'implies' is only logically consistent in one direction. This can be seen in a Table 3.1 in lines 1 and 3 for the condition **Y is Even** is **True**.

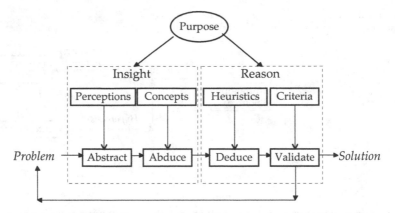

Fig. 3.2 The intelligence process

Table 3.1 Truth table for the hypothesis 'Implies'

	X is a vowel	Y is even	X implies Y
1	**True**	True	**True**
2	**True**	*False*	*False*
3	False	True	True
4	False	*False*	*True*

A simple computer program, **'confirm'**, can illustrate the process of choosing an action. This program will generate the correct minimum set of tests for any range of logic-based hypothesis using two sided cards. Three examples of its output are[1]:

QUERY > confirm that [vowel **implies** even] in list [' A' 'D' #4 #7]
　　　Try cards ['A' #7]

QUERY > confirm that [vowel **or** even] in list [' A' 'D' #4 #7]
　　　Try cards ['D' #7]

QUERY > confirm that [vowel **and** even] in list [' A' 'D' #4 #7]
　　　Try cards ['A' #4]

The program has been written in Clarity. Clarity is a Schematic Functional programming language. This language is fully described in the book *Addis & Addis Drawing Programs: The Theory and Practice of Schematic Functional Programming, Springer* (Addis and Addis 2010). The diagram below is the Clarity Schematic **'confirm'**. Such a diagram can be considered as a simple flowchart of linked processes as shown in Fig. 3.3.

---

[1] The command and responses have been made easier to read. The actual command for the first example is: > confirm [implies isvowel iseven] ['A' 'D' #4 #7] and the actual reply is simply ['D' #7]. In the other queries 'or' is '‖' and 'and' is '&&'.

Fig. 3.3 The function
'confirm' in the language
clarity

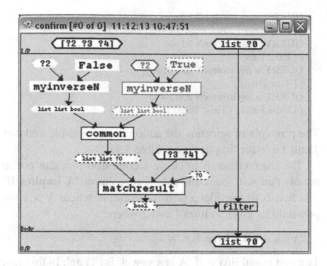

In Clarity, the method of 'running' a diagram is to type into a 'control' window the function 'name' followed by its appropriate parameters. This activates the function '**confirm**' where the answer for the 'QUERY' is given on the next line thus:

QUERY > confirm [**implies** isvowel iseven] ['A' 'D' #4 #7]
['A' #7]
or thus:
QUERY > confirm [**implies** iseven isvowel] ['a' 'd' #4 #7]
['D' #4]

The boxes in this diagram, whatever their colour, are either functions defined previously in the same way or library functions already provided by the system.

The function '**myinverseN**' will produce a subset of the truth values for the logic operator specified by the variable '?2' in the first parameter (this is 'implies' in our initial example but could also be 'or', 'and' etc). The variables '?3' and '?4' are the logic tests to be applied to a list of the items in **confirm**'s second parameter. The function '**myinverseN**' will list the Truth values (see Table 3.1) for the operator '?2' where the results are either **False** or **True** as requested by its second parameter. So for 'implies' the following combinations are **True** (see line 1, 3, 4 of the above Table 3.1).

QUERY > **myinverseN** implies **True**
[[False False] [False True] [True True]]

And in the following combination there is only one that is **False** (see line 2 of the Table 3.1).

QUERY > **myinverseN** implies **False**
[[True False]]

The function can also be used for other Truth operators such as 'or' (expressed as '||') and 'and' (expressed as '&&').

QUERY > myinverseN || True
[[False True] [True False] [True True]]
QUERY > myinverseN || False
[[False False]]
QUERY > myinverseN && True
[[True True]]
QUERY > myinverseN && False
[[False False] [False True] [True False]]

The principle of selecting the action is very simple and can be illustrated using the Truth Table for 'implies' (see Table 3.1).

The requirement is to chose a condition that can potentially give two possible results that will make the rule (last column '**A implies B**') either **True** or **False**. The first is to consider a positive example where A is a **vowel**. There are only two possibilities given in lines 1 and 2 where:

'**A is a vowel**' is **True**. E.g. 'A'

The first possibility is if '**A is a vowel**' is '**True**'. In this case there are two potential results for '**Vowel implies Even**', which depends upon the two possible truth-values of the statement '**B is Even**' given in lines 1 = True and 2 = False). Hence we need to examine the negative case in which B is odd, since the rule will not be supported if it turns out that '**A is a vowel**':

'**B is even**' is *False* (i.e. B is odd). E.g. #7

The two conditions { ['**A is a vowel**' is **True**] overlap when ['**B is even**' is *False* (i.e. B is odd)] }, and this only occurs when '**A implies B**' is *False(Line 2)*. So this is the line that should be used to test the hypothesis where we have the pattern [**True False**] for tests [**isvowel iseven**]. Thus 'A **isvowel = True**' or '#7 **iseven = False**'. In the function '**matchresult**' the variable?10 in the example below can be either **True** or **False**. Given a list of pairs of values (e.g. [[?10 False] [**True?10**]]), two truth tests (e.g. [isvowel iseven]), and a value (e.g. 'A'), the tests are both applied to the value, and the resulting pair of results is checked for a match against each pair in the list of possibilities. Only one of the possibilities needs to match for a result to be **True**. To make clear how this matching is taking place, the alternatives are expanded so that we have the following possibilities:

QUERY > matchresult [[?10 False] [**True?10**]] [isvowel iseven] '**A**'
True

Here it is **True** that '(**isvowel** 'A') is True'

QUERY > matchresult [[?10 False] [**True?10**]] [isvowel iseven] '**B**'
False

Here it is **False** that '(**isvowel** 'B') is True'

QUERY > matchresult [[?10 **False**] [True?10]] [isvowel **iseven**] **#4**
False

Here it is **False** that '(**iseven** #4) is False'

QUERY > matchresult [[?10 **False**] [True?10]] [isvowel **iseven**] **#7**
True

Here it is **True** that '(**iseven** #7) is False'

A Clarity function (Addis and Addis 1996) '**confirmTF**' applies '**matchresult**' to a list of values (e.g.['A' 'D' #4 #7]), resulting in a list of truth-values given the truth table of a logic operator. The logic operator '**implies**' in this case is the head of the list followed by the two truth tests, **isvowel** and **iseven**.

QUERY > confirmTF [**implies** isvowel iseven] ['A' 'D' #4 #7]
[True False False True]

The common patterns between the 'True' list and the 'False' list are found. These are then applied to the list that represents the card faces displayed (i.e. 'A' 'D' #4 #7), and those that satisfy the pattern are chosen. The function '**confirmTF**' is almost exactly the same as '**confirm**' (see Fig. 3.3) except that the '**filter**' is exchanged for '**map**'. **Filter** only lets through those values that are True (e.g. 'A' and #7) whereas '**map**' lists the truth-values [True False False True].

The function '**confirmTF**' shows only expected truth values for those given in the list ['A' 'D' #4 #7] that satisfy the two conditions for the function '**A implies B**' is **False**. So the function '**confirm**' will use this result to select the required items in the list to test for confirmation of the rule '**Vowel implies Even**'. In this case the items that are **True** in the list are 'A' and '7' we have:

QUERY > confirm [**implies** isvowel iseven] ['A' 'D' #4 #7]
['A' #7]

The function '**confirm**' uses the results of the logic tests '**isvowel**' and '**iseven**' given by function '**matchresult**' to select the matching values that are **True** from the list shown by '**confirmTF**' (also see Table 3.1).

This function 'confirm' represents the action part of the intelligence system shown in Fig. 3.4 and does not include the generation process of testable hypotheses. The hypothesis in this case is already given ('implies'), and so it is not inferred from observations. The only purpose of the function 'confirm' is to show how to validate a possible hypothesis against a given set of data.

The deduction process is used to expand all the potential possibilities of a given hypothesis (in this case the '**implies**' truth table), and the validation process has the built in criteria to examine every positive (**True**) and negative (**False**) case. What we have shown here is a mechanism that can infer a validation-testing scheme. So far, the insight must be provided externally as to what hypothesis needs to be confirmed. In our example the action to validate a hypothesis is the suggested test pattern ['A' #7].

So we now need a function that will suggest hypotheses to test. This is the prime process of abduction. A function 'abduce' can be constructed that will generate functions of the right form for validation. The approach taken is simple and certainly not very subtle; we will simply generate functions at random and test them by our validation process until a hypothesis is found that is validated. We then stop.

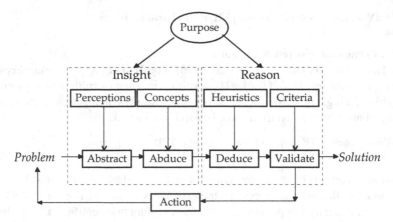

Fig. 3.4 Validation requirements trigger action

For this we create a function '**gen_function**' that randomly chooses a potential logic operator from a list of operators, and '**gen_feature_pair**' generates a pair of suitable parameters that may also include the logical operator '**not**'. For example, we can generate the pair of requirements thus:

QUERY > **gen_function** Implies	**QUERY** > **gen_feature_pair** [(isa "int") (isnot iseven)]
QUERY > **gen_function** Xor	**QUERY** > **gen_feature_pair** [(isnot (isa "char")) (isnot iseven)]
QUERY > **gen_function**	**QUERY** > **gen_feature_pair** [isvowel (isnot (isa "int"))]

We then combine these functions in '**abduce**' shown in Fig. 3.5. Examples of this function are[2]:

    QUERY > abduce
    [is_not vowel **and** is_not even]
    QUERY > abduce
    [is_not a vowel **or** is_even but_not_both]
    QUERY > abduce
    [is not even **implies** a vowel]

A more efficient abduction mechanism might have been written that ensures that the generated hypothesis has a good chance of success. For example, we might choose a method of generation that simulates the process of evolution. This might combine successful hypotheses to produce potentially better hypotheses.

The problem with the function '**abduce**', as defined in this program, is that it has no memory and will reproduce a hypothesis that has already been rejected or generate another hypothesis that has little to do with previous ones; in this function the hypotheses do not evolve from those that have gone before. To provide a mechanism

---

[2] The actual command is > abduce and the response is [&& (isnot isvowel) (isnot iseven)] etc.

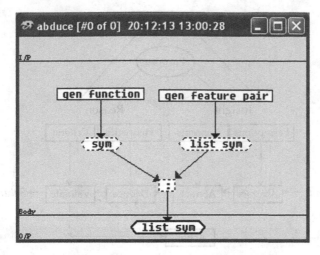

Fig. 3.5 The function abduce at top level

that will use experience, we need a *memory* of some sort. If we include memory then we will finally have a primitive construct of all the elements of an intelligent system as seen in Fig. 3.6.

The function **'add_idea'** uses a parameter as a memory shown in Fig. 3.7

QUERY > add_idea []
[[**xor** (isnot iseven) isvowel]]
QUERY > add_idea [[xor (isnot iseven) isvowel]]
[[**&&** (isnot iseven) (isnot isvowel)]
[**xor** (isnot iseven) isvowel]]
QUERY > add_idea [[&& (isnot iseven) (isnot isvowel)] [xor (isnot iseven) isvowel]
]
[[**&&** (isa "char") iseven]
[**&&** (isnot iseven) (isnot isvowel)]
[**xor** (isnot iseven) isvowel]]

The function 'getRule' (see Fig. 3.8) uses add_idea, which calls 'abduce' to add a single new hypothesis to a growing list of hypotheses saved in its parameter. The function 'get_rule' always gives the latest hypothesis (function **'head'**).

The function **'getRule'** is then used by **'giveR4S'** to generate new rules for testing as in Fig. 3.9. The testing involves the principles used in the function **'confirmTF'** described in Fig. 3.3.

QUERY > giveR4S [['a' #6] ['d' #2] ['e' #4] ['c' #7]] ['a' 'd' #4 #7]

Would ' **even OR consonant** ' be a good rule to try?
Yes, try this rule. . . ' **even OR consonant** '
Only these cards need be checked. . .
[a 7]
Both sides of the checked cards:-
[[a 6] [c 7]]

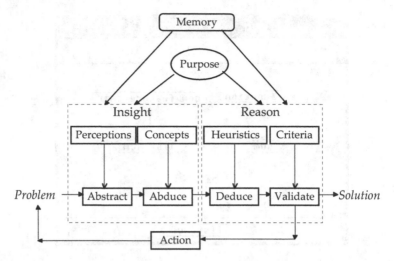

Fig. 3.6 Final form of intelligence

Fig. 3.7 The function
'add_idea' has memory

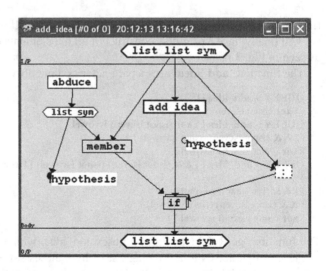

This is a rule that works. . . **' even OR consonant '**
Shall we try to find another rule? (y or n):- **y**
OK, trying again.
Would **' vowel implies even '** be a good rule to try?
Yes, try this rule. . . . ' **vowel implies even '**
Only these cards need be checked. . .
[a 7]
Both sides of the checked cards:-
[[a 6] [c 7]]
This is a rule that works. . . ' **vowel implies even'**
Shall we try to find another rule? (y or n):- **y**
OK, trying again. . . .

Fig. 3.8 The function 'get_rule' generates a new 'idea'

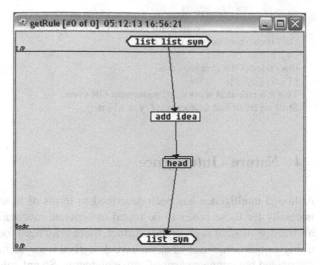

Fig. 3.9 The function 'giveR4S' generates tested potential rules

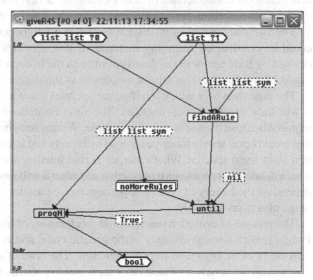

Would ' **vowel implies odd** ' be a good rule to try?
Yes, try this rule. . . . ' **vowel implies odd** '
Only these cards need be checked. . .
[a 4]
Both sides of the checked cards:-
[[a 6] [e 4]]
This rule will **not** fit, let's try another.
Would ' **even AND vowel** ' be a good rule to try?
parameters cannot be even or vowel
' **even AND vowel** ' is a rule that can't possibly work.
This rule will not fit, let's try another.

Would ' **consonant OR even** ' be a good rule to try?
Yes, try this rule. . . . ' **consonant OR even** '
Only these cards need be checked. . .
[a 7]
Both sides of the checked cards:-
[[a 6] [c 7]]
This is a rule that works. . . ' **consonant OR even** '
Shall we try to find another rule? (y or n):- **n**

3.4   Nature's Intelligence

Although intelligence has been described in terms of functional boxes there is no necessity for these boxes to be found as separate mechanisms. They represent an abstraction of what is observed. Further, there is no need for intelligence to reside in a single organism, since what we have described is a system and systems can be any distributed but connected set of active elements. So ant colonies or eco-systems are open for investigation.

The material form of an intelligent system is not important. An intelligent system could be constructed from any mechanism that provides constraints. Engines as devised by Babbage or the siphon system as in the Europa Water Clock (Berlin, See Fig. 3.10) could all potentially be employed as intelligent engines.

The time span over which intelligence operates is not a critical property, although it will have practical consequences. The time limitations imposed for IQ tests is required because the test is unique to people. We can imagine a very slow intelligence that would operate over many years or an extremely fast intelligence as might be found in a short lived species. What emerges is that intelligence has a set of parameters, which define what problems it may solve and what it will never solve. These solutions depend on the battery of concepts, perceptions, heuristics and criteria as well as the range of actions available.

The process of evolution has all of the mechanisms of intelligence (see Fig. 3.11). Insight is born through changes in the genetic code, and is the starting point for the generation of an organism (morphogenesis). The laws of complex systems govern the organism's structure. These laws form stable patterns that explain the shape of living things (Goodwin 1994). The success or failure of a species is judged by its ability to survive the current environment. The memory of the success is contained in the distribution of successful individuals in the population of the species. These individuals are the candidates for reproduction, and so the search for an optimum solution is automatically provided. In this way validation and memory are combined into a single concept.

The consequence of this view would suggest that not only will the same solution (type) be 'reinvented' from different starting points (see rabbits and their marsupial equivalents, the wallaby, in New Zealand) but the evolutionary system may well 'reinvent' the same species all over again. This might explain the rediscoveries of prehistoric animals, such as the 'thought to be extinct' fish the coelacanths. The

Fig. 3.10 The Water clock, Europa Centre, Berlin

intelligence of evolution, although confined to a specific activity and driven by the pressure of life, is a complete intelligence; except in its ability to change the level of abstraction; it is stuck at the level of the DNA sequences.

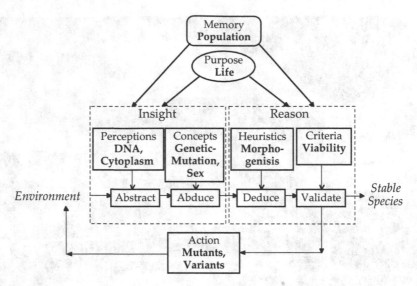

Fig. 3.11 Evolution as an intelligence process

We may speculate that the human species is an attempt by evolution to take a step beyond this limitation. Our inventions such as the car or computer seem to be following the same route as evolution; they might be considered a form of accelerated life.

The basic ingredients of intelligence have been identified through a review of different aspects of human problem solving. Intelligence must have all these ingredients to be called intelligence. The examination of IQ suggested that there is a set of discrete specialisations within which human intelligence can be effective. Information theory suggested that the recognition of the features or percepts, i.e. elements of perception, of a problem domain is critical, and that once these percepts are established an abduced hypothesis will emerge from one of the domain 'generators'. From a functional point of view these generators could be as unsophisticated as look up tables. The value of the hypotheses can be measured by the effective reduction of the perceived entropy. A hypothesis is evaluated through its use and effectiveness; wisdom can be assessed as the improvement in the choice of hypothesis from a viable set of potential hypotheses. Intelligence is driven by purpose and supported through memory.

The value of the speed with which problems are solved is only a peculiarity of the human condition. The potential to solve a problem is not altered by the platform on which intelligence is 'run'. In practice, speed is of vital importance specifically to living organisms, and we would expect that the biological architecture would evolve to cope. However, it is architecture we all share and although speed says something of the efficiency of our intelligence it does not define its bounds.

The notion of intelligence has really been constructed from the way people have used the term both formally (as in logic) and semi-formally (as in IQ tests). By exposing the way 'intelligence' is talked about and used, a set of mechanisms have been identified as the necessary components of intelligence.

What has been discarded is the necessity to rely upon human intelligence as a fundamental unit of performance. It has been used as the stone in the soup; however, to recognise intelligence requires the means of sharing the same abstractions and insights as well as the acknowledgement of purpose. The notion of intelligence has been extended beyond recognisable thought; there can, for example, be physical manifestations of the process. This model thus allows us to identify and assess objectively other potential forms of intelligence systems.

References

Addis T, Addis J (2010) Drawing programs: the theory and practice of schematic functional programming. Springer, Heidelberg, ISBN 978-1-84882-617-5, e-ISBN 978-1-84882-618-2

Goodwin B (1994) How the leopard changed its spots: the evolution of complexity. Weidenfield & Nicolson, London

Johnson-Laird PN, Wason PC (1977) Thinking: readings in cognitive science. Cambridge University Press, London

Shannon CE, Weaver W (1964) 'The mathematical theory of communication'. University of Illinois Press, Urbana (first published 1949)

Wason PC, Johnson-Laird PN (1968) Thinking and reasoning. Penguin Modern Psychology UPS 11. Penguin Books, London

Chapter 4
Knowledge Science

God knows what the Truth is

Anon

4.1 Introduction

Once we have defined and implemented a simple version of intelligence, the problem now arises as to how this might be extended to be useful. One way is to use it in conjunction with the expert knowledge of some professional. To capture this expertise on a computer is particularly important when it comes to rare, expensive or vanishing skills. Intelligence itself is of no real value unless it can be used in the world of human affairs; it is this view that stimulated the idea of an 'Expert System'. An Expert System is intended to capture the knowledge and skills of an expert in a computer program so that such a program can either replace an expert or amplify a novice's knowledge to the point of being equivalent to an expert. The questions then arise of how we might harvest this knowledge and represent it in a computer, and how we can use such knowledge.

Underlying the notion of an Expert System is the relationship between knowledge and technology. Computer technology has tended to force our perception of knowledge into specific categories (such as data and processes) that are often inappropriate for modelling our understanding of the world. Our inability to resolve this tension between knowledge and technology has been one of the major reasons that Expert Systems are confined to a narrow band of application types. There is also no standard Expert System, so the representation of expert knowledge can be widely different. In order to cope with these differences, we must form the bases of a technological science of knowledge. To understand formally the relationship between knowledge and technology in this more general sense I have taken, as stated earlier, a pragmatic stance; a stance that will highlight what is of *practical* value in our notion of knowledge. This approach, as we have argued previously, relates directly to our actions in the world and thus to our knowledge about the world. It is clear that knowledge underlies our actions, since it is through our knowledge of a situation that we are able to assess our response to it.

I present a view of knowledge in this chapter that shows how the tension between knowledge as we perceive it and the limitations of technology might be resolved. I will show that separate forms of knowledge must be identified and brought together

© Springer International Publishing Switzerland 2014
T. Addis, *Natural and Artificial Reasoning*, Advanced Information
and Knowledge Processing, DOI 10.1007/978-3-319-11286-2_4

by the human insight of an experienced designer (knowledge engineer) in order to create an Expert System. I will also demonstrate in this chapter why our current systems are limited and how this view will stimulate new frontiers of research.

The study of knowledge is usually referred to as epistemology, but this study is primarily concerned with the nature of people and their relationship to the world. It is not expressed in terms of computer emulations. In particular, the traditional concern is centred on the justification of knowledge. The difficulty in obtaining an absolutely confident answer to the question of whether a particular set of beliefs are 'true' can be seen through the works of the French philosopher Rene Descartes (see Sutcliffe 1968). He, having considered the possibility that even ones own senses are suspect (we could be living in a dream, or hallucinating, or God could be playing a game), was reduced to starting his philosophies with the unconfirmed belief that God in His benevolence would not deliberately mislead us. That is, our observations are directly related to what is 'True'.

Truth has thus been taken to be God's view of His world. Ironically, from this underlying foothold of belief in God, formal representations of knowledge, such as logic and predicate calculus have been created, both of which in their turn underwrite the technology of the computer and the modern theories of artificial intelligence. Certainly ever since the philosopher Immanuel Kant established that knowledge depends upon our concepts it has been recognised that knowledge is inseparable from the mode of its representation.

A 'knowledge engineer' is an expert who can elicit and thus capture the knowledge of a target expert in a way that can be used by an Expert System. A knowledge engineer will conceptualise expert knowledge in terms of their preferred method. It should be noted that there is no standard method of representation at this stage of knowledge capture. The process involves many hours of informal and semiformal discussions between a knowledge engineer and the target expert or experts. The results of these discussions are often sketched in terms of diagrams and a semi-formal language. However, since there is a strong dependency between representation and knowledge, such semiformal languages are developed within an engineering environment and are normally biased towards a particular view of a chosen Expert System design (Shaw and Woodward 1990). Because of this bias such representations obscure certain aspects of knowledge; in particular, the different roles of different kinds of knowledge. It is therefore important to step away from the Expert System and construct a general theory of knowledge representation. This representation should be cast to lie outside any particular Expert System design but appropriate to be used for all of them.

4.2 A Taxonomic Approach

The question "What is a knowledge representation?" was answered in part by Randal Davis et al. (1993), and a summary of his team's deliberations is shown in Table 4.1. The Roles of Knowledge Representation: (Davis et al. 1993). The important issue

Table 4.1 The roles of knowledge representation. (Davis et al. 1993)

Role	Description
Surrogate	A substitute for the thing itself. For reasoning about the world rather than taking action in it
Set of ontological commitments	In which terms should the world be thought about?
A fragmentary theory of intelligent reasoning	Expressed in terms of: 1. The conception of reasoning 2. The set of inferences sanctioned 3. The set of inferences recommended
A medium for effective computing	1. An environment in which thinking is accomplished 2. Guidance for organising information
A medium for human expression	A language which says things about the world

here is that it is a serious attempt at categorising knowledge by the role it has within a human, social and technological framework. However, the presumption here is that knowledge remains only within the human domain, and that it is a system whose parts must necessarily remain within that human world.

This restriction to the human domain is explicitly made through the warning, "*A knowledge representation is not a data structure*", where data structure may be some abstract representation scheme (such as a graph), usually created for eventual computer storage (Addis 1985). However, it is generally accepted that a 'semantic net', which is a directed graph of annotated boxes and arrows, does represent some components of knowledge. The reason for this distinction seems to be based upon the idea that semantic nets have 'semantics', where 'semantics' refers to the topological constraints that come from what the net represents rather than its construction rules.

This loses a clear understanding of what the difference is between nets and graphs since the difference is identified through a set of unspecified implicit constraints that are only obtainable through human interpretation. This pushes the nature of knowledge back from whence it came, into the minds of peoples, so calling this graphical representation a 'semantic' net does not, in itself, give it meaning.

If a proper study of knowledge is to be undertaken then the relationship between a representation and the world it represents must be investigated. What will need to be considered now is the place that a users of a representation have with respect to their interpretation of. It is only then that an understanding of engineering Knowledge Systems can evolve.

My theory of knowledge, expressed in part in this chapter, addresses this problem of engineering knowledge systems. This will include some mention of machine learning and scientific discovery (Addis 1985, 1989, 1990). The theory is based upon a knowledge taxonomy that identifies the different types of knowledge called into play when a system has to interact with the world to achieve some purpose. The taxonomy has been derived from how it is discussed and used by knowledge engineers. Thus, knowledge in this chapter is classified according to its role in a

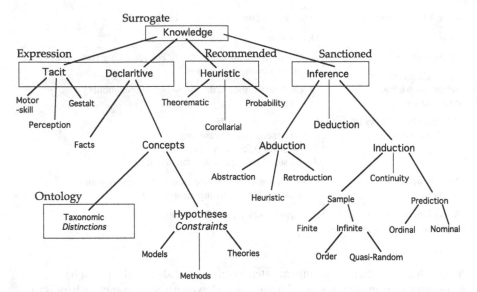

Fig. 4.1 A role-taxonomy of knowledge

system. Figure 4.1 shows the current status of this taxonomy, only part of which will be discussed here.

As boxes in Fig. 4.1, overlaid on this taxonomy are the roles, as identified by Davies et al. (Table 4.1), of the different categories of knowledge. All knowledge can act as a surrogate to the world. *Tacit* is understood from experience, *declarative* is defined knowledge, and both are primarily used via a representation as human expression and communication. Part of the declarative knowledge is the 'ontology' or *taxonomy* accepted by the participants of a conversation, and the range of possible *inference* mechanisms that can be sanctioned are shown. The *Heuristics* shown in Fig. 4.1 provides the guidance for problem solving within a representational scheme.

Figure 4.1 illustrates that knowledge can be divided into four broad categories. Davies et al.'s theory only provides three of these categories:

• Declarative
• Heuristic
• Inferential

These must be present in any operational system, though their inclusion is not, of course, a sufficient condition for intelligence. The *tacit* dimension remains outside of any symbolic system, but must be possessed by a human user for that system to be viable. Such knowledge is embodied partly in cognitive structures and partly in social ones; this is why so much of what people learn must be taught, ostensibly, by example and by other people (Collins 1975, 1985, 1990).

4.2.1 Tacit Knowledge

Tacit knowledge is a skill or understanding that can be demonstrated but cannot be represented by, say, a list of rules or instructions. Typical examples of tacit knowledge are:

- Riding a bike
- Playing the piano
- Laboratory skills
- Problem solving (e.g. factors of a simple polynomial through inspection).

Tacit knowledge may tentatively be divided into three distinct types:

Motor skill or kinaesthetic knowledge (the ability to interact physically with the world)

Perceptual knowledge (the ability to observe the world in an active sense)

Gestalt (the ability to recognise patterns or 'situations' in the world).

Though many of these can be transferred (e.g. by instruction), tacit knowledge is personal in that its acquisition requires first-hand experience of the situations in which it is applied (Polanyi 1958). Studies of scientific practice have also emphasised the importance of personal knowledge (Collins 1975, 1985; Gooding 1990b, c, 1992, 1993a, b; Shapin 1989). Tacit knowledge remains in the world of being human.

4.2.2 Declarative Knowledge

Declarative knowledge is the main result of the knowledge elicitation processes; it is a knowledge schema. Much of a knowledge engineer or analyst's work is concerned with identifying an appropriate taxonomy (often referred to within artificial intelligence as the 'ontology') of an expert's domain. This involves determining a set of distinctions made about the world, hypotheses or beliefs about that world, and facts taken to be 'True' of that world. The roles of knowledge are:

4.2.2.1 Facts

Facts are represented as propositions that ascribe specific properties to particular objects (or events). The ascription is based on observation. Thus, a fact is an instance of a concept and a concept is a generalisation from specific set of instances. Concepts can be used to imply new facts or to confirm known facts. *Facts* are 'known' observations, deductions or beliefs of or about the world.

Table 4.2 The role of truth in declarative knowledge

Types of declarative knowledge	Truth of the knowledge dependent upon
Fact	Observation, deduction or belief
Distinction (taxonomic)	Convention or definition
Hypothesis	Convenience

4.2.2.2   Taxonomic

The taxonomic class of concept consists of propositions that define general features, classes, categories, or types of objects or events. *Taxonomic knowledge* is concerned with the distinctions made in a domain.

These propositions are identified by the nature of the knowledge in that they are 'true' by convention or by definition. For example, the truth of the statement that "a bachelor is an unmarried man" depends upon a convention that the verbal token "bachelor" should represent the class of persons who are male and unmarried.

4.2.2.3   Hypotheses

Hypotheses are propositions that express constraints, laws or rules about the world rather than our modes of representing the world. Taking a pragmatic view, (Peirce 1958, 1966) wrote "*Hypotheses* are true if they are useful; they are useful if they make the world a less surprising place".

In conjunction with inference, *hypotheses* make predictions about the world so as to reduce the effective information content of incoming messages from or about the world. Without hypothesis formation, it would be impossible to develop new concepts about the world: learning could not happen.

Table 4.2 summarises the distinctions between different types of declarative knowledge. Note that the role of 'Truth' here is to characterise an abstraction of the world that is person or people centred. Thus the set of facts, distinctions, and hypotheses assert a view of the world that is in part influenced by the world itself (observations), part by the individual (beliefs), part by society (conventions), and part by purpose (convenience). 'Truth' reduces to a parameter that really has a role only for *deductive inference*.

Hypotheses may be either theories or models. Although these are often represented visually, i.e., as visual hypotheses (Gooding 1992; Thagard and Hardy 1992; Trumpler 1992), in the first instance I will only be concerned with the declarative and verbal forms of hypotheses. Later we will wish to extend the notion of a hypothesis to form part of a mechanism (a machine, or a physical structure or natural system).

Models, in conjunction with an inference system and heuristic knowledge, make predictions about a limited part of the world, and are derived from theories and perceptions that encompass a greater view than any model. Associated with a model is a set of inference mechanisms so that the model may be activated (driven). Many different models may be derived from a single theory. Thus, a set of models is the extension of a theory in the same way that a set of facts is an extension of a concept.

An extension is a relationship between a set of symbols and a symbol which is not itself a member of the set. The meaning of the symbol *is* the set. Since every symbol of the set can itself have an extension, the relationship of a concept to a set of facts (or a theory to a set of models) is relative and not absolute (Addis 1990).

4.2.3 Heuristic Knowledge

Heuristic knowledge is that knowledge which indicates how a deductive process should be performed. Given a number of facts and hypotheses, many potential paths of deduction are possible. The heuristic knowledge uses extra-logical information to guide the deductive process towards 'useful' results. What is useful depends upon the purpose of the system.

4.2.4 Inferential Knowledge

C. S. Peirce pointed out there are three types of *deduction*. Since there is only one formal process of deduction based upon 'modus ponens' (although there are many mechanisms such as resolution that can achieve the same result), the distinctions he identified can be related to the different classes of heuristics identified in Fig. 4.1. Exactly how these may be identified within a knowledge system is yet to be understood.

We can note that *inference*, in general, can be divided into two styles:

- *Open*: 'Open' inference does not necessarily have identifying formal mechanisms associated with it. In general, open inference is related to the creation or the construction of insights.
- *Closed*: Closed inference identifies the process of selection from pre-formed or pre-determined set of insights.

The problem with most artificial intelligence systems is that it simulates intelligence through an inference that appears open (capable of learning) but which is in fact closed. Closed inference is usually found in both intelligent mechanisms and many established skills (such as navigation, engineering and mathematics).

Inference, as Peirce observed, has three distinct forms. These are *abduction*, *induction* and *deduction*. Their roles are simply described as:

Generate a hypothesis (*abduction*) - >
Validate a hypothesis (*induction*) - >
Infer new facts from a hypothesis (*deduction*).

4.2.4.1   Abduction

In its most general form, abduction is the process behind insight. It is involved in three classes of activity:

- *Retroduction*: *Open retroduction* is the *creation* of a new hypothesis and *closed retroduction* is the *selection* of a hypothesis from a pre-defined set. Often only closed retroduction is referred to as 'abduction' in the literature, and this limited view depends upon the notion of *reverse implication*. Thus, if (A implies B) then we can say that if we observe B then A is a possible cause. However, this inference is closed because it depends upon the pre-existence of propositions such as (A implies B). Such a predefined system is closed.
- *Abstraction*: *Open abstraction* is the process of creating or observing new taxonomic concepts and *closed abstraction* is the process of selecting taxonomic concepts from a pre-defined set.
- *Heuristic*: *Heuristic abduction* is the insight that creates or selects the process (the heuristic) of how to solve a problem. The heuristic tells the inference process how to continue with deduction. Whereas heuristic knowledge, as defined earlier, selects a path of reasoning, the heuristic abductive inference proposes how such a decision should be made.

4.2.4.2   Induction

Open induction, taken in the context of the other forms of inference defined here, is the *process of validating a hypothesis*. Validation involves induction that is not enumerative, that is, does not involve generalising from a set of particulars, as it is normally understood. *Induction* here requires the pre-existence of a hypothesis, a deductive procedure and a set of criteria. The categories of criteria are shown in Fig. 4.1.

The normal definition of induction, and one not fully supported here, is based upon the principle of generalisation from a given set of instances. In practice this view *combines the notions of validation with retroduction* (Strawson 1952). 'Induction' in this combined sense is the process of reasoning where the conclusions are not entailed by the premise (i.e. truth is not guaranteed to be preserved). Thus statements like:

He's been travelling for 24 hours, so he'll be very tired

can be explained by a suppressed premises (undeclared hypotheses) such as:

People who travel for 24 hours will be very tired

Such suppressed premises allow us to reconstruct the 'inductive' inference *as a form of deductive inference*. However, the suppressed premises do not appear as conclusions to deductive arguments based on particular instances (examples drawn from the extensions of the premises). 'Induction', as held by this common view, involves the generation of a suppressed premise (retroduction) and its validation (induction as defined here).

On the view of Addis et al. (1993) *validation* and thus the induction of a hypothesis should involve the assessing the utility or viability of the hypothesis, given a particular purpose. *Closed induction* validates by comparing the inferred results with an established model (e.g. the null hypothesis in statistics).

Induction, as I have defined here, takes on three categories of criteria:

- sample,
- continuity, and
- prediction.

For example, the 'sample' criteria is concerned with testing a hypothesis against a set of examples (which may be finite or infinite).

The validation of a hypothesis through its ability to make predictions (that is, to reduce the apparent entropy of the given set with respect to a set of classes; it infers an order in the state of affairs) is well defined for a finite set. Validation of an infinite set given only a finite set of examples must make some assumptions about the stability of the infinite set's properties.

4.2.4.3   Deduction

Deduction is valid through formal proof. It is the process of inferring conclusions that must follow from the premises; it preserves Truth. Truth here is an abstract property assigned to the propositions and their Truth-value (True or False) may not necessarily relate to the world. Closed deduction uses known (i.e. pre-determined) solutions.

4.3   Intelligent Inference

Within this framework we define as 'intelligent' any system that has the capacity to use all three forms of inference (abduction, induction and deduction) together (NB. Abstraction and Retroduction are classed together as Abduction in this definition[1]). Intelligent processes typically keep these forms in tension. The dynamics are more complex than the logical dialectic of 'generation' and 'testing' as studies of knowledge-creation processes in a science show. The characteristic of knowledge-creation processes has been shown to be changing continually (Gooding 1992; Pickering 1989; Twieney 1985; Twieney and Gooding 1992).

The main cycle of activity may be described as follows (also see Table 4.2):

---

[1] It is not clear to the author if the process of Abstraction is necessary for some kind of 'pure' intelligence where the elements of the world are given or predefined.

Fig. 4.2 The cycle of
intelligence and the
interaction between the
different types of inferences

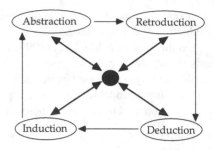

- *Abstraction* of relevant features ensures that a germane hypothesis can be retroduced.
- *Retroduction* attempts to create a hypothesis (or set of hypotheses) that is framed in terms of the abstracted features and fits given knowledge and understanding. The creation process is dependent upon some mechanism (possibly some kind of meta-concept) that is influenced by experience. In this way only feasible hypotheses are generated.
- *Deduction* from this hypothesis will provide the essential information for induction.
- *Induction* validates the deduced results according to a set of criteria that depend upon purpose. The result of induction influences further abstraction, and so on.

Figure 4.2 illustrates the process of intelligence described above. The creation and validation of hypotheses is performed by interacting and co-operating abstraction, retroductive, deductive and inductive inferences. As suggested this process in its simplest form is similar to the simple 'generate and test' procedure often quoted by others. However, the process is more complex than this simple cycle in that the results at each stage influence the way in which each element in the cycle behaves. There is a "tension" among the three inferences and this "tension" provides feedback data from one inference to another in order to improve the quality and credibility of a potential hypothesis.

The black solid circle in Fig. 4.2 indicates the flow of information (thick arrow) between the four inferential mechanisms. The tension is created when the four inferential mechanisms cooperate to formulate a viable hypothesis. Communications between the mechanisms involves a cycle of abstraction, retroduction, deduction and induction and the feeding-back of information that will ensure a hypothesis is applicable. Thus features from the world are abstracted that serve the overall purpose of the system and lead towards viable hypotheses. Hypotheses are abduced that will, in their turn, serve the criteria of induction, and deduction will form conclusions that can be validated and useful (e.g. solve the problem). Abstraction is unique in that it depends to a large extent on close activity with the world; it is sense based (i.e. sight, touch, hearing, taste and smell as well propriaception). Abstraction depends upon involving people.

For a given set of facts (e.g., a sequence of numbers) it is the role of retroduction to create a reasonable hypothesis for those facts (e.g. the sequence). Deduction exercises the hypothesis and returns a prediction of a new fact (e.g., the next number in the series). The validation of the retroduced hypothesis is the function of induction that ensures that the hypothesis is suitable for the purpose (e.g., the prediction is correct, the calculation was not too complex, it fits all or most of the facts and the form of the hypothesis is simple).

The interaction of the three forms of inference explains why, given that many possible hypotheses can be generated, we tend to generate only a small set for evaluation. In the Faraday simulations done by Gooding and Addis (see Chaps. 6 and 7, Addis et al. 1990, 1992; Gooding 1990a, b, 1992) one example of this appears as the Construe-Experiment-Clarify (C-E-C) cycle. It should be possible to identify different reasoning styles (or different qualities of intelligence) according to the mix or range of different kinds of inference.

4.4 Knowledge Acquisition

The knowledge engineer's task is to represent and model expert knowledge. This involves negotiating a path from the informal and pre-articulate state of an expert's (or experts') knowledge towards a formal model of it. Each stage of this process has its own representation scheme and associated techniques.

It was argued by Addis et al. (1993) that because a functional database language (FDL) explicitly represents all the different declarative roles of knowledge, it will therefore provide a formal representation that is best suited for an unbiased elicitation method. They then argued that a graphical approach to formal modelling exploits the advantages of visualisation and offers a median way between the extremes of rules-oriented and data-intensive approaches. By combining the two argued points in a Visual Functional Program (VFP language Clarity[2]) they provide the justification that VFP is an ideal environment for knowledge acquisition.

4.4.1 Abstracting to a Representation

An emphasis on the linguistic form (i.e., text) in most knowledge representation defers to the traditional philosophical bias towards propositional knowledge. In practice, most conceptual modelling representations involve an essential pictorial or diagrammatic representation, even though these may be defined in terms of a language. Systemic networks, semantic nets, SFD graphs, KADS diagrams and repertory grids express conceptual models within a two-dimensional diagram. Relational analysis uses a diagrammatic scheme to show the elementary items (attributes, objects and entities) that are recognised by a business. However, many

---

[2] A version of Clarity is available through the author or from http://www.clarity-support.co.uk/.

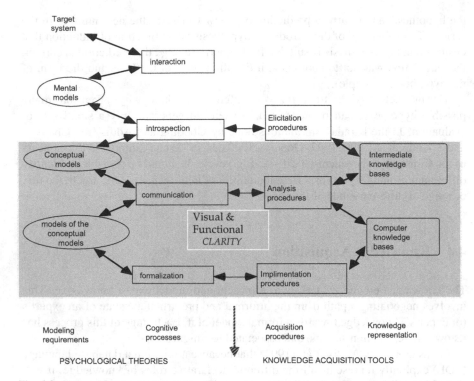

Fig. 4.3 Abstracting to a representation (The processes that link elicitation, modeling and formal representation are shown (modified from Shaw and Woodward). The non-verbal representations typically used in moving from conceptual models to formalized implementation ones are absent.)

diagrams are too informal to translate directly to a formal structure that can be implemented as a program. For these, where the target system (implementation) forces a representational bias, an extra stage in modelling is required.

Figure 4.3 shows the processes linking elicitation, modelling and formal representation (modified from reference Shaw and Woodward 1990). The non-verbal representations typically used in moving from conceptual models to formalised, implementable ones, are not shown.

It is well known to AI workers that sketches and diagrams are good guides to implementation. Nevertheless, accounts assume that all diagrammatic modelling reduces to linguistic representation. Thus an account by Shaw and Woodward, in which diagrammatic representations are not even identified as part of the process, shows how quickly visualisations are replaced by linguistic representations. They therefore underestimate the importance of diagrams to communication and conceptualisation during the elicitation process (Fig. 4.3). Of course, the machine representations sought by knowledge engineers, like Maxwell's famous field equations, must be symbolic in form. However, this fact does not require us to assume that all representations reduce to linguistic ones. Images were just as important to Maxwell as they had been to Faraday (Wise 1979). Many modes of scientific investigation are irreducibly graphical (Griesemer 1991; O'Hara 1992).

Formal representation is essential to computational representation; nevertheless it may prematurely displace informal, diagrammatic working during the elicitation process (Shaw and Woodward's summary 1990 of the process, pp. 189–190, suggests that this is the case). Addis et al. give the diagrammatic representations used in knowledge elicitation a more prominent and more enduring role by showing that it is possible to combine the accessibility, flexibility and exploratory capacity of diagrams with the disciplines of formal representation. It is possible to have your cake and eat it because it is achievable to generate program code directly from diagrams.

Moreover, since a functional database language (FDL) is used, it is possible to model at any level of abstraction, combining different levels of complexity in the same representation. Further advantages of this approach emerge from a consideration of the recent history of hardware and systems software design.

4.5 Knowledge as Data and Processing

Influenced by earlier conceptions that the world can be split into two categories, data (information) and processing (action), computer technology has dictated that all knowledge (including models of skills and the world) should be divided between storage (data) and processing. Work on rule extraction from data using 'inductive' techniques has demonstrated equivalence between these two forms of knowledge (Quinlan 1979). Models of skills (such as the skilful playing of a chess endgame) can be represented either as a large database processed by a simple pattern matching algorithm or as a set of rules that is processed by a deductive inference system.

Similarly, software engineering has tended towards design methods that emphasise either the data or the process form of representation. Systems analysis, in particular, is oriented toward database designs. These use graded methods that first consider the domain directly and then move the abstraction of the domain towards a mass data storage solution. The steps involved are:

- Relational Normalisation,
- Conceptual Model,
- Logical Model and
- Physical Model (see Fig. 4.4).

Other methods, largely independent of database analysis, develop the associated software (process). These methods include:

- Function Charts,
- Data Flow and
- Nassi Schniederman Charts (Fig. 4.4).

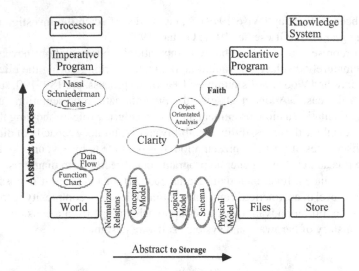

Fig. 4.4 Dimensions of abstracting to a representation. (The diagram illustrates the emphasis of the two main software engineering methods on process (vertical axis) and information (horizontal axis). Any model of knowledge can be represented at some level of abstraction as a point in this space. The scales of abstraction indicate the order that each method (enclosed in an *oval*) is used to implement a system.)

The advantage of these approaches is that each can provide a method: an explicit procedure that ensures a reliable design that can be justified. However, these methods are appropriate only for the imperative programming of data. Because of their influence, there is a tendency for knowledge analysts to bifurcate knowledge into (see Fig. 4.5) taxonomic structures (suitable for storage) and processes (appropriate for imperative programming), as a matter of course.

However, as D. Michie pointed out, people do not naturally conceive their own knowledge in either of these extreme forms of data and processing. Representation of people's knowledge is best understood in terms of some intermediate form that combines data and rule. Many practical skills use such a mixture: navigators, statisticians, architects and electronic engineers all use tables as well as rules. Michie called this intermediate form "the human window" (Michie 1979). It is the shaded area in Fig. 4.5. Interactive systems—whether used by experts or by novices—should operate within these limits.

The diagram (Fig. 4.5) implies that knowledge can be considered as something apart from its representation. The same knowledge can thus be described in different forms in the same way that music can be represented as the physical undulations on a disc, or the magnetic orientations on tape, or the musical notations on paper. The inverse relationship between process and data for a single source of knowledge is also illustrated here. The curved line indicates the many different mixes of data and process. The spheres denote a single source of knowledge represented in different ways (Addis 1980). Michie's 'Human Window' is labelled as the 'Area of Conception'.

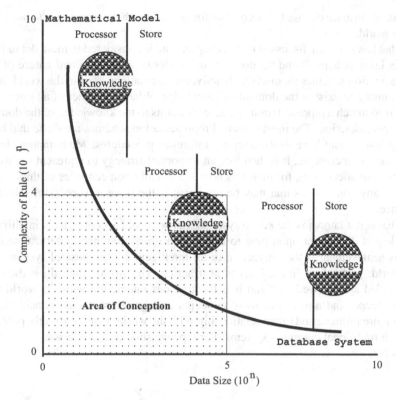

Fig. 4.5 The interchange of data with rules. (Michie 1979)

A knowledge system consists of a balance between a pure store and a processor. The role of object-oriented analysis is to keep the balance between data and processes for any particular knowledge source. This balance ensures that the designer can conceive of his model more easily, in the form of the object. The notion of 'Frames', where a kind of form (a frame) is created for a generic object, was an original conception that led to object analysis. The frame has been developed from experience in the field. The object frame therefore lacks the coherence and completeness that might be expected had it been derived from a formal theory of a knowledge representation.

4.6   The Boundaries of Knowledge Representation

Knowledge of the world is a human and social affair. However, it does have identifiable elements that allow us to create hypotheses, represent knowledge and discuss the nature of intelligence. Given such a study it is possible, within the human framework, to attribute knowledge to inanimate objects such as computers and other machines.

This is because *we* choose to interpret its form in a way that corresponds to *our* view of the world.

What has not been discussed in this chapter, and is considered in more detail later in this book (Chaps. 8 and 9, also see Addis 1990), is the role and nature of the representation schemes themselves. Briefly, representations exist in the world, have constraints and exist in the domain of knowledge. What a designer of a system has to do is to match a representation and its constraints to the knowledge of the domain under consideration. The most powerful representation schemes are those that have a long history and have evolved strong inference procedures. Mathematics, in all its forms, is an example. It is therefore an important strategy to represent the world in a mathematical form, for then it is possible to call upon centuries of thinking to support any conclusions that may be drawn; it is the route to successful scientific advance.

What is not known is the key to systems that we could accept as truly intelligent. This key is dependent upon how to achieve an *open* inference system. One clue to this achievement is the interaction of an intelligent and purposeful system with the world; particularly at the level of abstraction. The world, after all, is the only unbounded system we have, and it is through our interaction with the world that new concepts and novel systems of concepts emerge. Here we are considering a much more intimate and direct relationship with the world than is currently possible through traditional computer systems. Perhaps we should consider something akin to a robot.

References

Addis TR (1980) Towards an expert diagnostic system. ICL Tech J May:79–105

Addis TR (1985) Designing knowledge-based systems. Originally Kogan Page, then Prentice Hall (1986) ISBN 0-13-201823-3, and also Chapman & Hall, October. Hardback: ISBN 0 85038 859 7. Soft back: ISBN 1 85091 251 3

Addis TR (1989) The science of knowledge: a research programme for knowledge engineering. In: Proceedings of the third European Workshop on Knowledge Acquisition for Knowledge-Based Systems (EKAW '89), Paris, June

Addis TR (1990) Knowledge for design. Knowl Acquis 2:95–105

Addis T, Gooding D, Townsend J (1990) A functional description of Faraday's discovery of the electric motor. Working Paper, Science Studies Centre, University of Bath

Addis T, Gooding D, Townsend J (1992) Knowledge design from natural intelligence: an interactive representation of Faraday's experimental researches. Poster, Joint Councils Initiative Workshop, Imperial College, March 1992

Addis TR, Gooding DC, Townsend JJ (1993) Knowledge acquisition with visual functional programming. In: Knowledge acquisition for knowledge-based systems, 7th European workshop, EKAW '93, Toulouse and Caylus, France. 6–10 Sept. Springer, ISBN 3-540-57253-8, ISBN 0-387-57253-8. Lecture Notes in AI 723. Bibliography

Collins HM (1975) The TEA set: tacit knowledge and scientific networks. Sci Stud 4:165–185

Collins HM (1985) Changing order. Sage, Englewood Cliffs

Collins HM (1990) Artificial experts. MIT, Cambridge

Davis R, Shrobe H, Szolovits P (1993) What is a knowledge representation. AI Mag 14(1):17–33, Spring

Gooding D (1990a) Mapping experiment as a learning process. Sci Technol Hum Values 15:165–201

Gooding D (1990b) Experiment and the making of meaning. Kluwer Academic, Dordrecht

Gooding D (1990c) Rediscovering skill in science. Bath 3: Technology and Medicine, Bath: Science Studies Centre

Gooding D (1992) Putting agency back into experiment. In: Pickering A (ed) Science as practice and culture. Chicago University Press, Chicago, pp 65–112

Gooding D (1993a) Visualisation in and of science. In: Joint HSS-BSHS-SHOT conference, Toronto, July 1992 and Princeton University workshop on visualisation in science, February

Gooding D (1993b) What is experimental about thought experiments? In: Hull D, Forbes M, Okruhlik K (eds) PSA 1992, vol 2, 1993 (in press)

Griesemer JR (1991) Must scientific diagrams be eliminable? The case of path analysis. Biol Philos 6:155–180

Michie D (1979) Problems of the 'Human Window'. Presented at the AISB summer school on expert systems, Edinburgh, July

O'Hara RJ (1992) Telling the tree: narrative representation and the study of evolutionary history. Biol Philos 7:135–160

Peirce CS (1958) Science and philosophy: collected papers of Charles S. Peirce', vol 7. Harvard University Press, Cambridge

Peirce CS (1966) Charles Peirce: selected writings, edited by Wiener PP. Dover, New York

Pickering A (1989) Living in the material world. In: Gooding D, Pinch TJ, Schaffer S (eds) The uses of experiment: studies on the natural sciences. Cambridge University Press, Cambridge, pp 275–297

Polanyi M (1958, 1998) Personal knowledge: towards a post critical philosophy. London: Routledge, p 428

Quinlan JR (1979) Discovering rules by induction from large collections of examples. In: Michie D (ed) Expert systems in the micro electronic age. Edinburgh University Press, Edinburgh, pp 168–201

Shapin S (1989) The invisible technician. Science 77:554–563

Shaw LG, Woodward JB (1990) Modelling expert knowledge. Knowl Acquis 2:179–206

Strawson PF (1952) Introduction to logical theory. Methuen, London

Sutcliffe FE (1968) Descartes: discourse on method and meditations. Penguin Classics, ISBN 0 14 0444.206 5

Thagard H, Hardy S (1992) Visual thinking in the development of Dalton's atomic theory. In: Proceedings of 9th Canadian conference on AI, Vancouver

Trumpler M (1992) Converging images: techniques of intervention and forms of representation of sodium channel proteins in nerve cell membranes. Paper for Princeton history of science workshop series on visualisation in the sciences, October 1992

Tweney RD (1985) Faraday's discovery of induction: a cognitive approach. In: Gooding D, James F (eds) Faraday rediscovered. Macmillan, London, pp 189–209

Tweney RD, Gooding D (1992) "Introduction", Michael Faraday's 'Chemical Notes, Hints, Suggestions and Objects of Pursuit' of 1822. IEE, London

Wise MN (1979) The mutual embrace of electricity and magnetism. Science 203:1310–1318

Chapter 5
Modelling Experiments

The art of being wise is the art of knowing what to overlook

William James,
Principles of Psychology, 1890.

5.1 Introduction

Professor David Gooding (Nov 1947–Dec 2009), a science historian, and I worked together for many years on the topic of modelling the science process. These models were validated from examples drawn from history. This chapter presents some of these examples.

I have suggested in Chap. 4 that the induction component of inference can involve experimentation as a validation method. The purpose of validation is to confirm that a particular model conforms to the world. The implied syntactic and structural elements of models specify relationships between their constituents, but they cannot show what outcomes that their interaction would produce over time. Simulation, in general, consists of iterating the states of a model so as to produce behaviour over a period of simulated time. This stepping through the states of models enables us to trace the implications and outcomes of inference rules and other assumptions implemented in the models that make up a theory. We can apply this method to experiments, which we treat as models of the particular aspects of reality they are designed to investigate.

Scientific experiments are constantly being designed and re-designed during implementation and use. The role of experiments is to mediate between our theoretical understanding and the world. It also involves the practicalities of engaging with both the empirical and social world. In order to model experiments we must identify and represent features that all experiments have in common. We will treat these features as parameters of a general model of an experiment so that by varying these parameters different types of experiment can be modelled.

© Springer International Publishing Switzerland 2014
T. Addis, *Natural and Artificial Reasoning,* Advanced Information
and Knowledge Processing, DOI 10.1007/978-3-319-11286-2_5

5.2   Experiment, Inference and Theory Change

Experimentation is one of the key features of science and technology, yet it is often treated as simply an adjunct of the construction and revision of theories. Similarly, the impact of evidence in theory acceptance and revision has traditionally been modelled in terms of one of the logical or statistical rules of inference. In this chapter we will draw on studies of experimental work in the history of science to develop a model of experimentation conducted by agents who interact with each other as well as with the phenomenology of their experiments. This approach to discovery aims to integrate formal, empirical and ethnographic methods in order to include some of those features of science that philosophers, historians, and social and cognitive scientists identify as important for understanding the process of science and the conduct of scientists.

5.2.1   Experiments and Experimenters

We will develop the view that experiments can be considered as models of the particular aspects of reality they are designed to investigate. Therefore, in order to model experiments I must identify and represent in our simulation those features that all experiments have in common as well as features that researchers have in common (Gooding and Addis 1999). We will treat these features as parameters of a simulation model that enables us to vary some of them to represent different types of experiment, different actors, and the fact that making inferences about evidence is a contingent and socially mediated activity. We can then model experiments ranging from compelling, idealized thought experiments and decisive or crucial experiments to those that are exploratory, ambiguous or controversial, as are most cutting-edge research experiments.

> When *modelling a person* and in particular a scientist
> I will refer to them as '*actors*' or '*agents*'.

This is so we will never confuse a real person with a simulated person during this discussion. I can vary the sensitivity of actors in our model to new data, their receptivity to the opinions of other actors, their access to experimental resources, and their contact with other actors.

Recent philosophical work, by Giere (2004), Cartwright (1999), and others argue that to show how theoretical claims actually engage with the world we must move beyond a purely semantic conception of scientific theories. Experiments are constantly designed and re-designed in the context of implementation and use, so they can be considered as types of models which mediate between abstract, theoretical understanding and the practicalities of engaging with the empirical and social world (Morgan and Morrison 1999). Our computer implementations of the model have included features such as design, transparency or ambiguity of phenomena produced by the design, plasticity of descriptors, scope for interpretation and construction, role of communication in establishing a result, and the explicitness and strictness of rules that define the compatibility of observations and hypotheses. Each experiment is treated as an instance of the model. We will describe the generalized model and how it integrates properties of experimentalists as social actors, and will provide examples showing how single- and dual-actor instantiations behave under simulation.

5.3 Rationality, Inference Rules and Epistemic Practices

Traditional approaches to scientific inference model belief-revision use rules that relate observational data to confidence in one or more hypotheses. The relationship can be modelled by logic (as in the case of hypothetico-deductive and falsification- ist models) or probabilistically (as with inductivist and Bayesian models). Statistical approaches allow for changes in the probability of an hypothesis as evidence accumu- lates, while Bayesian models approximate to learning systems in which evidence is evaluated in a context of judgments about the prior probability of the evidence being considered (Hesse 1974; Salmon 1990; Matthews 2004). Our approach challenges three assumptions of all these approaches. These are:

- *Firstly* that a logical and statistical model treat evidential support as an objective, a-temporal relationship between hypotheses and data. Here a scientific theory or model is considered as a unique and unchanging representation of the world.
- *Secondly* that in specifying how data should affect confidence in a hypothesis such models also assume an ordered stream of data.
- A *thirdly* that scientific rationality is a wholly mental, 'internal' affair, whether conducted according to logical rules such as falsification (Wason 1960) or Bayesian updating (an assumption also shared by experimental and cognitive psychology). This makes rational choice a purely individual matter.

However, none of the above assumptions is true of real science. First, empirical stud- ies of theory acceptance do not support the philosophical ideal of a single, definitive set of rules governing scientific inference. Comparative studies designed to iden- tify a set of scientific inference rules and heuristics showed instead that each case demands additional rules or amendments to existing rules (Laudans et al. 1986; Donovan et al. 1988). As the set of instances expands, so does the set of rules and conditions on rules (Gooding 1989). Contrary to the second assumption about evi- dence, scientists do not always 'receive' data in a predetermined form or in a fixed order. As for the third assumption, scientists constantly interact with others whose opinions are often divergent and also fluctuate over time. The impact of the opin- ions of others introduces other variables, such as 'trust'. This means that inferences by individuals about hypotheses cannot be modelled solely in terms of empirical evidence.

These considerations explain the failure of attempts to model theory-change solely in terms of inference rules operating on observational data. More generally, they indicate the difficulty of reconciling a universal, principled account of science with the variability and contextual nature of practice in the many domains of science. To understand how any rule of inference would work in practice, it would have to be implemented in a way that reflects the contingent and socially situated character of scientific thinking. Simulation methods allow us to do this. We can then evaluate the assumptions of our models of science by playing out the consequences of the properties of a situation, of inference rules and of the attributes of actors. For example, an actor may be biased, or insensitive to the opinions of others, or have access only to certain other actors or to certain experiments. We will advance a stronger argument that introducing communication into a model of science produces a degree of complexity that cannot be handled by models defined only as static, semantic structures.

The context in which beliefs are formed and confirmed or rejected includes multiple networks of epistemic practices. Science studies recognize the existence of a range of influences, constraints and sources but reject the notion of a single set of procedures, rules, norms or institutions sufficient to explain in general terms how the sciences work. The sciences do produce results—some of which turn out to be robust—without being constrained by centralized authority, or by standardized protocols, or exclusively by consensual factors, or by an objective world that determines outcomes. Each actor, site or node of a scientific community has a viewpoint, a partial view consisting of beliefs, local practices, local constraints, norms and resources. None of these are fully shared across all sites. For example, experimental results often cannot be replicated unless expertise (tacit knowledge) is also transferred (Collins 1985). Nevertheless, there is sufficient transfer of descriptors, concepts, methods and expertise to allow for communication between domains and between differing theoretical positions (Star and Griesemer 1989; Galison 1997; Gorman 2005), and for negotiation leading to the aggregation of elements from different viewpoints (Star 1989, p. 45). This explanation emphasises the diversity and context of practices, styles, and discourses (Galison and Stump 1996). It does not follow that there are no common methods and strategies, but if many communities of practitioners conduct science then we cannot expect a finite set of unambiguous rules to govern belief-revision and theory change.

5.4 Dynamic, Socially Mediated Inference

If complexity and variability defeat formal and semantic models, must we then conclude that scientific processes cannot be modelled? Here we adopt an alternative approach. This involves modifying some assumptions of traditional computational models and of philosophical theories about how confidence in hypotheses relates to experimental evidence. Drawing on findings of science studies about the social aspect of belief, we propose a way of modelling the dynamical rationality of science.

Simulation methods are not only advantageous, they are necessary (Ahrweiler and Gilbert 1998).

We use an agent-based approach in which every agent or actor can investigate a world of experiments and communication with other agents. Agents are defined by their capacity to interact with this world and not solely by inherent or 'personal' features. This follows from the view of science studies and with an insight of Herbert Simon. He remarked that 'we cannot explain the path of an ant without reference to properties of the terrain (such as chemical messages left by other ants)'. He goes on to argue that human intellectual processes may, in fact, be relatively simple in that most of the complexity of human behaviour may be drawn from a created environment of objects designed to assist our intellectual endeavours (Simon 1981, p. 159). Research into how cultures provide for a cognitive environment bears out this insight (Baird 2004; Heintz 2004; Hutchins 1995) in a way, oddly enough, that Simon and Newell's implementation of it (Newell and Simon 1973) failed to do (Collins 1990; Gorman 1992; Ahrweiler and Wörman 1998). It is clear that to design the material environment of science we must also add the social environment of other actors.

Our simulated actors are therefore characterized by their responsiveness to opinion (receptivity), responsiveness to data (flexibility), access to experiments, ability to communicate with other actors, and by a belief profile. This profile specifies an actor's confidence in each of a range of given hypotheses and allows us to represent bias. Beliefs are formed by an actor's interaction with other actors and (*via* procedures) with instruments that produce observations. Each actor revises its view of the world on the basis of the data and opinions it encounters. What an actor does will depend on which hypotheses it believes. Thus we treat beliefs as Peirce did, as dispositions to act; that is, to make an experiment, or consult another actor, self-consult or does nothing.

Like Simon's ants, scientists do not encounter a predictable, ready-made world: they shape and enhance the world to make it more conducive to science. Whereas ants must use chemical messaging, scientists cannot always apply ready-made terms, concepts or procedures to interpret new or surprising features of the world. Studies of visualization and modelling show that where science is producing new knowledge, people are dealing with a world that is only partially described, using images or concepts whose meaning is being worked out according to methods that were investigated (Gooding 2004; de Chadarevian and Hopwood 2004; Lynch and Woolgar 1988). Traditional views of science have emphasized the established, accepted, finished product—the clearly expressed, predictable, experimentally proven knowledge of textbooks and monographs. This approach hides the extent to which scientists invent and negotiate ways of representing aspects of the world they are investigating (Kuhn 1961). Engaging with the natural world is both an *adaptive* and an *inherently a social* process (Gorman et al. 2005).

We have identified several aspects of science that should be included in a model of inference: in particular, plasticity of representations and the inherently social character of these tokens of meaning. Plasticity can be handled according Wittgenstein's analysis in the *Philosophical Investigations*. The meaning of a term is not given by a finite, fixed set of necessary and sufficient conditions for its application (as assumed in analytical philosophy), nor by stipulating an exact set of referents (Addis and Gooding 2004). Rather, meaning is given by sets of objects and associations that are invoked when a term is used. Membership of these sets can change (Hesse 1973; Kuhn 1974). In science—as in everyday life—words and phrases often emerge from concrete situations in which participants jointly work out ways of describing what is going on (Arrighi and Ferrario 2004). New terms, symbols or images are created that acquire meaning through collective use in real situations (Gooding 1990; Suchman 1987; Goodwin 1995). Even after terms or symbols have acquired an established usage that does conform to semantic rules, experts must sometimes validate judgements about correct usage or the validity of an inference. It is the scientific counterpart of establishing the authenticity of a painting or whether an ornament is made of real gold (Putnam 1975). This is the context in which we shall argue that experiments function as models. These models mediate between the emerging language of description and the explanation of the changing phenomenology of a domain.

5.5   Experiments as Mediating Models

Scientists use experiments to constrain the variability of a complex world by selecting certain features and processes and excluding others. The desired level of control can be difficult to achieve, so experiments develop over time; they have histories. Sometimes experiments become autonomous of the theories they are meant to test (Hacking 1983). During the twentieth century the character of experiment changed, from bench-top activities conducted within a single space by a very few people, to being complex arrangements of detecting and measuring machines, data flow, data analysis, and control procedures for managing the machines, information and large numbers of people (Galison 1997; Pickering 1995). Experiments were absorbed into distributed cognitive systems (Giere 2004; Nersessian 2005). Nevertheless, one aspect of experiments did not change: their design, use, interpretation and validation all involve seeking a consensual view through negotiation between individuals and groups of individuals.

Experiments are social objects constructed *via* epistemic practices. They are not simply ways to display facts. The way in which an experiment is perceived, no less than the way its results are interpreted, will vary according to context. Similar points have been made about models: models are abstractions that select features of the world and mediate between the abstract concepts of a community and the dappled, complex world they are theorizing (Cartwright 1999). Models have histories showing that their complexity varies according to function and context. Models are also investigative instruments, and like experimentation, modelling can become an autonomous activity (Morrison 1999). As with experiments, there is no unified method for modelling (de Chadarevian and Hopwood 2004). Models and experiments facilitate mutual adjustment of theories in relation to empirical evidence, networks of theoretical assumptions, and the material exigencies of acquiring data. Experiments

Fig. 5.1 Simulation shares features with *theory* (explicit, articulated concepts and rules), *experiment* (empirical data and a range of outcomes) and *demonstration* (rigorous argument according to rules) yet remains distinct from each of them

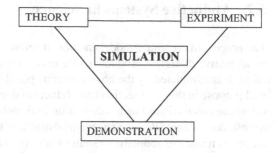

can be regarded as mediating models because experiments sometimes *are* models—simplified, abstractions of more complex processes—and because experiments often have the same cognitive *function* that models do in theorizing: they are integral to the process of inventing, constructing, negotiating and validating beliefs about the world.

5.6 Static and Iterative Models

Our simulation aims to capture this mediating function of experiments (as sets of *devices and procedures* that produce *observational results*) in relation to theories (as sets of *hypotheses*) and to scientific communities (as sets of *actors*). This requires a model that can be iterated in order to draw out the consequences of the assumptions it implements. A static model specifies the form and structure of its constituents, but cannot show what their interaction would produce in time and in the world.

The key difference between a model and a simulation is that a simulation iterates the states of a model, to produce behaviour over a period of time. Simulation differs from mathematical process models in science, which use procedures such as integration or differentiation to calculate end-states. These linear methods generate outcomes that are determined by the starting parameters. By contrast, iteration enables us to trace the implications of structural and other assumptions of the models that make up the theory, by exploring the range of outcomes that occur for a given set of starting parameters. In this respect simulations are similar to experiments and to theories (Fig. 5.1).

Because our simulation involves an adaptive belief system, the only way to discover, say, how a model of inference works out in a particular context is to run the simulation many times in order to ascertain the range of behaviours and outcomes. Variability of event-sequences and their outcomes represents unpredictability due to the outworking of social and other contingencies. Simulation makes it possible to evaluate such assumptions experimentally, not solely in relation to logical, semantic or other criteria. Historical, ethnographic and cognitive studies provide empirical benchmarks against which the behaviour of the simulation is evaluated. This sets simulations apart from models (as static structures of propositions arranged according to syntactic rules) and from experiments (as material components arranged according to physical, chemical or other constraints).

5.7 Abductive Systems in Science

The process of creating a model and how it relates to the experimentation is initiated by abductive inference. Abductive inference proposes a set of models for consideration. It is stimulated by the observation of puzzling phenomena (Peirce C. S.). We will propose in this next section that abduction does not work in isolation from other inference mechanisms (such a deduction and induction), and illustrate this through an inference scheme designed to evaluate multiple hypotheses. We will also use game theory to relate the abductive system to actions that produce new information. This will provide us with a formal link between inference and action. To enable evaluation of the implications of this approach we have implemented the procedures used to calculate the impact of new information in a computer model. Experiments with this model display a number of features of collective belief-revision observed in the field that lead to consensus-formation, such as the influence of bias and prejudice. The scheme of inferential calculations invokes a Peircian concept that:

> 'belief' is the propensity to choose a particular course of action.

Of the three types of inference proposed by Peirce, deduction is the one most widely accepted and understood (Peirce 1966, p. 92 ff.). In the semantic tradition, scientific models are reducible to formal systems of propositions. Formal systems invoke deduction because inferences can be made without reference to anything except the model itself. Deduction is a self-contained syntactic process in that validation of an inference depends simply upon a priori semantic truths and the preservation of truth-values. These can be specified in a truth table. Thus deduction appears to free us from the vagaries and changeability of an external world.

What makes this possible is that deduction relies upon the existence of well-defined sets. The members of such sets are known without ambiguity. However, what is often ignored is how the rules that specify set membership are established. In practice, it is left to the user of a formal system to devise rules that can be applied to test a candidate element for membership of a set. If this can be done with a finite set of rules and without reference to context, then the formal model is considered unambiguous. Following the model of Wittgenstein's Tractatus, we consider such sets to be 'rational' (Wittgenstein 1921; Addis and Billinge 2004).

By contrast, Peirce's notion of 'abductive' inference does not depend upon truth-values. Instead, the process of validation depends upon 'induction', the third type of inference that Peirce recognized. First, abduction generates a model (a hypothesis) that is used together with deduction to explain some surprising facts and to predict new ones. Where these are successful, this reduces our uncertainty about the world or, as Peirce put it—'makes the world a less surprising place'. However, any reference to the world requires a form of validation that depends upon observation of the world. Peirce's version of induction involves comparison of expected and actual outcomes to validate the abduced model of the world. Traditional 'induction', when considered as generalization from given instances, converges to the combination of the two Peircian inferences of abduction and validation (see Chap. 3 and Addis 2000).

The cycle 'abduction (generation) deduction (prediction) induction (validation) the inference abduction' reflects something of the scientific process of interpreting new or surprising findings by generating a hypothesis whose consequences are then evaluated empirically (Hanson 1958; Gooding 1996). However, an abduction cycle calls for sensitivity to empirical context. This in turn calls for variability in the set of descriptors and for some plasticity in their meaning (for examples see Gooding 1990). This plasticity of meaning requires a kind of set for which there is no finite collection of rules that establish membership of an element; we must be able to change membership by adjusting the set of rules that can be applied. Such sets mediate between the stable language of formal models and the changing, often uncertain contexts to which they apply. Scientists work out the rules governing set-membership as they develop the experimental and theoretical methods of a domain.

We will call such dynamic and flexible sets *irrational*.

We will illustrate this through a computational model of beliefs represented as the level of confidence in each of a set of hypotheses. These beliefs can be revised in the light of new information (Addis and Gooding 1999; Gooding and Addis 1999, 2004). This model will show how abduction, as part of a larger inference system, can make the world a less surprising place. In order to implement it as an iterative model, we must first articulate the notion of abduction in terms of a measure of expectation.

The most appropriate measure of *expectation*[1] is called *entropy*[2].

However, we found that when we try to minimize this measure through an agent's actions so as to make the world a less surprising place then this measure produced implausible behaviour. In particular, simulated agents will become locked into fixed patterns of belief and behaviour.

The entropy measure works only if it is:

  i. continually validated and adjusted
 ii. incorporates random actions based upon game theory.

Our simulation experiments suggest, therefore, that rules governing membership in irrational sets require:

  i. a continuous reappraisal and revision
 ii. the possibility of actions that appear irrational.

The set of beliefs is irrational in that its membership can change (e.g., to include new descriptors for surprising or anomalous information, Gooding 1990), even without recourse to definitions or correspondence rules (Kuhn 1974, pp. 310–312). Behaviour

---

[1] Also referred to as *surprise*

[2] As described by Shannon and Weaver, 1964

may also be irrational as suggested by game theory. Game theory is used in our model of science to dictate the selection of an experiment or alternatively to talk to another agent. These selections are not always warranted by the current set of beliefs of an agent, since it will sometimes choose an action that is counter to the firmest of beliefs. If the agent does not do that then, as mentioned previously in this chapter, the agent becomes inflexible and will remain firmly stuck in what is possibly an incorrect belief.

In the next chapter we will step through the formal theory that supports irrational action.

References

Addis TR (2000) Stone soup: identifying intelligence through construction. Kybernetes 29:849–870
Addis T, Billinge D (2004) 'Music to our ears: a required paradigm shift in computer science' presented at ECAP04. University of Pavia, Italy
Addis TR, Gooding DC (1999) Interacting agents: simulating a community of scientists. Int J Hum Comput Interact (submitted)
Addis TR, Gooding DC (2004, 2008) 'Simulation methods for an abductive system in science', in MBR04: model-based reasoning. In: Science and engineering, abduction, visualization, and simulation. University of Pavia, Italy, December 2004. Also in Foundations of Science, Vol 13, No 1, March 2008.
Ahrweiler P, Gilbert N (eds) (1998) Computer simulations in science and technology studies. Springer, Berlin
Ahrweiler P, Wörman S (1998) Computer simulations in science and technology studies. In: Ahrweiler P, Gilbert N (eds) Computer simulations in science and technology studies, Springer, Berlin, pp 33–52
Arrighi C, Ferrario R (2004) 'Abductive reasoning, interpretation and collaborative processes', in MBR04: model-based reasoning. In: Science and engineering, abduction, visualization, and simulation, University of Pavia, Italy, December 2004
Baird D (2004) Thing knowledge: a philosophy of scientific instruments. University of California Press, Berkeley
Cartwright N (1999) The dappled world: a study of the boundaries of science. Cambridge University Press, Cambridge
Collins HM (1985) Changing order. Sage, Englewood Cliffs
Collins HM (1990) Artificial experts. MIT Press, Cambridge
de Chadarevian S, Hopwood N (eds) (2004) Models: the third dimension of science. Stanford University Press, Stanford
Donovan A, Laudan L, Laudan R (eds) (1988) Scrutinizing science: empirical studies of scientific change. Reidel/Kluwer Academic, Dordrecht
Galison P (1997) Image and logic, a material culture of microphysics. Chicago University Press, Chicago
Galison P, Stump D (1996) The disunity of science: boundaries, contexts, and power. Stanford University Press, Stanford
Giere RN (2004) The problem of agency in scientific distributive cognitive systems. J Cogn Cult 4:759–774
Gooding DC (1989) How to be a good empiricist. Br J Hist Sci 22:419–27
Gooding DC (1990) Experiment and the making of meaning. Kluwer Academic, Dordrecht
Gooding DC (1996) Creative rationality: towards an abductive model of scientific change. In: Meheus J (ed) Philosophica: creativity, rationality and scientific change, vol 58. pp 73–101
Gooding DC (2004) Cognition, construction and culture: visual theories in the sciences. J Cogn Cult 4:551–594

Gooding DC, Addis TR (1999) A simulation of model-based reasoning about disparate phenomena. In: Magnani L, Thagard P, Nersessian N (eds) Model based reasoning, Kluwer/Plenum, London

Gooding DC, Addis TR (2004) Modelling scientific experiments as mediating models, model-based reasoning in science and engineering, abduction, visualization and simulation, MBR'04. Pavia, Italy, December 16–18

Goodwin C (1995) Seeing in depth. Soc Stud Sci 25:237–274

Gorman ME (1992) Simulating science: heuristics, mental models and technoscientific thinking. Indiana University Press, Bloomington

Gorman ME (2005) The essential and the accidental. Ratio 18(3):276–289

Gorman ME, Tweney RD, Gooding DC, Kincannon AP (eds) (2005) Scientific and technological thinking. Lawrence Erlbaum Associates, Mahwah

Hacking I (1983) Representing and intervening. Cambridge University Press, Cambridge

Hanson NR (1958) Patterns of discovery. Cambridge University Press, Cambridge

Heintz C (ed) (2004) Studies in cognitive anthropology of science. J Cogn Cult 4(3–4)

Hesse MB (1973) Models of theory change. In: Suppes P et al (eds) Proceedings, 4th international congress of philosophy, logic and methodology of science, Bucharest, pp 379–391

Hesse MB (1974) The structure of scientific inference. Macmillan, London

Hutchins E (1995) Cognition in the wild. MIT Press, Cambridge

Kuhn TS (1961) The function of measurement in modern physical science. In: Woolf H (ed) Quantification: a history of the meaning of measurement in the natural and social sciences, Bobbs-Merrill, New York, pp 31–63

Kuhn TS (1974) Second thoughts on paradigms. In: Suppe F (ed) The structure of scientific theories, University of Illinois Press, Urbana, pp 459–82

Laudans L, Donovan A, Laudan R, Barker P, Brown H, Leplin J, Thagard P, Wykstra S (1986) Scientific change: philosophical models and historical research. Synthese 69:141–223

Lynch M, Woolgar S (eds) (1988) Representation in scientific practice. MIT Press, Cambridge

Matthews R (2004) Opposites detract. New Sci 181(2438):39–43

Morgan M, Morrison MS (1999) Models as mediating instruments. In: Morrison MS, Morgan M (eds) Models as mediators: perspectives on natural and social science, Cambridge University Press, Cambridge, pp 10–37

Morrison M (1999) Models as autonomous agents. In: Morrison MS, Morgan M (eds) Models as mediators, Cambridge University Press, Cambridge, pp 38–65

Nersessian NJ (2005) Interpreting scientific and engineering practices: integrating the cognitive, social and cultural dimensions. In: Gorman M et al (eds) Scientific and technological thinking, Erlbaum, Hillsdale, pp 17–55

Newell A, Simon HA (1973) Human problem solving. Prentice-Hall, Englewood Cliffs

Peirce C (1966) The fixation of belief. In: Weiner PP, Charles S (eds) Peirce: selected writings, Dover, New York, pp 92–260

Pickering A (1995) The mangle of practice: time, agency and science. Chicago University Press, Chicago

Putnam H (1975) The meaning of meaning. In: Gunderson K (ed) Language, mind and knowledge. University of Minnesota Press, Minneapolis, pp 131–93

Salmon W (1990) Rationality and objectivity in science or Tom Kuhn meets Tom Bayes. In: Savage CW (ed) Scientific theories. University of Minnesota Press, Minneapolis, pp 175–204

Simon HA (1981) The sciences of the artificial. MIT Press, Cambridge

Star SL (1989) The structure of ill-structured solutions. In: Gasser L, Huhns M (eds) Distributed artificial intelligence, vol 2. Pitman, London, pp 37–54

Star SL, Griesemer J (1989) Institutional ecology, 'translations' and boundary objects: Amateurs and professionals in Berkeley's museum of vertebrate zoology, 1907–39. Soc Stud Sci 19:387–420

Suchman L (1987) Plans and situated actions. The problem of human machine communication. Cambridge University Press, Cambridge

Wason PC (1960) On the failure to eliminate hypotheses in a conceptual task. Q J Exp Psychol 12:129–140

Wittgenstein L (1921) Tractatus logico-philosophicus (English edition 1961). Routledge and Kegan Paul, London

Chapter 6
Modelling Inference

When the torrent sweeps a man against a boulder, you must
expect him to scream, and you need not be surprised if the
scream is sometimes a theory
Robert Louis Stevenson, Virginibus Puerisque, 1881.

6.1 Simulation Methods

Historians and students of scientific method know that scientists evaluate hypotheses and theories comparatively, not in isolation (Kuhn 1977; Salmon 1990). In the early stages of the development of a new field, many hypotheses may be proposed. Scientists generally seek to narrow down the range of potential hypotheses while increasing their precision. Nevertheless, attempts to improve the empirical adequacy of theories via experiments sometimes lead to further hypotheses, introduced to protect other, more fundamental assumptions of a theory. For example, evidence against the existence of luminiferous ether arose through Michelson and Morley's experiments, which were designed to produce a definitive empirical support for this core assumption of the wave theory of light. The Lorentz-Fitzgerald contraction hypothesis was introduced to *save* the ontological commitment to the ether in the face of this evidence because the ether was considered essential to the wave theory of light (Swenson 1972; Siegel 1981).

In order to capture a scientist's view of the world we have introduced the notion of a confidence profile (Gooding and Addis 1999). This is a set of values representing an agent's confidence or belief in each of a range of hypotheses. Some of these will be alternatives to others and, where they are sufficiently specific, some may also contradict others. Scientists inhabit a changing world of information-bearing experiments and social interactions, so the probability of a particular hypothesis being true must reflect both empirical information and the opinions of others, as well as the probability of other hypotheses that make up the current view of the world. This probability is calculated dynamically in the light of the results of experiments and consultations. We use a modified version of Bayes' Rule to calculate the impact of recent evidence, converting an observed experimental result into a set of modifiers for a confidence profile. Note that we will not use Bayes' Rule, as is normally the case, to calculate the accumulated evidence for a hypothesis.

© Springer International Publishing Switzerland 2014
T. Addis, *Natural and Artificial Reasoning,* Advanced Information
and Knowledge Processing, DOI 10.1007/978-3-319-11286-2_6

We first consider the Bayesian equation from the point of view of an agent who performs experiments in order to determine which hypothesis (or model) is most likely. We determine the confidence in a hypothesis H 'given' (shown as '/') a result R_e from an experiment 'e' thus:

$$E_{n-1}(H/R_e) = E_{n-1}(R_e/H)/E_{n-1}(R_e)$$

where

$$E_{n-1}(R_e/H) = [E_{n-1}(H) * P(R_e/H)]$$

- $P(R_e/H)$ is the a priori probability that R_e will occur given the hypothesis H for a given experiment 'e' as perceived by an agent.
- $E_{n-1}(H)$ is the confidence that an agent has in a hypothesis H at time $n-1$. The confidence value ranges from 0 to 1 and represents the probability of the agent acting as though H is the only hypothesis.

This generic equation represents a personalized view of the world for a specific agent. (For simplicity, we present these equations in a generic rather than in an agent-specific form). Here R_e is the result of an experiment 'e' given H. The expected result for any experiment will depend upon the perceived probability of each hypothesis and an a priori understanding of the probability of a result for the hypothesis supposing it reflected the behaviour of the world at the time of the experiment. The confidence profile reflects only past experience. In order to represent an agent's overall view of the world we must also calculate a unified value that characterises the agent's expectations about the outcomes of future experiments. In particular, we can determine an agent's view of the expected result for the its set of beliefs in all hypotheses as $E_{n-1}(R_e)$.

6.2 Confidence Adjustment

Many have argued the advantages of a Bayesian approach to the understanding of theory-selection in scientific change. Central to Salmon's argument for Bayesian methods is the contention of post-Kuhnian philosophy of science, that formal, hypothetico-deductive methodologies cannot provide a rational account of theory change in science (Kuhn 1977; Salmon 1990, p. 258;). Although our dynamic model of belief-revision incorporates a Bayesian calculation, and we retain the Bayesian assumption of the independence of each item of evidence, our model is *not* Bayesian. This is because:

- *First*, whereas Bayes' Rule assumes a constant and unchanging world we are simulating the impact of a world in which even what counts as evidence can change; hence the need for flexible (irrational) sets of descriptors. We take the view that changes in the world will be gradual relative to the number of events that can occur during an inference cycle. A useful feature of our model is that it

allows us to specify the impact of recent evidence and consultation for each agent.
This allows a hypothesis to remain available for consideration despite a run of
apparently falsifying observations (for example see Gooding and Addis 2004).
This important virtue is in keeping with scientific practice (see, e.g., Kuhn 1977;
Lakatos 1970).
* *Second*, we reject the Bayesian assumption that the order in which events occur is
  irrelevant, insofar as changes in belief will change the set of hypotheses available
  for the interpretation of results (see Sect. 6.4).

Changes in belief can be induced by consultation as well as experimental evidence.
So different sequences of action performed by the agent will produce different patterns of belief-revision in that agent (Gooding and Addis 2004). Even in the case of
a single (non-consulting) agent, the order in which evidence appears is not predetermined. Iterative, simulation-based methods allow us to explore the effects of what
sociologists of science call 'contingency' (Knorr-Cetina 1975). Thus, they offer a
huge advantage over single-step discussions of the implications of a particular inference rule or confirmation strategy applied to a single sequence of events (Gooding
and Addis 2004).

6.3   The Impact of Evidence: Hypotheses

It follows that we cannot use an inductive inference rule (such as Bayes rule) to
calculate the accumulation of evidence for a hypothesis. There is a long tradition
(dating from the work of Ramsey and de Finetti in the 1930s) of associating disbe-
lief with a prior probability of (or near) zero and certainty with a probability near
one. However, hypotheses do not achieve absolute certainty and they should always
remain hypothetical; scientists will re-classify them as a necessary postulate (as in
the case of the luminiferous ether), as a principle (as both Galilean-Newtonian and
Einsteinian relativity were), or as facts (e.g., elements transmute, species mutate).
Nor can a hypothesis be wholly, irretrievably disbelieved and still be hypothetical;
without belief, a hypothesis will be re-labelled as an artefact, a fiction or non-fact,
as a non-existent entity (phlogiston, the ether), or as a false (though once-believed)
principle (e.g., the immutability of chemical elements and of biological species).

To call something a hypothesis, H is to say that there is some empirical support for
H given evidence R_e. This support is $E_{n-1}(H/R_e)$, and is a value that lies between 0
and 1 for each hypothesis H. Given a new result R_e from carrying out an experiment
'e', the probability which represents an agent's confidence concerning a particular
hypothesis can be modified to $E_n(H)$ by adapting the above equation to the following
one (see Addis 1985, p. 260):

$$E_n(H) = [(N - 1)E_{n-1}(H) + E_{n-1}(H/R_e)]/N$$

We can thus define a concept *flexibility* which ranges from 0 to 1 for each agent such that:

$$\text{flexibility} = 1/N$$

Flexibility represents an agent's responsiveness to new observational evidence. Flexibility is considered to approximate to a window of N events within which belief has adapted to the current position. The larger the window the less responsive the agent becomes to the current event.

6.4   The Impact of Opinion: Consultation

We assume that one agent consulting another is equivalent to accessing the consulted agent's complete range of confidence values. This access has the effect of modifying the consulting agent's confidence in each hypothesis as if it had performed its own experiment. (Bayes' Rule is not applied in consultations; it is needed only to update confidences based on experimental results). The confidence value of each of the hypotheses, which make up the consulting agents belief profile, will be modified according to the following equation:

$$E_n(H) = [(M - 1)E_{n-1}(H) + E_{n-1}(H_{\text{Consultee}})]/M$$

M ranges from 1 to infinity. The larger M, the smaller the effect any evidence has on the change in confidence. We can thus define concept receptivity. This ranges from 0 to 1 for each agent as:

$$\text{receptivity} = 1/M$$

Receptivity reflects the consulting agent's receptiveness to the beliefs of any consultee.

6.5   A Simple Example of Confidence Adjustment

Given a coin that is to be tossed, we might consider two possible hypotheses:

- **H1**. The coin is good (e.g., has both a head and a tail)
- **H2**. The coin is double headed (or tailed)

Result	P (Result/H1)	P (Result/H2)
Heads	0.5	1.0
Tails	0.5	0.0

According to Peirce, knowing that one of these hypotheses is true "makes the world a less surprising place". Treating entropy as a form of a measure of surprise, as did

Shannon and Weaver, we can calculate the difference made by 'knowing' H2 is the case from the difference in entropy of the two situations:

$$\text{Entropy of H1} = -(0.5\text{Log}_2(0.5) + 0.5\text{Log}_2(0.5))$$
$$= -((-0.5) + (-0.5)$$
$$= 1\text{bit}$$

$$\text{Entropy of H2} = -(1.0\text{Log}_2(1.0) + 0.0\text{Log}_2(0.0))$$
$$= -((-0.0) + (-0.0)$$
$$= 0 \text{ bit}$$

So the difference made by 'knowing H2 rather than H1 is the case' is $(1-0) = 1$ bit.

The effect of the new information is mediated by an agent's current beliefs about the world. Suppose an agent's initial confidence has in each of these hypotheses is:

Agent	
$E_{n-1}(\text{H1})$	0.8
$E_{n-1}(\text{H2})$	0.2
Total	1.0

Then we can calculate the effect of an experiment (tossing the coin) as follows. Using:

$$E_{n-1}(\text{H/Re}) = E_{n-1}(\text{Re/H})/E_{n-1}(\text{Re})$$

Agent			
$E_{n-1}(\text{R}_e/\text{H}) =$ $En - 1(\text{H}) * P(\text{Re/H})$	E (Head/H)	E (Tail/H)	Total
$E_{n-1}(\textbf{H1}) * \textbf{P(Result/H1)}$	0.8 * 0.5 = **0.4**	0.8 * 0.5 = **0.4**	**0.8**
$E_{n-1}(\textbf{H2}) * \textbf{P(Result/H2)}$	0.2 * 1.0 = **0.2**	0.2 * 0.0 = **0.0**	**0.2**
$E(\text{R}_e)$	**0.6**	**0.4**	**1.0**

We can then calculate:

Agent		
$E_n(\text{H/R}_e)$	Head occurs	Tail occurs
$E_n(\textbf{H1/R}_e)$	0.4/0.6 = **0.67**	0.4/0.4 = **1.0**
$E_n(\textbf{H2/R}_e)$	0.2/0.6 = **0.33**	0.0/0.4 = **0.0**
Total	**1.0**	**1.0**

So from the update-equation we have:

$$E_n(H) = [(N - 1)E_{n-1}(H) + E_{n-1}(H/R_e)]$$

If we let $N = 4$ so that

$$(N - 1)/N = 3/4 = 0.75$$

and also
$1/N = 0.25$ for an agent's flexibility then:

Agent $E_n(H)$	Head occurs	Tail occurs
$E_n(H1)$	$0.75 * 0.8 + 0.25 * 0.67 = \mathbf{0.77}$	$0.75 * 0.8 + 0.25 * 1.0 = \mathbf{0.85}$
$E_n(H2)$	$0.75 * 0.2 + 0.25 * 0.33 = \mathbf{0.23}$	$0.75 * 0.2 + 0.25 * 0.0 = \mathbf{0.15}$
Total	**1.0**	**1.0**

It is important to note that whereas on a purely Bayesian model the appearance of a tail could eliminate the belief that the coin is double headed (H2), our model does not produce this conclusion. This response is not as irrational as it might appear: it keeps open the possibility of alternative explanations (e.g. that there has been a switch of the coin, say, for a double-tailed coin, or an observational error). This is more like what is required for the abductive cycle and for scientific investigation in general (Tweney 1985; Matthews 2004).

6.6   Confidence, Indifference and Change

The number of hypotheses actively considered by scientists varies. During the exploratory stages of an investigation scientists are rarely in a position to consider just two well-defined alternative hypotheses. Nevertheless, the tendency is always to reduce the number of hypotheses in play, and to make them as specific as possible. This means that confidence in a particular hypothesis is affected, not only by experiments and consultations, but also by the number of hypotheses available for consideration.

In order to allow for changing numbers of hypotheses, we introduce a dynamic threshold, the indifference value. This defines hypotheses that are under active consideration (or are believed to be possibilities). Thus, we have a variable set of hypotheses that implicates a changing ontology and phenomenology.

To calculate the indifference value we need a function that changes smoothly between limiting values and is easily to calculate for any number of different hypotheses. A quantity that suits our purpose and varies in time as required is the inverse of entropy.

Entropy indicates an expectation; it is a measure of the 'surprise' value of an event. Here 'surprise' is measured as the log of the inverse probability of that event (or $-\log_2 p$). So:

$$\text{Surprise} = -\log_2 \cdot p$$

In information theory, entropy (given by $-\sum p \log_2 p$) is the *average degree of certainty* (surprise) of being able to predict the next bit of information in a stream, e.g. the next character in a string of characters. (The logarithmic scale used in keeping with other human sense sensitivities (Shannon and Weaver 1949). So:

> The more unlikely the event the greater the surprise.

We use this in a general measure of an agent's confidence about its current view of the world and its ability to respond correctly to event n. In the equation below we will use 'A' and subscript 'a' to denote a particular agent. Because the hypotheses under consideration in this example will be assumed mutually exclusive, the average surprise will increase as an agent becomes more confident about a smaller number of hypotheses. We call this general confidence measure for an agent the *model entropy*. The term model denotes the set of hypotheses that make up the agent's view of the world. Model entropy is given by:

$$\text{Entropy}(\text{Agent}_a) = -_a \sum_H E_n(H_a) * \text{Log}_2(E_n(H_a))$$

and from this we can obtain an inverse of the entropy which gives an expected value for $E_n(H)$. This will be denoted by $I_n(A)$. $I_n(A)$ will be called an *Indifference Threshold* for the agent A at event (time) n:

$$\text{IndifferenceThreshold}(a, n) = -\log_2{}^{-1}(\text{Entropy}_n(A_a))$$

$$= I_n(A)$$

The expression $E_n(H)$ is the expected probability of a hypothesis. Values of $E_n(H)$ above $I_n(A)$ are considered to be significant, i.e., the hypothesis is actively believed by the agent[1].

$I_n(A)$ can be treated as a generic confidence over all the hypotheses. If we consider the case that all hypotheses had this confidence value as one possible state that could occur we can say that the agent is *indifferent* to them all, thus the name *Indifference Threshold*. $I_n(A)$ indicates a level of general confidence an agent has about its view of the world at time n.

---

[1] Since most of the calculations are done by natural logarithms, it is useful to note that: $2^x = e^{(x.\log 2)}$

We will propose that the agent says it *believes* in all those hypotheses that have a greater confidence value than I_n (A) and *disbelieves* all hypotheses that have a lesser value.

Therefore, from our simple example with the coins we have:

Initially (before the coin toss):

Agent 1s belief in

$$H1 = 0.4 + 0.4 = 0.8$$

And its belief in

$$H2 = 0.2 + 0.0 = 0.2$$

So :

$$\text{Entropy (Agent)} = -(0.8 * \text{Log}_2(0.8) + 0.2 * \text{Log}_2(0.2))$$
$$= 0.26 + 0.46$$
$$= 0.72$$

Since we require our indifference threshold to be in terms of a probability but the entropy measure is in terms of a log of a probability then this result needs to be converted. So the *indifference threshold* **I** will be the:

$$\{\text{inverse} - \log_2(\mathbf{0.72})\}, = \mathbf{0.61}(\text{approximately}).$$

This is because:

$$-\text{Log}_2(\mathbf{0.61})\text{is approximately equal to } \mathbf{0.72}.$$

If a **tail** occurs then Agent 1's belief in **H1** and **H2** becomes:

$$\text{Entropy (Agent)} = -(0.85 * \text{Log}_2(0.85) + 0.15 * \text{Log}_2(0.15))$$
$$= 0.2 + 0.41$$
$$= 0.61$$

The indifference threshold I will be **0.66** since $-\text{Log}_2 (\mathbf{0.66}) = \mathbf{0.61}$ (approximately).

We can say that when the result of the coin toss is tails, the general agent's confidence has gone up from 0.61 to 0.66. Given a string of **tails** this confidence will eventually reach 1.0, whence the remaining hypothesis (H1 in this case) would be re-designated as a fact. Nevertheless, in our game theory model the agent is not so certain of the world that it never acts to test for alternative hypotheses. No matter how 'certain' they become of a hypothesis, the agents in our model remain open to conflicting (negative) evidence. (For examples, see Gooding and Addis 2004).

6.7 Agents and Groups

The aim of every agent is to raise its general confidence in some view of the world by discovering facts about the world. A group of agents has a similar aim; to obtain new information to minimize their collective uncertainty about the world. For a collection of agents a similar group-confidence value can be derived from the Group Entropy:

$$\text{Entropy(Grp)} = \sum_A \sum_H \sum_n (H/A) * \{\text{Log}_2(E_n(H/A)) - \text{Log}(|A|)\}/ |A|$$

This expression represents the expected result of a single sampling of the confidence in any hypothesis of an agent randomly chosen from the group.

Similarly, the inverse of the group entropy represents the significance threshold for the group of agents in terms of an expected probability. We can also calculate the inverses of entropy for an agent $I(A)$, a group of agents $I(G)$ and for a set of experiments $I(E(A))$ as perceived by a single agent or a group of agents $I(E(G))$, where an experiment 'e' is defined in terms of the probabilities of results R that are considered possible for a given range of hypotheses H.

These dynamic threshold values are independent of the number of hypotheses or experiments, so we can define the indifference level of a group of actors independently of particular hypotheses that happen to be in play. This is important for two reasons. It allows us to use these dynamic values in agent-based decision-making about the next action to take (see Sect. 6.6). It also allows us to represent the processes whereby scientists respond to changing evidence by altering their view of the world, e.g. a hypothesis changes from being a mere possibility, to being considered plausible, to being generally accepted and, finally, coming to have the status of a fact, law or principle. If all hypotheses were to be eliminated except one, both $I(A)$ and $E(A)$ would equal unity (implying certainty). If this happens, it can be said of the agents that they are both indifferent to the hypothesis as well as certain of it.

6.8 The Choice of an Action

6.8.1 Evaluating Actions

Agents decide whether to experiment or to consult by evaluating each of the possibilities offered by each kind of action. We represent an experimental setup as a table of real numbers that indicate the a priori probability of a result occurring, given that a hypothesis (or model) is a correct description of the world's constraints. We refer to the hypothesis that is active within a simulation run as the objective model. Simulated experiments have those outcomes that are most probable in a world in which the objective model is true (see Gooding and Addis 1999). This list of occurrence probabilities defines each possible experiment. The list will sum to unity for each hypothesis, since at least one of the results must occur in a world of which that model is the best available description. Experiments differ in producing different sets of results, so where the set of occurrence probabilities for an experiment is the same for any hypotheses, it is the same experiment, regardless of the physical apparatus used.

In our model, the choice of an experiment is derived from its effectiveness, as perceived by an agent, in discriminating between hypotheses. This choice is governed by the agent's initial confidence $E_{n-1}(H)$. We represent an agent's view of an experiment by the entropy, represented for each experiment as:

$$\text{Entropy}(e) = \sum R_e \sum_m H_m\{E_{n-1}(R_e/H_m)\} * \text{Log2}(E_{n-1}(R_e/H_m))$$

This equation describes the confidence of a result given a hypothesis as perceived by an agent, i.e. the choice of experiment is affected by an agent's bias. The experiment with the lowest entropy is the experiment most likely to be chosen by the agent in that it will have the clearest and most decisive results for supporting or negating each of the hypotheses in the agent's confidence-profile. Thus, the choice reflects both a property of the experiment and a property of the experimenter.

Even so, the experiment with the lowest entropy is 'most likely' to be selected. This is because the actions of agents are governed, Monte Carlo fashion, by a probability distribution based upon belief, and because we apply game theory in the decision procedure (Luce and Raiffa 1957). Suppose in our simple example we choose to 'ask' for a head or a tail. Then allowing for mishearing, we could write a table of probabilities for H1 thus:

Hypothesis: the coin is good—H1	Head	Tail	No response
Exp1: Ask for a Head	0.9	0.05	0.05
Exp2: Ask for a Tail	0.05	0.9	0.05

But even with mishearings for H2 we would have:

Hypothesis: the coin is double headed—H2	Head	Tail	No response
Exp1: Ask for a Head	0.9	0.00	0.1
Exp2: Ask for a Tail	0.1	0.0	0.9

The initial beliefs of the agent about the different hypotheses is as before:

Agent	
$E_{n-1}(H1)$	0.8
$E_{n-1}(H2)$	0.2
Total	1.0

The experimental setup (here, calling for a coin to be tossed) is defined by a table of real numbers. To obtain a vector of expectations we multiply an agent's *confidence*

profile by the matrix representing the result probabilities of all experiments that are
possible. This calculation generates a *biased perception* for each agent of each of the
experiments. The results can now be made into expectations of results for the agent
thus:

0.8 * Hypothesis: the coin is good—H1	Head	Tail	No response
Exp1: Ask for a Head	0.72	0.04	0.4
Exp2: Ask for a Tail	0.4	0.72	0.4

* multiply

0.2 * Hypothesis: the coin is good—H1	Head	Tail	No response
Exp1: Ask for a Head	0.18	0.0	0.02
Exp2: Ask for a Tail	0.04	0.0	0.16

* multiply

Note that the total confidence over both hypotheses for each experiment is equal to
one. So for the agent we have:

Exp 1

$$= -\{0.72 * \text{Log}_2 (0.72) + 0.04 * \text{Log}_2 (0.04) + 0.04 * \text{Log}_2 (0.04)$$
$$+ 0.18 * \text{Log}_2 (0.18) + 0.0 * \text{Log}_2 (0.0) + 0.02 * \text{Log}_2 (0.02)\}$$
$$= 1.27 \ (\text{entropy for H1 and H2})$$
$$\text{I (Exp 1)} = 0.41 \ (\text{approximately})$$

Exp2

$$= -\left(0.04 * \text{Log}_2 (0.04) + 0.72 * \text{Log}_2 (0.72) + 0.04 * \text{Log}_2 (0.04)\right.$$
$$\left. +0.04 * \text{Log}_2 (0.04) + 0.0 * \text{Log}_2 (0.0) + 0.16 * \text{Log}_2 (0.16)\right)$$
$$= 1.32 \ (\text{entropy for H1 and H2})$$
$$\text{I (Exp 2)} = 0.40 \ (\text{approximately})$$

Taking this criterion alone, experiment 1 ("Ask for a Head") is a marginally better
choice because it has lower entropy. However, according to the logic of falsification
that many have attributed to science (Popper 1959; Wason 1960; Lakatos 1970), this
is not the best experiment to choose. The exposure of a Tail would eliminate H2, so
we ought to "Ask for a Tail". There is a way of avoiding an apparent conflict between
confirmatory- and non-confirmatory strategies so that our agents can employ both.
The clue is to note that the Indifference levels (0.40, 0.41) do not sum to unity. This
suggests that these 'probabilities' are not giving the complete story. Something more
needs to be done.

Our agents do not update their beliefs in a simple Bayesian fashion. In the most general terms, a Bayesian agent moves through time and evidence having a set of beliefs. Each time it learns a new fact, the agent revises its degree of belief in each hypothesis by adapting to the new fact. For a Bayesian agent, 'confirmation' is analogous to a new fact making a hypothesis more probable than it was before; 'disconfirmation' is analogous to new evidence making a hypothesis less probable than before. Close analysis of scientists' behaviour suggests that they sometimes behave as Bayesians (Gooding and Addis 2004), however, recent evidence shows that this is not the only factor at work.

6.9   Choosing Actions

In what we have modelled, each agent perceives the potential outcome of an experiment differently because each has a different confidence profile, just as in real life. It follows from our definition of an experiment that each agent perceives a subtly different experiment being performed. The result of the multiplication (belief profile × result probabilities) is then used to modify each agent's a priori confidence value for each hypothesis. The degree of modification to the belief profile depends upon the agent's flexibility (see Sect. 6.2.1). A similar process occurs when there is a decision to consult another agent rather than experiment. The cycle of learning through consultation is similar to that for an experiment, except that there is no need to involve Bayes' Rule because the confidence values in the profiles of consulters and consultees are already expressed in the same terms; that is belief or perceived probability.

The Peircian, pragmatic notion of belief implies that the numerical confidence value attached to each hypothesis by an agent represents the probability, given available each state of affairs, of its performing an action. Under certain conditions Game Theory favours a 'mixed strategy' approach where a mix of actions are tried according to some probability distribution (Luce and Raffia 1957, pp. 67–70). We use an agent's belief profile to calculate personalised *entropies* for each experiment (see Evaluating Actions). The decision mechanism deploys this profile as a set of probabilities to act. We will illustrate this using the simple coin experiment.

Indifference represents the expected probability of an event (as implied by a hypothesis). The gain for choosing 'correctly' would be increased confidence in one's view of the world. If we assume the expected loss for acting on a wrong belief is one unit and expected gain is zero then we can express the payoff in a two person zero sum matrix (Table 6.1, 6.2).

- I_h is the expected 'belief' that some hypothesis represents a particular state of affairs. It does not matter which hypothesis, since this represents an average.
- Expected Gain in Exp1 is $I_h * (0) - (1 - I_h) * (-1) = (1 - I_h)$.

The equations in Table 6.1 can be generalized for any number of hypotheses and actions.

Table 6.1 A payoff matrix for a 'two person zero sum' game

Action (frequency)	Expected hypothesis	Expected NOT hypothesis
Exp1 (f_h) Ask for Head	$I_h * (0)$	$(1 - I_h) * (-1)$
Exp2 (f_t) Ask for Tail	$I_t * (0)$	$(1 - I_t) * (-1)$

Table 6.2 An example of a payoff matrix

Action (frequency)	Expected hypothesis	Expected NOT hypothesis
Exp1 (f_h) Ask for Head	$0.41 * (0)$	$0.59 * (-1)$
Exp2 (f_t) Ask for Tail	$0.40 * (0)$	$0.60 * (-1)$

We iterate this mixed strategy in each cycle of the belief-revision process. Inclusion of this strategy makes the application of game theory to science and to learning more appropriate than a single-step decision procedure would be. If f_h is the frequency of applying the strategy 'ask-for-head' and f_t is the frequency of 'ask for tail', then we can calculate for each actor the gain (maximum-security or minimum possible loss) between the agent's two options, as:

$$f_h = (1 - I_t)/[(1 - I_h) + (1 - I_t)]$$
$$= 0.59/[0.59 + 0.60]$$
$$= 0.496$$
$$f_t = 1 - f_h$$
$$= 0.504$$

So for optimum results the frequency of 'Ask for a Head' should be **0.496** and 'Ask for a Tail' should be **0.504**. Having only a slight bias towards asking for head reflects the strong prior belief that the coin is good; the coin is fair. This course of action would be more rational than asking for a tail every time, given that the agent believes that the coin is good.

The above equations are extended to deal with decisions about which experiment to perform or which agent to consult. Agents evaluate a distribution of choices in order to select those most likely to maximize the gain (confidence in the overall view of the world). A consultee is chosen by extending the calculations to consider the entropy of every pair of agents', including the agent making the decision, average confidence in each hypothesis. Self-consultation then becomes an option. As with evaluating experiments, the payoff should invoke a 'maximum security' level from the entropy pairings. So an agent's best bet is to decide which other agent it is to be influenced by in order to gain a greater overall confidence. The mechanism of a 'conversation', where agents infer each other's internal views of music, has been investigated by Addis and Billinge (2004) and described in Chap. 13.

Fig. 6.1 Agent 'Tom' starts
with belief that the coin is
good (*red line*) but is
persuaded by the evidence
that the coin is double
headed. Note that the *green*
line (mislabelled
'actor-entropy') actually plots
the Indifference level

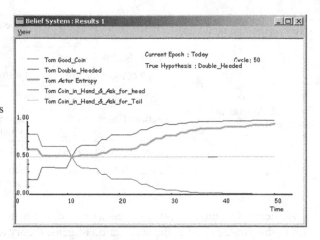

Fig. 6.2 Agent 'David' starts
with an unbiased view

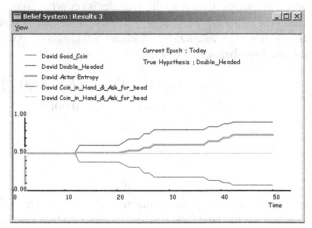

6.10   Running the Program

The belief revision program that implements this model was run using our simple
example for three agents. In this simulation the agents have no communication with
each other. Their flexibility and receptivity (Sect. 6.2.1 and 6.2.2) was 0.25 as in our
illustrative example. However, all agents had access to all the experiments (two in
this simple case). The agent 'Tom' started with the 'belief' of 0.8 in 'good coin' and
a belief of 0.2 for a 'double-headed coin'. A typical run is shown in (Fig. 6.1) where
Tom's overall confidence level falls at first then rises as more evidence is obtained.

Figure 6.2 shows agent 'David' starting with no bias. The number of cycles needed
to develop a suspicion that the coin is double headed varies but is typically about
eight cycles.

Fig. 6.3 Agent 'Jan' starts with a positive bias

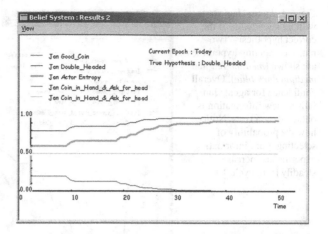

Agent 'Jan' in Fig. 6.2 believes 0.2 that the coin is good and 0.8 that it is double headed. The result is a steady increase in confidence towards the final conclusion that it is a 'fact'.

The flat centre plotlines in these figures indicate that in all cases the actions 'Ask for head' and 'Ask for tail' remain equally likely (probability of 0.5). From an information point of view the options are about the same, no matter what the agent's belief might be. This is due to the simplicity of the situation. In more complex cases a genuine bias between the actions will become apparent as belief changes (see Gooding and Addis 2004) (Fig. 6.3).

6.11 Other Examples

We have also run this simulation using an extension of Wason's four-card problem (Wason 1960; Wason and Shapiro 1971). In the original task sets of four cards are displayed, two showing integers and two characters (e.g., A, D, 4, 7). The subject is asked to turn a card (or cards) to show that the rule 'An even number implies a vowel on the other side'. Wason was testing whether subjects reasoned so as to falsify the rule (so the expected action is to turn an even number and just one other card (Johnson-Laird and Wason 1977)). We adapt this problem by providing our agents with 100 cards and, in some scenarios, access to other agents. Each card represents a possible experiment, although there are only four distinct choices (to turn a vowel, a consonant, an odd or an even). The entropy-driven mixed strategy (see Evaluation Actions—Choosing Actions) implies that the rule should be discovered with a minimum number of turns.

This scenario allows for ten possible logically distinct rules (or hypotheses; see Addis and Gooding 1999, pp. 23–24). The simulated agents 'home in' on the correct rule within ten or so moves (see Fig. 6.4). They also correctly eliminate the redundant

Fig. 6.4 Agent 'Jan' starts
with no knowledge of the
correct hypothesis. Two
major competing hypotheses
are shown (*medium red* and
medium dark blue). Overall
confidence for agent 'Jan'
falls as new information is
obtained then rises. Notice
how the probability of
selecting more informative
experiments increases
steadily from cycle 10

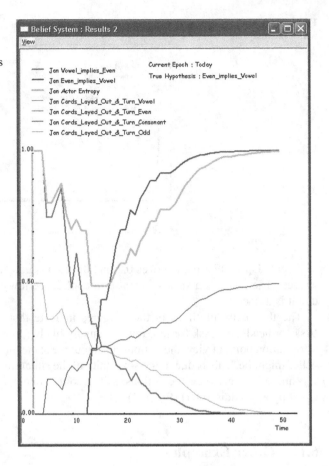

actions (e.g. A, 7), reducing their probability to a very low value. There is a corresponding increase in the probability of selecting the best moves (e.g. D, 4). Figure 6.4 also illustrates the effect of biasing an agent against the correct rule by initiating a run with Jan's confidence in the correct rule set at zero. This makes a different set of actions more probable, so that the agent Jan is less likely to discover the correct rule in the early stages. However, agent 'Jan' gets to know about the 'correct' hypothesis from fellow agents. As soon as this new hypothesis is recognised Jan's confidence increases, different cards are selected and the 'new' idea takes rapid hold.

6.12   Belief and Truth

If agents are prevented from consulting, they take longer to arrive at a correct outcome than agents that combine experiments with consultation. This endorses the post-Kuhnian view that science is an inherently social process. Consultation also moderates the impact of evidence: agents with high flexibility (i.e. great sensitivity to recent events) display more erratic behaviour than similarly flexible agents that consult (Chap. 7 and Gooding and Addis 2004). As Fig. 6.1 indicates, a strong negative bias can be overcome. However, three things are needed:

1. frequent consultation (to be made aware of new information, as illustrated in Fig. 6.4),
2. a strong commitment to an alternative view held by at least some participants (so that peer pressure alone does not force a consensus—see Fig. 6.4, where the actor-entropy (indifference) dips before rising steadily),
3. experimental evidence supporting an alternative view during the time of change.

The three-part inference system of abduction, deduction and induction as defined by Peirce takes into account the possibility of change and error. For this to work, no particular form of inference can act alone. Deduction unaided cannot deal with the irrational sets needed to capture the phenomenology of a changing world and of human responses to it. We have not used the abductive cycle strictly as a hypothesis generator (Gooding 1996; Hanson 1958; Magnani 1998, 2001). Rather, we have emulated abduction through look-up tables representing the experimental phenomenology for each hypothesis. These models differ inferentially and cognitively, but from a functional point of view, the two methods are indistinguishable (Addis 2000). For either method of implementation to work, abduction also needs to be made part of a larger system of different, interacting inference and decision mechanisms. In such an inference-system, the notion of 'Truth' is confined to the internal workings of deduction. In its place, we have 'Belief'—the confidence an individual has in statements that influence his or her actions—as a dynamic indicator of the evaluation of a particular worldview. The notion of 'belief' as a propensity to act displaces truth. A consequence of our approach is that actions that would be deemed irrational according to traditional models of inference and of ontology can be valuable in that they help agents continually test the world for change.

References

Addis TR (1985) Designing knowledge-based systems. Kogan Page, New York
Addis TR (2000) Stone soup: identifying intelligence through construction. Kybernetes 29:849–870
Addis TR, Gooding DC (1999) Learning as collective belief-revision: simulating reasoning about disparate phenomena. proceedings AISB'99 Symposium on Scientific Creativity, University of Edinburgh, pp 19–28
Addis T, Billinge D (2004) 'Music to our ears: a required paradigm shift in computer science' presented at ECAP04. University of Pavia, Italy
Addis TR, Gooding DC (2004, 2008) Simulationmethods for an abductive systemin science. MBR04: model-based reasoning. Science and engineering, abduction, visualization, and simulation. University of Pavia, Italy, December, 2004. Also in Foundations of Science, March 2008. Vol. 13, No 1, pp 37–52

Johnson-Laird PN, Wason PC (1977) A theoretical analysis of insight into a reasoning task. In: Johnson-Laird PN, Wason PC (eds) Thinking: readings in cognitive science. Cambridge University Press, Cambridge, pp 143–157

Knorr-Cetina K (1975) The manufacture of knowledge. Pergamon Press, Oxford

Kuhn TS (1977) Objectivity, value judgement and theory choice. In: Kuhn (ed) pp 320–339

Lakatos I (1970) Falsification and the methodology of scientific research programmes. In: Lakatos I, Musgrave A (eds) Criticism and the growth of knowledge. Cambridge University Press, Cambridge, pp 91–196

Luce RD, Raiffa H (1957) Games and decisions: introduction and critical survey. Wiley, New York

Matthews R (2004) Opposites detract. New Sci 181(2438):39–43

Popper KR (1959) The logic of scientific discovery. Routledge, London

Salmon W (1990) Rationality and objectivity in science or Tom Kuhn meets Tom Bayes. In: Savage CW (ed) Scientific theories. University of Minnesota Press, Minneapolis, pp 175–204

Shannon CE, Weaver W (1964) The mathematical theory of communication. University of Illinois Press, Urbana (first published 1949)

Siegel DM (1981) Thomson, Maxwell and the universal ether in Victorian physics. In: Cantor GN, Hodge MJ (eds) Conceptions of ether. Cambridge University Press, Cambridge, pp 239–260

Swenson LS (1972) The etherial ether: a history of the Michelson, Morley, Miller experiments. University of Texas Press, Austin

Tweney RD (1985) Faraday's discovery of induction: a cognitive approach. In: Gooding D, James F (eds) Faraday rediscovered. Macmillan, London, pp 189–209

Gooding DC (1996) Creative rationality: towards an abductive model of scientific change. In: Meheus J (ed) Philosophica: creativity, rationality and scientific change, vol 58. pp 73–101

Gooding DC, Addis TR (1999) A simulation of model = based reasoning about disparate phenomena. In: Manani L, Nersessian NJ, Thagard P (eds) Scientific discovery: model-based reasoning. Kluwer Academic, New York, pp 103–123

Gooding DC, Addis TR (2004, 2008) 'Modelling scientific experiments as mediating models', MBR04 Proceedings. In: Magnani L (ed) MBR'04 proceedings. Reproduced in foundations of science, vol 13, Number 1, March 2008

Hanson NR (1958) Patterns of discovery. Cambridge University Press, Cambridge

Magnani L (1998) Model-based creative abduction. In: Magnani et al (eds) pp 219–237

Magnani L (2001) Abduction, reason and science. Kluwer Academic, Dordrecht

Wason PC (1960) On the failure to eliminate hypotheses in a conceptual task. Q J Exp Psychol 12:129–140

Wason PC, Shapiro DA (1971) Natural and contrived experience in a reasoning problem. Q J Exp Psychol 23:63–71

Chapter 7
Simulating Belief and Action

Reason's last step is the recognition that there are an infinite number of things which are beyond it

Pascal, Pensées, 1670.

7.1 Modelling Inferences About Observations

In Chap. 6 we noted that the concept of 'truth' was limited to deductive inference only. For other kinds of inference we have introduced the new concept of 'belief' to replace 'truth'. Our approach is now to represent experiments with a computer model that allows for variability in four key components of the scientific process:

- *hypotheses* which are 'believed' or 'disbelieved' by agents,
- where each hypothesis implicates a *phenomenology*
- that the agents produce by performing *experiments*
- made up of *procedures and apparatus.*

Thus, we have the interacting sets of hypotheses, results and experiments. The membership of each set can vary according to the hypotheses favoured by the agents. An example illustrates the approach.

In Gruber's shadow box experiments, subjects are able to see an image that is a 2-D shadow projection of an object hidden inside it (Fig. 7.1). Different subjects may see different shapes cast as different projections of the object (Gruber 1985). A cylindrical object can project a circle (endways), a rectangle (sideways), or a range of capsule shapes (by oblique projection). Gruber was testing subjects' ability to modify a construction based on their own perception (e.g., of a circular shape) by the different perception of another subject (e.g. a triangular shape). This required individuals to set aside the implicit presumption of the superiority of their own perceptions (Gooding 1990). In some cases subjects could generate a correct solution only by exchanging observations and conjectures with other subjects. Gruber found that adults are better at collaboration (trusting the observations of others) than adolescents or children, and that few subject groups generated more than one construct, even for simple (implied) objects.

We use tables to relate such constructs (hypotheses) to the observations (data) via the probability of observing (say) a triangle if the box contains (say) a cone. The box works by projection so the simplest phenomenology will be that of a perfectly

© Springer International Publishing Switzerland 2014
T. Addis, *Natural and Artificial Reasoning,* Advanced Information and Knowledge Processing, DOI 10.1007/978-3-319-11286-2_7

Fig. 7.1 A shadowbox is where subjects may exchange information about images in order to identify an object from its *shadow* projection(s)

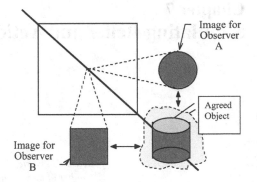

Table 7.1 Relationship between a set of observations and a set of hypothesized objects

Phenomenology hypothesized objects	Circle	Triangle	Square	Point-circle (oblique)	Circle-point (oblique)	Point-square (oblique)	Square-point (oblique)	Items in phenom-enology
Sphere	Yes	No	No	No	No	No	No	1
Cone	Yes	Yes	No	Yes	Yes	No	No	4
Pyramid	No	Yes	Yes	No	No	Yes	Yes	4
Objects implied	2	2	1	1	1	1	1	–

symmetrical object. A sphere has only one 2-D projection, a circle (see Table 7.1). But if an observer then sees, say, a triangle, the sphere hypothesis must be set aside in favour of an object (or set of objects) that could have both circular and triangular projections.

In this example, the experimental procedure is rudimentary. Making an experiment involves looking at one or more faces of the box. This approximates to the epistemic ideal of direct (i.e. unmediated) observation. Since the phenomenology can be described using simple, ordinary language descriptors, the example also eliminates another source of complexity in science, miscommunication. Nevertheless, the example illustrates the essentials of our approach: subjects make *experiments* that mediate between two partially defined domains: a variable set of *hypotheses* and a variable set of *phenomena*. They can also *communicate* with other subjects to acquire additional observations and hypotheses.

Table 7.1 illustrates that the cone and pyramid hypotheses have a richer phenomenology than the sphere. This makes the sphere an easier hypothesis to rule out. The Venn-diagram in Fig. 7.2 (Venn 1880) displays this phenomenology as sets of observables for each hypothesised object, showing where sets overlap or are mutually exclusive. For example, a sequence of observation reports containing anything other than a circle will rule out the sphere; similarly, observation of a square will rule out sphere and cone. The order in which observations are encountered will of course affect the pattern of belief-revision.

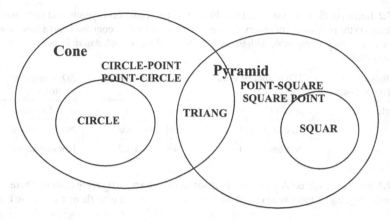

Fig. 7.2 Venn diagram illustrating unique projections (e.g., *circle* for sphere and *square* for pyramid) and the shared phenomenology of hypothesized objects (e.g., sphere and cone can both have a *circle* projection; cone and pyramid can both have a *triangle* projection)

This process of negotiating hypotheses about objects compatible with the observed projections can be specified in terms of our analogy to variable or *irrational* sets (Chap. 5, Addis and Gooding 2004). Possibilities for observation depend on which experiment is selected. But this depends in turn on which hypothesis is most believed and whether doing an experiment seems more likely to reduce an actor's uncertainty about the world than would consulting another actor. So the process is far more complex than can be captured by applying a single inference rule to a set of observations.

This process of negotiating hypotheses about objects compatible with the observed projections can be specified in terms of our analogy to variable or *irrational* sets (Chap. 5, Addis and Gooding 2004). Possibilities for observation depend on which experiment is selected. But this depends in turn on which hypothesis is most believed and whether doing an experiment seems more likely to reduce an actor's uncertainty about the world than would consulting another actor. So the process is far more complex than can be captured by applying a single inference rule to a set of observations.

7.2 Why Inference Can't be Modelled

We remarked above that the order in which observations are encountered would affect the pattern of belief-revision. This process is also influenced by the order in which an agent consults other agents. Different patterns of observation and consultation will produce different states in each of the agents. The order in which such events occur is not predictable. An iterative approach—a *simulation*—can capture this aspect of science in a way that static, structural or semantic models do not.

Table 7.2 Initial position of subject A. The table relates the constructs (hypotheses) to the observations (data) via the probability of observing (say) a triangle if the box contains (say) a cone. Each of the three constructs is compatible with the only available data, so each datum is assigned an equal probability of 1.0

Hypothesis: Observed shape:	2D: triangular card	3D: cone	3D: triangular section bar
Triangle	$p = 1.0$	$p = 1.0$	$p = 1.0$
Circle	Not envisaged	Not envisaged	Not envisaged
Cross	Not envisaged	Not envisaged	Not envisaged

Table 7.3 Position of subject A after consulting subject B, who reports seeing a circle. There is now some ambiguity, e.g. if there is a cone in the box, observation of a triangle or a circle are equally probable

Hypothesis: observed shape:	2D: triang. card	3D: cone	3D: triang. bar	2D: disc	3D: sphere	3D: rod
Triangle	1.0	0.5	1.0	0.0	0.0	0.0
Circle	0.0	0.5	0.0	1	1	1
Cross	Not seen	Not seen	Not seen	Not seen	Not seen	Not seen

Table 7.4 Position of subject A after first consulting subject C who reports seeing a cross

Hypothesis: observed shape	2D: triang. card	3D: cone	3D: triang. bar	2D: flat cross	3D: intersecting sheets
Triangle	1.0	1.0	1.0	0.0	0.0
Cross	0.0	0.0	0.0	1.0	1.0
Circle	Not seen	Not seen	Not seen	Not seen	Not seen

In Gruber's experiments, if a subject interprets a triangular shadow as being compatible with (say) 'the existence of a solid cone in the box' then this hypothesis would be ruled out by a second subject's report of a circular image. Consider the situation of one of three subjects, A, as shown in Table 7.2. A has postulated three objects compatible with the evidence. The observations of subjects B and C are not yet known. On the basis of this one observation A could postulate a 2-D object (a flat triangular card) or two 3-D objects (an opaque cone and a triangular bar).

New objects are postulated to explain new kinds of observation. Suppose A first consults B, who reports seeing a circle. A could postulate or negotiate with B the construction of three further objects (a disc, a sphere, and a rod). A's situation at this point is shown in Table 7.3.

Suppose A first consults C, who reports seeing a cross. Then, as indicated in Table 7.4, A invokes a different set of hypotheses and phenomena than if B is consulted first.

In recognising the social dimension of inference, we accept that patterns of belief revision depend not only on evidence, but also on the influence of others. This introduces order effects. Similar sets of tables would be needed for subjects B and C, detailing the pattern of construction and the probabilities of each possible observation, for every possible sequence of observation and consultation. For this very simple case the first iteration would require two observation-construction tables for each subject and could be calculated by hand. But for even a modest degree of complexity simulation methods must be used. In science there are well-defined pathways of communication and constraints on communication, but there are also many sources of contingency (Knorr-Cetina 1981). When we factor in real-science contingencies such as access to experimental setups and the accessibility of other observers, the situation becomes more complex still.

Confirmation theories and cognitive models of inference do not encounter such difficulties because they treat agents in isolation, as do experimental designs based on such models (e.g. Wason 1960). These approaches fail to represent one of the most important features of learning and belief-formation—its social character. It could be argued that scientists use rules of inference and heuristic principles that constrain variability due to social interaction and individual personality so that (say) actor A would always choose to make the most decisive experiments or to consult the most competent actors.

This objection simply reasserts an article of faith of traditional philosophies of science: for rationalists, that there are objective (i.e. universal or non-contextual) principles of reasoning about observations, and for empiricists, that evidence eventually eliminates false hypotheses in favour of the true one. A further objection might be that inference rules (other than the Bayes rule) apply only when all the evidence is in. The entire set of hypotheses and associated observations could be included in a single table that relates hypotheses to phenomena *via* sets of probabilities, representing a final state of pooled knowledge. But this requires that all actors have simultaneous access to reports of every type of observation. It would reveal nothing about the dynamics of the process according to which each actor revises its beliefs in response to each observation or consultation. Tables 7.2–7.4 illustrate a sequence whereas information is acquired so hypotheses are introduced, amended or rejected.

7.3 A Historical Example

Simulated experiments will have those outcomes that are most probable in a world in which the active, objective hypothesis is true. We argued in Chap. 5 that scientists change the world by improving their experiments and engaging with other researchers. In practice, even where an experiment is designed to test a particular hypothesis, this development turns up additional hypotheses relating to other processes that are implicated by the method of investigation. An example is the Michelson-Morley-Miller experiments to detect ether-effects between 1880s and the 1930s. These experiments were designed to detect a difference in the velocity of light due to

Table 7.5 Non-historical, retrospective view of the role of the interferometer experiments

Result	Hypothesis:	
	Lorentz hypothesis + Newtonian relativity	Special relativity
No displacement	0.01 (error)	0.90
Small displacement	0.09	0.09 (error)
Predicted displacement	0.90	0.01 (error)

Table 7.6 Early stages of the development of the interferometer experiments

Result	Hypothesis		
	Apparatus effect (temperature, vibration)	Ether drag (no apparatus effects)	No ether drag
No displacement (Helmholtz)	0.50	0.1	0.9
Small displacement (error)	0.50	0.1	0.1
Predicted displacement (Michelson, Lorenz)	0.00	0.8	0.0

differences in the relative velocity of the earth and the luminiferous ether (Swenson 1970). Michelson and Morley's experiments showed a much smaller effect than that predicted. In 1905 Einstein's special theory of relativity made the ether unnecessary. It included the radical proposal that the velocity of light is a constant so that if the ether existed the velocity-dependent effects could not detect it. Table 7.5 assigns a small probability to the occurrence of all three types of result (including the result predicted by the rival hypothesis).

The Michelson-Morley experiment is often presented as a crucial experiment that confirmed Einstein's theory (Holton 1973a). Yet for many, the non-existence of 'ether' (and therefore, an interaction with light) remained beyond consideration. There is a long history of hypotheses about the behaviour of the apparatus and ad-hoc hypotheses dealing with the negative result before and after 1905. In the early stages of his search for evidence of ether-drift, Helmholtz advised Michelson that unless temperature gradients within the interferometer apparatus could be eliminated, differential expansion of the material would mask any effects indicating ether effects. Fitzgerald later proposed a similar effect of the ether on the interferometer arms in order to explain the null-results. Table 7.6 summarises this simplified version of the early situation. It illustrates the range of possibilities that could be expected from the Michelson-Morely experiment. Here we treat the Helmholtz' criticism as a hypothesis about the experimental apparatus (no displacement). Fitzgerald introduced an ad-hoc explanation of the negligible result; according to this the ether affects the length of the interferometer arms.

Table 7.7 Hypotheses in play prior to 1905

Result	Hypothesis:			
	Apparatus effect (temperature, vibration)	Ether drag + Lorenz-Fitzgerald contraction applied to apparatus	Ether drag (no apparatus effects)	Velocity of light is constant (some apparatus effects)
No displacement	0.45	0.1 (error)	0.1 (error)	0.9
Small displacement	0.45	0.9	0.1 (error)	0.1 (error)
Predicted displacement (may indicate experimental error)	0.10	0.0	0.8	0.0

Table 7.8 The situation after 1905

Result	Hypothesis:			
	Apparatus effect (temperature, vibration)	Ether drag + Lorenz-Fitzgerald contraction applied to apparatus	Ether drag (no apparatus effects)	No ether drag: velocity of light is constant
No displacement (Helmholtz)	0.45	0.1	0.1	0.9
Small displacement (error)	0.45	0.9	0.1	0.1
Predicted displacement (Michelson, Morley, Lorenz-Fitzgerald	0.10	0.0	0.8	0.0

Fitzgerald's suggestion is included in Table 7.7 along with relativistic alternatives mooted in a textbook by Föppl in 1894 (Holton 1973b, pp. 208–212) and by Poincare in 1904 (Poincare 1905). For those who accepted the argument of Einstein's 1905 paper, the null results confirmed his postulate of special relativity. Yet, the search for ether-drag effects continued long after 1905. By the 1930s D. C. Miller finally concluded, that Helmholtz had probably been right all along (Swenson 1970, 1972). Rejecting the explanation provided by Einstein's relativity postulate of 1905, he continued to believe that the experiments confirmed some conjunction of Helmholtz's surmise and the Lorenz-Fitzgerald contraction hypothesis (see Table 7.8).

This method of representation introduces each hypothetical possibility in historical sequence and shows how its probability varies for each scientist, according to each scientist's knowledge of experimental results and of another scientist' beliefs. To tell the full story we would need a set of matrices showing the probability of each set of outcomes of each set of experiments for each set of hypotheses, for each of the developments that can be discerned according to historical evidence. We would also programme changing sets of probabilities to govern actors' access to existing and new apparatus and techniques, and to other actors as these enter or leave the scene (e.g. Lorentz, Fitzgerald, Poincare, Einstein, Miller).

7.4   Simulating Experimental Science

We argue elsewhere (see Chaps. 4 and 5, also Addis and Gooding 2004) that there is no *a priori* reason to prioritise either the hypotheses (treating phenomena as deductive consequences) or the phenomena (from which hypotheses are induced or abduced). In science, hypotheses and phenomena develop jointly by a dynamic that combines inductive, abductive and deductive forms of inference. To consider the dynamics we shall examine examples based on simulation of the Gruber shadowbox. In Gruber's experiments, subjects have the option of consulting another subject. At every iteration stage of our simulation, each agent decides whether to experiment, consult or do nothing, and must select an experiment to perform or an agent to consult. The decision procedure is complex. An agent is motivated to reduce the uncertainty in its view of the world (see Chap. 6, Addis and Gooding 1999; Gooding and Addis 1999). This view consists of the agent's changing belief profile (a set of confidence values) and dynamic variables derived from this (e.g. scientist's belief entropy or indifference, or probability of consulting another scientist is reduced). Uncertainty consists of not knowing which hypothesis best describes the world. A scientist with a flat belief profile (having no bias towards a particular hypothesis) is less confident of his view of the world than is a scientist who is confident about only one or two hypotheses.

The belief-revision simulation tracks and reports agent (a simulated scientist) behaviour in two ways: as macro-behaviour, a trajectory of changing confidence in each hypothesis (a changing *belief-profile*, as plotted in Fig. 7.3) and as micro-behaviour, a narrative or *history of actions*. In Figs. 7.4 and 7.5, Table 7.10 the agent's display which of two experiments are selected (and the outcome) or which of two agents is consulted. During the process of experimenting or consulting an agent's indifference levels changes and is shown as a dynamic threshold $I_n(A)$. This dynamic threshold defines which of the hypotheses are believed (see Chap. 6).

7.5   How Experiments Mediate Between Hypotheses and Phenomenology

An experiment consists of a physical setup that is acted on by an agent procedure. Each apparatus-procedure pairing can produce a range of results. Which results can occur also depends on which hypothesis is being considered. So in our computer simulation, the range of possible results is expressed as a probability distribution for

Fig. 7.3 Single agent, flexibility 0.3; 3 hypotheses, negative bias: sphere 0.45, pyramid 0.45, cone 0.1; object in box: cone

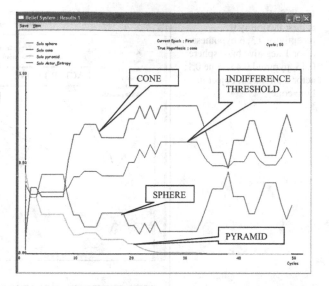

Fig. 7.4 The effect on belief of maximum responsiveness to new data. Single agent, 2 hypotheses, negative bias: sphere 0.8, cone 0.2; flexibility 1.0, object in box: cone

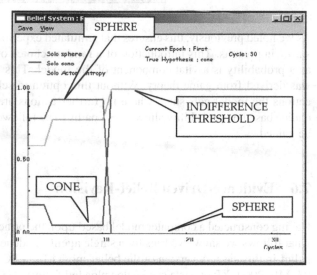

each combination of < hypothesis + setup + procedure > . The 'belief' (action probability) for each hypothesis adds up to 1.0 since the agent must act even if the action is 'do nothing'. This representation treats an experiment as mediating between four sets of objects: hypotheses, procedures, physical setups and observable outcomes. In selecting an experiment our agents will prefer those having more decisive outcomes. However, such an agent does not 'know' the specific outcome of any experiment beforehand. When the agent selects an experiment, its results in our simulation are generated 'Monte Carlo' fashion according to the probability distribution of the outcomes that are possible for each hypothesis (see, for example, Tables 7.7 and 7.8).

Fig. 7.5 Two communicating actors; flexibility 0.3, receptivity 0.3; 3 hypotheses; actor 1 negative bias: sphere 0.45, pyramid 0.45, cone 0.1; actor 2 unbiased; object in box: cone

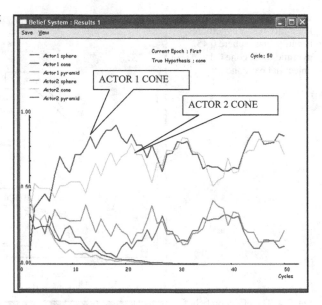

As we noted previously, this ensures that simulated experiments can sometimes have surprising results. This introduction of a random choice of actions based on belief as a probability is a vital component of the model. This method of action choice was derived from game theory. Without this option to select apparently irrational actions the model gets stuck where no further actions are possible. Introducing a choice based on probability allows fresh paths to be followed and new knowledge to be gained.

7.6   Evidence-Driven Belief-Revision

Having constructed a computer model based upon the principles described above, in what follows we show two runs for a single agent. Evidence is the only influence on belief in this case. A version of the belief model for a PC running Windows[TM] 95, 98, ME, 2000, XP or Vista can be downloaded from:

   http://www.clarity-support.co.uk/products/belief/index.html

We then compare the belief model with an otherwise identical starting scenario for two agents in which beliefs are also mediated by the other agent's opinion. This comparison illustrates how consultation:

1. produces order effects, in that consultation creates greater variability in the sequence of events and resulting belief-states
2. can also 'smooth' belief-revision.

7.6.1   Non-consultation Run (Solo)

In the following run there is just one actor ('Solo') with access to a simple (single-image) shadowbox. In this case the act of 'consultation' will be equivalent to 'no experiment'. On each cycle the object may be observed as either a circle, triangle or circle point. The plot (Fig. 7.3) indicates that an initial bias in favour of the pyramid hypothesis is quickly overcome by increased confidence in the sphere hypothesis. By cycle 8 both have been displaced by the cone hypothesis. Cone and sphere are again considered almost equiprobable later in the sequence (cycles 35–40). This indicates that an emerging bias may be overcome by new evidence. The pattern of events (self-consultation, experimentation or inaction) that shapes these patterns of belief is shown in the narrative sequences in Tables 7.9 and 7.10. At cycle 38, following a sequence of 'circle' observations, the actor is for the moment undecided between them.

These narratives (in Tables 7.9 and 7.10) also illustrate how revising confidence in hypotheses based on experimental evidence produces behaviour that *appears* to switch between confirmatory behaviour (as between cycles 32 and 38) and falsifying behaviour (as between cycles 7–10 and 38–42). Although this fits with strategies used by scientists (Tweney 1985), it is misleading to construe the simulation behaviour in these terms.

The inference process updates confidence in light of recent events (in this run the event-window $= 3.3$ events). Reducing the event-window further to just a single event (flexibility $= 1.0$) produces more abrupt changes in belief (Fig. 7.4). However, even with a single-event window an agent's behavior does not reflect simple falsification.

The narrative (Table 7.10) shows that the changes plotted in Fig. 7.4 are due to two experimental results separated by a series of self-consultations. It may seem that the sphere hypothesis is 'confirmed' at cycle 2 prior to being 'falsified' at cycle 9, given that a sphere could produce the circle seen at cycle 2 but cannot produce the pointed oblique projection seen at cycle 9.

However, when an actor can also consult other actors we cannot interpret these behaviours simply in terms of such rules. This is because actors' belief profiles will reflect other opinions as well as experimental evidence. Whereas logical models of confirmation (or falsification) exclude influences other than observational data, our simulation calculates the consequences of allowing actors to consult. This can be shown by comparing the 'solo' sequences Table 7.9 with a similar scenario in which there are two consulting actors in Tables 7.11 and 7.12.

7.6.2   Consultation Run for Two Agents (Actor1 & 2)

We argued in the section '**Why Inference can't be modelled**' that consultation complicates belief-revision models based on inference rules because consultation introduces the influence of opinions (rather than evidence) and introduces order

Table 7.9 Belief System 2.0– narrative for first 10 cycles in Fig. 7.3. Threshold value for action in cycle n is recorded in cycle $n +$

Cycle: agent	Actions	Setup or consultee	Result	Threshold	Preferred hypothesis
0: Solo	Single-image	Make_observation single_image	Circle_point	0.33871	Pyramid, sphere
1: Solo	Consultation	Solo		0.334326	Cone
2: Solo	Single_image	Make_observation single_image	Circle	0.334326	Cone
3: Solo	Consultation	Solo		0.346915	Sphere
4: Solo	Consultation	Solo		0.346915	Sphere
5: Solo	No_experiment			0.346915	Sphere
6: Solo	Consultation	Solo		0.346915	Sphere
7: Solo	Single_image	Make_observation single_image	Circle_point	0.346915	Sphere
8: Solo	Single_image	Make_observation single_image	Circle_point	0.371482	Cone
9: Solo	No_Experiment			0.430718	Cone
10: Solo	single_image	Make_observation single_image	Triangle	0.430718	Cone
30: Solo	No_experiment			0.628526	Cone
31: Solo	Consultation	Solo		0.628526	Cone
32: Solo	Single_image	Make_observation single_image	Circle	0.628526	Cone
33: Solo	Single_image	Make_observation single_image	Circle	0.567274	Cone
34: Solo	Single_image	Make_observation single_image	Circle	0.520047	Cone
35: Solo	No_experiment			0.492474	Cone
36: Solo	No_experiment			0.492474	Cone
37: Solo	Single_image	Make_observation single_image	Circle	0.492474	Cone
38: Solo	Single_image	Make_observation single_image	Circle_point	0.48467	Cone, sphere
39: Solo	No_experiment			0.514958	Cone
40: Solo	Consultation	Solo		0.514958	Cone
41: Solo	Single_image	Make_observation single_image	Circle_point	0.514958	Cone
42: Solo	No_experiment			0.569498	Cone

Table 7.10 Belief system 2.0—narrative for cycles 0–10 in Fig. 7.4

Cycle 1: Solo—Consultation Solo 0.606287 sphere
Cycle 2: Solo—single_image
Make_observation single_image *circle* 0.606287 sphere
Cycle 3: Solo—No_Experiment 0.788873 sphere
Cycle 4: Solo—No_Experiment 0.788873 sphere
Cycle 5: Solo—No_Experiment 0.788873 sphere
Cycle 6: Solo—No_Experiment 0.788873 sphere
Cycle 7: Solo—No_Experiment 0.788873 sphere
Cycle 8: Solo—Consultation Solo 0.788873 sphere
Cycle 9: Solo—single_image
Make_observation single_image *point_circle* 0.788873 sphere
Cycle 10: Solo—No_Experiment 1.000000 cone

effects. Figure 7.5 shows how the confidence of two agents in each of the three hypotheses changes, as consultations and new observations are made. Actor 1 starts with negative bias (see Fig. 7.5) while actor 2 is unbiased. They are otherwise identical as to flexibility, receptivity and access conditions.

Consultation has several effects:

- First, comparing actor 1 in Figs. 7.4 and 7.5 shows a jagged but less erratic trajectory.
- Second, the actors converge to the same conclusion. Multiple runs of this scenario show that the sequence of events producing agreement varies in each run (compare the two narratives in Table 7.11, which also show that self-consultation occurs less frequently than for a solo actor).
- Third, consultation can also moderate the effects of bias.

To understand the macro-behaviour displayed in the plots we would need to examine the actions of each actor and their outcomes in each of their iterations in more detail.

7.7 Conclusions

We have shown in this chapter how simulation methods enable us to model the interaction of hypotheses; experiments and an emerging phenomenology and that iterative modelling can represent the combined influence of evidence and opinion on inferences about hypotheses. Studies made with the belief-revision system show some behaviour that is stable over variation of parameters. These include convergence of beliefs to the objective hypothesis, that an emerging consensus is often interrupted and then restored, and that an optimum balance between the impact of evidence and the influence of opinions is achieved for an event-window of 2–3 events.

Table 7.11 Variability: the first six cycles of run plotted in Fig. 7.5 for comparison

S71_Run1					
Cycle: agent	Actions	Setup or consultee	Result	Belief threshold	Preferred hypothesis
0 Actor1	Single_image	Make_observation single_image	Point_circle	0.387161	Pyramid
Actor2	Single_image	Make_observation single_image	Point_circle	0.333366	[None]
1 Actor1	Consultation	Actor2		0.334326	Cone
Actor2	Consultation	Actor1		0.362669	Cone
2 Actor1	Single_image	Make_observation single_image	Triangle	0.338693	Cone
Actor2	Consultation	Actor2		0.353348	Cone
3 Actor1	Single_image	Make_observation single_image	Circle	0.351404	Cone
Actor2	Consultation	Actor2		0.353348	Cone
4 Actor1	Single_image	Make_observation single_image	Circle_point	0.344057	Cone
Actor2	Single_image	Make_observation single_image	Circle	0.353348	Cone
5 Actor1	Single_image	Make_observation single_image	Circle_point	0.390810	Cone
Actor2	Consultation	Actor1		0.355291	Cone sphere
6 Actor1	Single_image	Make_observation single_image	Circle	0.459860	Cone
Actor2	Consultation	Actor2		0.370988	Cone

Table 7.12 Variability: the first six cycles repeated again of the run plotted in Fig. 7.5 and shown for comparison with yet another run having identical parameters and starting conditions as shown in Table 7.11

S7I_Run3

Cycle: agent	Actions	Setup or consultee	Result	Belief threshold	Preferred hypothesis
0 Actor1	Consultation	Actor2		0.387161	Pyramid sphere
Actor2	Consultation	Actor1		0.333366	[none]
1 Actor1	Single_image	Make_observation single_image	Circle_point	0.356598	Pyramid sphere
Actor2	Consultation	Actor1		0.335216	Pyramid sphere
2 Actor1	Single_image	Make_observation single_image	Circle	0.338693	Cone
Actor2	Consultation	Actor1		0.333409	Pyramid sphere
3 Actor1	Single_image	Make_observation single_image	Triangle	0.347505	Sphere cone
Actor2	Consultation	Actor1		0.334583	Sphere cone
4 Actor1	Single_image	Make_observation single_image	Point_circle	0.345018	Cone
Actor2	Single_image	Make_observation single_image	Circle_point	0.335773	Cone sphere
5 Actor1	Consultation	Actor2		0.395465	Cone
Actor2	Single_image	Make_observation single_image	Coint_circle	0.372651	Cone
6 Actor1	Consultation	Actor2		0.387918	Cone
Actor2	Single_image	Make_observation single_image	Triangle	0.437254	Cone

Other robust results are that evidence-driven agents with a very small event window behave like naïve falsificationists, and abandoned hypotheses can be revived. Most important, given the argument of section '**Why Inference can't be modelled**', is that experimenters perform better when communicating with others.

References

Addis TR, Gooding DC (1999) Learning as collective belief-revision: simulating reasoning about disparate phenomena. In: Proceedings: AISB'99, Symposium on scientific creativity, pp 19–28

Addis TR, Gooding DC (2004) Simulation methods for an abductive system in science, in MBR04: model-based reasoning in science and engineering, abduction, visualization, and simulation, University of Pavia, Pavia, December 2004

Gooding DC (1990) Experiment and the making of meaning: human agency in scientific observation and experiment. Kluwer, Boston

Gooding DC, Addis TR (1999) A simulation of model-based reasoning about disparate phenomena. In: Magnani L, Nersessian N, Thagard P (ed) Model-based reasoning in scientific discovery. Kluwer, New York, pp 103–123

Gruber H (1985) From epistemic subject to unique creative person at work. Arch Psychol 53:167–185

Holton G (1973a) Einstein, Michelson and the "Crucial" experiment. In: Holton G (ed) The thematic origins of scientific thought: Kepler to Einstein. Harvard University Press, Cambridge, pp 261–351

Holton G (1973b) Influences on Einstein's early work. In: Holton G (ed) The thematic origins of scientific thought: Kepler to Einstein. Harvard University Press, Cambridge, pp 197–217

Knorr-Cetina K (1981) The manufacture of knowledge. Pergamon Press, Oxford

Poincaré H (1905) The value of science. English Trans. by G. B. Halstead 1913. Reprinted, Dover 1958, p 104

Swenson LS (1970) The Michelson—Morley—-Miller experiments before and after 1905. J Hist Astron 1:56–78

Swenson LS (1972) The Etherial Ether: a history of the Michelson Morley Miller experiments. University of Texas, Austin

Tweney RD (1985) Faraday's discovery of induction: a cognitive approach. In Gooding D, James F (ed) Faraday rediscovered. Macmillan, London, pp 189–209

Venn J (1880) On the diagrammatic and mechanical representation of propositions and reasonings. Philo Mag Ser 5 10(59):1880

Wason PC (1960) On the failure to eliminate hypotheses in a conceptual task. Q J Exp Psychol 12:129–140

Chapter 8
Programming and Meaning

Rules are for the obedience of fools and the guidance of wise men

Douglas Bader (1910–1982)

8.1 A Grand Challenge

During April 2005 at the University of York, an international workshop was held called *'The Grand Challenge in Non-Classical Computation'*. The purpose of the conference was to stimulate those doing research and development in Computer Science to consider new approaches to computing. The stimulation for this challenge was triggered by the novel concept of *'Quantum Computing'*, which seemed to offer the potential for ultra fast parallel processing using quantum mechanical principles such as superposition and entanglement. The organisers thought that there might be other mechanisms that could be harnessed based upon, say, biology, alternative physical principles or probability. They considered that by moving away from the architecture of computers there might be some benefits. It was put to the science community to consider and propose alternative computational mechanisms that might lead to some conceptual extensions of computer science.

The mass of proposals put before the workshop were concerned mainly with new engines of computing. However, another important challenge of the time was how people and communities could more easily interact with the computer. The problem, as David Gooding and I saw it, was embodied in the phrase *'socially sensitive computing'* and was included as another issue that was different from the mechanics of computation. This area of socially sensitive computing was also covered by the two existing studies of Informatics and Cybernetics.

A definition of *'Informatics'*, given by Edinburgh University (February 2014), is the study of the structure, the behaviour, and the interactions of natural and engineered computational systems. The central focus of Informatics is the transformation of information—whether by computation or communication or by organisms or artefacts. It was considered that the understanding of the informational phenomena, such as computation, cognition, and communication as a single combined subject, would enable technological advances and also provide insights into many natural and artificial systems.

© Springer International Publishing Switzerland 2014
T. Addis, *Natural and Artificial Reasoning,* Advanced Information and Knowledge Processing, DOI 10.1007/978-3-319-11286-2_8

However, long before informatics was offered as a course of study, the subject of '*Cybernetics*' was taught as part of the theory and practice of programming in the MIT Electronic Systems Laboratory (Wiener 1948). Its founder, Norbert Weiner, taught this course. He defined it as the study of control and communication in the animal and the machine. This also included social and other multi-element systems that involve feedback (e.g. control) and objectives (e.g. survival).

The studies of Informatics and Cybernetics seem to be similar and both include the objectives of the Grand Challenge (2005) as described next.

8.1.1 Meeting the Criteria

The organisers of the Grand Challenge (2005) gave 13 criteria for the grand challenge so that it would help potential authors to address the right issues. Each one of the criteria related to social or people sensitive issues. The study of behaviour in society is linked to the grand challenge specification and argued for as follows:

1. *It arises from scientific curiosity about the foundation, the nature or the limits of a scientific discipline.*

The proposal of socially sensitive computing, oddly enough, arises from the question of why, after 60 years of effort, millions of man hours and technology including silicon machines that do $1000+$ Giga-flops with $1000+$ Terabytes of storage, we have still not even addressed many of the important functions of a human brain. The brain is a device that looks like a bowl of porridge and consists of only 15 Gigacells working at about 50 cycles per second (Edwards 2014).

2. *It gives scope for engineering ambition to build something that has never been seen before.*

The proposal of socially sensitive computing could suggest new ways of looking at current problems. New types of computation might arise, and thus new engines could be created along different principles; notions such as 'a structure malleable program' that will reform its processes (say, between parallel and sequential) to best create a single efficient solution.

3. *It will be obvious how far and when the challenge has been met (or not).*

The challenge will have been addressed when it is no longer a problem that the world cannot be classified or partitioned. This need to predefine the world is a necessary starting point for all current computer programming. Once done it confines the possibilities of the program to a very limited point of view. Because of this limitation the challenge will never be met, but it is still worth trying in order to see how far we can get.

4. *It has enthusiastic support from (almost) the entire research community, even those who do not participate and do not benefit from it.*

Although at the time there was a growing group of people at Sussex University (Informatics) who responded very positively to the grand challenge, we are still a long way from producing human style intelligence.

5. *It has international scope: participation would increase the research profile of a nation.*

It clearly has worldwide implications but Artificial Intelligence has benefited most from faster and more compact computers. No new principles have evolved from or since the grand challenge.

6. *It is generally comprehensible, and captures the imagination of the lay public, as well as the esteem of scientists in other disciplines.*

Many of the problems people had at the time of the challenge have been ameliorated by 'iPads' and 'Apps'. What was really meant by this criterion is the excitement about the 'idea' proposed. The notion would strike at the very heart of how we organise ourselves and accept hypotheses. The accelerated growth of laws and regulations is derived from the misapprehension that concepts can be perfectly captured through definition. The rejection of this idea would release us all from the inappropriate constraints imposed by those in authority; it would give us a rationale on which to reject nonsense. Sadly, this has never happened.

7. *It was formulated long ago, and still stands.*

If 'long ago' means 'in the early part of the twentieth century', then it does still stand.

8. *It promises to go beyond what is initially possible, and requires development of understanding, techniques and tools unknown at the start of the project.*

This promise seemed to be the case. A new technology and science could stem from this proposal. As noted for 6, in some limited way it has in the form of iPads and Apps.

9. *It calls for planned co-operation among identified research teams and communities.*

It will require a wide range of specialisation ranging from psychologists, philosophers, linguists, sociologists and computer scientists of many fields (e.g. networking, systems, architecture and interface design). However, it never really happened except in very isolated places.

10. *It encourages and benefits from competition among individuals and teams, with clear criteria on who is winning, or who has won.*

I did not like to see this happen. It could do, but I would discourage it. Competition in science is generally counter-productive because it involves secrecy and ownership of knowledge.

11. *It decomposes into identified intermediate research goals, whose achievement brings scientific or economic benefit, even if the project as a whole fails.*

In some isolated cases this happened. A simple, working solution to such tasks as information retrieval could be of considerable benefit to the community as a whole. Google and other public search engines have clearly demonstrated this point. Many of the objectives already pursued and abandoned from lack of practical success (such as natural language understanding and adaptive interfaces) were re-examined due to this new paradigm. They achieved very little and have become irrelevant.

12. *It will lead to radical paradigm shift, breaking free from the dead hand of legacy.*

It is a radical paradigm shift. The question is: "would we be able to go against our own training and start thinking within this new framework?" The answer seems to be 'No!'

13. *It is not likely to be met simply from commercially motivated evolutionary advance.*

Socially Sensitive Computing is not a simple evolution from where we stand, and that is a problem (see last point above).

I will argue from the Church-Turing thesis (Kleene 1967) in this chapter, that:

- A computer program can be considered as equivalent to a formal language similar to predicate calculus where predicates can be considered as functions.

This can be related to such a calculus in Wittgenstein's first major work, the Tractatus (Wittgenstein 1921). The Tractatus's theory and its relationship to the world can be used as a model of a formal classical definition of a computer program. It was originally intended to explain how meaning and language were tied together via a 'referential' semantics; that is each word in the language was associated with some object or action in the world.

8.1.2 Problems with Referential Semantics

A problem arose from using referential semantics, since most everyday objects are complex. Objects, such as a 'car' or a 'garage' can be described in terms of other objects. This makes them propositions rather than simple primitive objects. Further, if 'my' red car were to be destroyed then the proposition:

  My red car is in the garage

would suddenly cease to have meaning, or if all cars were scrapped, then all sentences containing 'car' would become nonsense. This sudden loss of meaning is unlikely to be the case.

The problem with nonsense is that it cannot even be assigned a truth-value. Therefore, Wittgenstein, in his Tractatus, set out to identify the simple primitive objects by specifying their necessary characteristics. One of the objects that do fit his criteria is the 'bit' as used in a computer. A 'bit' is really a primitive distinction, which may be realised, for example, as a voltage difference or a bead position on a wire or a counter placed in a square. Obviously, the electronic version of a 'bit' has many practical advantages; it is compact, fast and computationally viable. Other objects that fit are space, time, colour (being coloured), force and mass (as per Newton).

Although Wittgenstein's Tractatus satisfied formal languages, such as predicate calculus, he found that it did not completely explain natural language. The referential paradigm of meaning cannot cope with the human use of a language. For example, you can take the notion of a 'game' and explain this by pointing to examples of games. But what defines a game? Is there any definition that will both contain the idea of all games and exclude all that are not games? The answer seems to be no. Yet this negative case cannot happen within the bounds of the Tractatus.

This indeterminacy of meaning in natural language seems to be a flaw in his initial great work. Recognising this he then went on to explore these flaws in his second great work 'the Philosophical Investigations' (Wittgenstein 1953). Here he expands the principles of meaning to include the flexible way language is used. This involves what he called 'a language game' where the rules of the 'game' can be changed. The challenge we make is *"can computer science make the same leap?"* Can we extend the computer interactions to also include a programming game?

I propose that because of this essential flaw identified by Wittgenstein, computers are unlikely to have the possibility of natural communication with people unless we apply a different approach to program design. I will come to this conclusion by considering the two major works on the philosophy of language by Wittgenstein. I will show that such a lack of natural communication with machines is related to same reason that Wittgenstein made the paradigm shift away from his first work— the Tractatus. I will explain why the Tractatus clearly aligns with formal computer modelling and that his second work, the Philosophical Investigations, best fits the more flexible requirements of human communication. How his second work might be used to make computer communication more human becomes another question to be answered.

8.2   Inferring Internal Experience

As we have discussed, classical linguistic philosophy suggests that language understanding arrives from denotational (referential) semantics. If we examine what people talk about, we find that many of the conversations are descriptions of our own internal lives. Since nobody can have direct access to another's internal experiences, then the only way in which such experiences can be understood is indirectly through inference. We can infer each other's experience because we share the state of being a person, in the same culture, using a common language and in the context of similar external events (such as a musical performance; see Chap. 6 and Billinge and Addis 2003). It is hence possible through conversation to build an internal model of another person's view of the world. The only requirements for this model is to be able to make predictions from conversations about:

- one's own possible future experiences
- the way one should respond to another person
- an interpretation of what is said
- new ideas and ways of looking at the world

For example, if the non-technical music literature is examined, such as record reviews, concert reports, descriptive, as opposed to analytical, music histories and biographies, it becomes evident that the common experience does not have to be even the music itself in order for one person to describe an experience to another. The rich and extensive use of metaphor suggests that emotional resonance and association to a commonly understood situation can be employed to trigger what, to the author of the description, is his "accurate" emotional response to a piece of music. Communication, in this case, will depend mostly upon our shared humanity, sometimes upon our personal experiences but unlike computers, little upon any external referential semantics. This point is explained in Chap. 13.

8.3 A Philosophical Paradigm of Meaning for Computing

The implications of such observations on the communication of internal experience are radical. They have led us to take Wittgenstein's *Tractatus* as a paradigmatic description of the current state of computer science. We will treat the tractatus as theory of formal computer languages and use it to describe how programming languages have meaning. We can take this step because the Church-Turing Thesis shows that the Turing Machine (the classical computer) is equivalent to Lambda calculus and recursive functions. Lambda calculus and recursive functions together form the description of functional programming languages (e.g. ML, LISP).

David Gooding (University of Bath, private communication 2004) notes that:

> The Tractatus was modelled on Hertz' Principles of Mechanics. Hertz believed that his book would be a full and final statement of the principles of mechanics; Wittgenstein thought that Frege, Russel and Whithead had done the same for mathematics and that he would do the same for language.

In the Tractatus Wittgenstein creates a formal analysis of language and in particular, shows how it relates to the world through 'objects'. What exactly an object is emerges from exploring its role in a language. I now look at the statements in the Tractatus labelled **Tn** where n is a number indicating the statement's level in an argument. There are seven major statements (e.g. **T2**) and the point indicates a branch of further statements made from the initial statement (e.g. **T2.01, T.02**).

- **T2**, What is the case—a fact—is the existence of states of affairs.
- **T2.01**, A state of affairs (a state of things) is a combination of objects (things)
- **T2.02,** Objects are simple.
- **T2.021,** Objects make up the substance of the world. That is why they cannot be composite.
- **T2.0251,** Space, time and colour (being coloured) are forms of objects.

It was from *Tractatus* that predicate calculus emerged. This is a formal language for describing states of affairs or facts. Pure functional programming languages, such as ML and LISP, have evolved from predicate calculus. Wittgenstein describes predicate calculus in the *Tractatus*. His early work encapsulated a formal and logical representational schema into a descriptive form that was based upon denotational (or referential) semantics. Such a semantics link the meaning of a symbol to an object in the world. A 'symbol' can only have one meaning and a 'sign' can represent two or more symbols. The distinction between symbols is inferred by how the sign is used.

- **T3.32,** A sign is what can be perceived of a symbol
- **T3.321,** So one and the same sign (written or spoken) can be common to two different symbols—in which case they signify in different ways.

Thus, a symbol's physical representation is a sign and it is usually a recognisable mark on the page such as a word or character, but it can be a spoken word or any other physical display. This display (the sign) refers through a symbol to an object in the world. Wittgenstein also referred to these signs presented in some kind of relationship as 'pictures'.

- **T3.221,** Objects can only be *named*. Signs are their representatives. I can only speak *about* them: I cannot *put them into words*. Propositions can only say how things are, not what they are.
- **T3.27,** A name cannot be dissected any further by means of a definition: it is a primitive sign
- **T3.3,** Only propositions have sense: only in the nexus of a proposition does a name have meaning.
- **T3.32,** A sign is what can be perceived of a symbol.

The idea here is that the meaning of the symbol is to what it points (its referent), and so it can only have one meaning. A sign can represent more than one symbol and its distinction may be inferred as to how it is used. A 'name' is a primitive sign.

A sign may also represent other signs in relationship; these are signs that represent propositions, or states of affairs. For example, the sign 'father' refers to a sign that refers, in turn, to the proposition 'A man who has an offspring'. Thus, the sign 'father' refers to the symbol that is the object of being a father. These are propositions and refer to a state of affairs.

8.3.1   Objects

Wittgenstein was after a set of primitive and simple objects in the world. These objects would form the base from which everything else could be expressed in terms of propositions. In this case, the referents (the objects) will have some logically strange properties. Objects must be:

1. *independent* in that they can freely combine to form "states of affairs" that can
   be described. This is supported by the statements:
   a. **T2.01**, A state of affairs (a state of things) is a combination of objects (things)
      1. **T2.0122**, Things are independent in so far as they can occur in all possible
         situations, but this form of independence is a form of connection with states
         of affairs, a form of independence.
      2. **T2.0124**, If all objects are given, then at the same time all *possible* states
         of affairs are also given.
   b. **T2.0272**, The configuration of objects produces states of affairs.
2. *atomic* in that there are no smaller constituents:
   1. T2.021, Objects make up the substance of the world. That is why they cannot
      be composite.
   a. **T2.02**, Objects are simple.
3. *in all possible worlds*
   1. **T2.022**, It is obvious that an imagined world, however different it may be from
      the real one, must have *something*—a form—in common with it.
   2. **T2.023**, Objects are just what constitute this unalterable form.
4. *immaterial*
   1. **T2.0231** The substance of the world *can* only determine a form, and not
      material properties. For it is:
      1. only by means of propositions that material properties are represented
      2. only by the configuration of objects that they are produced.
   2. **T2.0233**, If two objects have the same logical form, the only distinction
      between them, apart from their external properties, is they are different.
5. *indescribable* except by their behaviour (form)
   1. **T2.0121**, It would seem to be a sort of accident, if it turned out that a situation
      would fit a thing that could already exist entirely on its own, this possibility
      must be in them from the beginning.
      1. If things can occur in states of affairs, this possibility must be in them from
         the beginning.
      2. (Nothing in the province of logic can be merely possible. Logic deals with
         every possibility and all possibilities are its facts.)
      3. Just as we are quite unable to imagine spatial objects outside space or
         temporal objects outside time, so too there is *no* object that we can imagine
         excluded from the possibility of combining with others.
      4. If I can imagine objects combined in states of affairs, I cannot imagine
         them excluded from the *possibility* of such combinations.
   2. **T2.021**, Objects make up the substance of the world. That is why they cannot
      be composite.
   3. **T3.0271**, Objects are what is unalterable and subsistent; their configuration is
      what is changing and unstable.
6. *self-governed* in that they have their own internal rules of behaviour
   1. **T2.0141**, The possibility of its occurring in states of the affairs is the form of
      an object.
   2. **T2.0121**, see above

3. **T2.0123**, If I know an object I also know all its possible occurrences in states of affairs.
   1. (every one of these possibilities must be part of the nature of the object)
   2. A new possibility cannot be discovered later.
      a. **T2.01231**, If I am to know an object, though I need not know its external properties, I must know all its internal properties.
4. **T2.03**, In a state of affairs objects fit into one another like links of a chain.
   1. **T2.033**, Form is the possibility of structure.

These referents (objects) are intended to be more than just elements of description; they form the real world:

T2.04, The totality of existing states of affairs is the world.

T2.06, The existence and non-existence of states of affairs is reality. (We also call the existence of states of affairs a positive fact, and their non-existence a negative fact).

From these referents, the full force of logic, predicate and propositional calculus retains stability of meaning and sense. Such a stance results in the position that everything is potentially unambiguously describable:

T2.225, There are no pictures that are true a priori.

T2.224, It is impossible to tell from a picture alone whether it is true or false.

T7. What we cannot speak about we must pass over in silence.

8.3.2 A Rational Set

I now introduce here the idea of a 'rational' set. The idea of rational and irrational sets was proposed first by Jan Townsend Addis (private communication February 2004), who related the irrational sets to Cantor's (1845–1918) irrational numbers. In the case of rational numbers the rule was that a member number could be expressed as a ratio of integers. Examples of irrational numbers are $\sqrt{2}$ and π. There are infinitely more irrational numbers than rational numbers. So we will define a *'rational' set is a set where there is a finite set of rules that unambiguously includes any member of that set and unambiguously excludes any non-member of that set.*

It should be noted that all the sets referenced by the Tractatus are rational, where set membership is always specifiable and context independent or has an explicit context that is also rational. This, as discussed above, was the formal limitation imposed on the *Tractatus*.

The *Tractatus* provides an extensive and useful description of computer programming languages. The argument is that signs (the visible part of an expression) in propositions do not always refer to primitive objects but are themselves referencing propositions. This is expressed by the following *Tractatus* statements:

T3.14, What constitutes a propositional sign is that in its elements (the words) stand in a determinate relation to one another.

A propositional sign is a fact.

T3.31, I call any part of a proposition that characterises its sense an expression (or symbol)
(A proposition is itself an expression)
Everything essential to their sense that propositions can have in common with one another
is an expression.
An expression is the mark of 'a form' and 'a content'.
T4.03, A proposition must use old expressions to communicate a new sense.
A proposition communicates a situation to us, and so it must be essentially connected with
the situation.
And the connection is precisely that it is its logical picture.
A proposition states something only in so far as it is a picture.
T4.22, An elementary proposition consists of names. It is a nexus, a concatenation, of names.
T4.221, It is obvious that the analysis of propositions must bring us to elementary
propositions, which consist of names in immediate combination.
This raises the question how such combination into propositions comes about.
T5.135, There is no possible way of making an inference from the existence of one situation
to the existence of another, entirely different situation.

This notion of meaning being related to its use rather than just reference is also
discussed in his next great work the Philosophical Investigations 43–60 (Wittgenstein
1953).

These states of affairs, in turn, are complexes that finally end up as compound
statements whose ultimate referent in computing is the bit. For example, in computer
languages we may have seven bits of the ASCII code identifying 1000001 as the
character A and 1000010 as the character B, etc. There are also special characters
such as 'delete' 1111111 and 'start' 0000001.

Here the bit is the mechanical equivalent of Wittgenstein's referent objects. The
bit, if taken as a detectable distinction, has all the strange properties of Wittgenstein's
object. For example, a world cannot exist (or at least be detectable) unless it contains
at least one distinction. A 'bit' is a concept that can only be embodied in a distinction.
A particular 'bit' is an argument place.

* **T2.0131,** A spatial object must be situated in infinite space. (A spatial point is an
  argument place.) A speck in the visual field, though it need not be red, must have
  a colour: it is, so to speak, surrounded by colour-space. Notes must have *some*
  pitch; objects of the sense of touch *some* degree of hardness, and so on.

Further, it is at the bit that the program links to the world and has meaning. It is
this meaning that allows the program to have "sense" with respect to the computer.
This formal semantics and the ability for programmers to create procedures and sub-
routines (sub-propositions or expressions) is the primary characteristic of all high
level and assembler programming languages.

The consequence of such a formal model is that any set of signs can be used in
a program to represent a proposition. All that is necessary is that there is a formal
definition that gives the sign meaning within the program in terms of the proposition
it represents. Since a proposition can take on an infinite number of forms through the
use of tautologies and other formal equivalences then there is an infinite but bounded
set of possible organisations that can be adopted for a program. Such a set is bounded
by the meaning of the term 'essential program'. An essential program is a theoretical
idea and refers to the base or minimum program. However, the additional adopted

structure is also represented, in the end, by bits on a computer. This will appear as a program overhead that is used to support a chosen program organisation or structure and in this sense only the program interpretation has changed. We can say that within the referential paradigm:

- The only strictly formal and unique meaning a computer program can have is found within a computer.

However, we know that computer programs have some other relationship to the world. This will be explored in the next chapter.

8.3.3   Social Consequences

There are also social consequences of the view adopted by the Tractatus in that it is assumed that rules can be created for all situations and as such, these rules can bypass human judgement. It also assumes that there is only one correct way of seeing the world and so all human existence can be governed by some finite set of laws. It is because there is a tendency to support such a 'rational' view that we now have all the measures of performance and rules of assessment in the modern work environment. It was this rational view that was the driving force behind Artificial Intelligence during the 1960s and it was the major reason for the demise of Cybernetics as a serious science.

References

Billinge D, Addis T (2003) The functioning of tropic communication: a mechanism for consistent figurative descriptions of artistic effect. In: AISB'03 symposium on artificial intelligence and creativity in arts and science. University of Wales, Aberystwyth

Edwards C (2014) Billion core brains. Eng Technol 9(3):62–65.

Kleene SC (1967) Mathematical logic. Wiley, New York

Wiener N (1948) Cybernetics: or control and communication in the animal and the machine. MIT, Cambridge, ISBN 0262 230070, ISBN 026273009X

Wittgenstein L (1921) Tractatus logico-philosophicus (English edition 1961). Routledge and Kegan Paul, London

Wittgenstein L (1953) Philosophical investigations. Blackwell, Oxford

Chapter 9
Irrational Reasoning

> *The intellect is not a serious thing, and never has been. It is an instrument on which one plays, that is all*
>
> Oscar Wild (1854–1900)

9.1 Dual Semantics

In Chap. 8 referential semantics was shown to fit a computer programming language since the meaning of a word could be related to the bit as an object in the machine. This is not the complete story. This is because computer languages have a *dual semantics* in that the program signs (e.g. the names/labels given to data items, procedures and sub-routines) at the highest level also have referents in the world other than the computer (Fig. 9.1).

This other source of objects is found in the analysis of the problem domain in terms of records (as in database and program structures), relations (as in normalised data structures) and objects (as in object-orientation). It is the role of the analysis done by a computer expert (a System Analyst) to identify and create a logical picture. This logical picture is a description of the user's world that will be used to implement a set of programs. It is this analysis that will identify constructs (objects) in the world that are meant to be stable and unchanging (as per *Tractatus* referents—Wittgenstein 1921) to which names can be given within the computer programs and their meaning assigned.

Now it is acceptable that propositions can represent material properties:

- **T2.0231**, The substance of the world can only determine a form, and not any material properties. For it is only by means of propositions that material properties are represented—only by the configuration of objects that they are produced.

and relationships between objects:

- **T2.031**, In a state of affairs objects stand in a determinate relation to one another.

and any complex model of the world:

- **T3.1,** In a proposition a thought finds an expression that can be perceived by the senses.

© Springer International Publishing Switzerland 2014
T. Addis, *Natural and Artificial Reasoning,* Advanced Information
and Knowledge Processing, DOI 10.1007/978-3-319-11286-2_9

Fig. 9.1 The problem with dual semantics

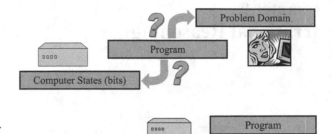

Fig. 9.2 The only rational interpretation of a computer program

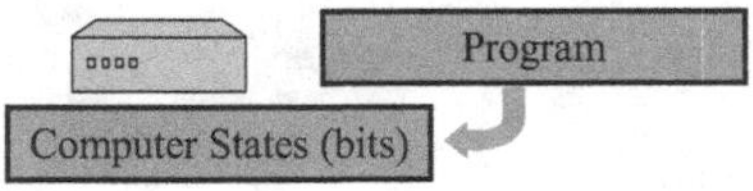

- **T3.11,** We use the perceptible sign of a proposition (spoken or written, etc.) as a projection of a possible situation. The method of projection is to think of the sense of the proposition.
- **T3.32,** A sign is what can be perceived of a symbol.
- **T4.01,** A proposition is a picture of reality. A proposition is a model of reality as we imagine it.
- **T4.021,** A proposition is a picture of reality: for if I understand a proposition, I know the situation that it represents. And I understand the proposition without having had its sense explained to me.

and a proposition can have one and only one complete analysis:

- **T3.25,** A proposition has one and only one complete analysis.

Such an analysis is dependent upon only the essential features of the proposition (the program) that link it to the referent objects (which is the bit in our case).

A computer program, as we have already seen, has such an analysis with respect to the computational engine (Fig. 9.2), so the 'alternative' interpretation of a program, the problem domain, depends upon its accidental features.

- **T3.34,** A proposition possesses essential and accidental features. Accidental features are those that result from the particular way in which the propositional sign is produced. Essential features are those without which the proposition could not express its sense.

This develops a peculiar tension in program design that is hard to keep stable, particularly with respect to the informal, and often undefined, mechanism which links the program names with the user's domain. Further, the 'objects' that are usually chosen to be referenced in the informal analysis of the problem domain do not normally have all the features required of Wittgenstein's objects. For example, they usually cannot be unambiguously defined. This is because no set of rules can be formulated to identify completely most objects that exist in the world as recognisable entities. Simple distinctions such as the computer bit are possibilities provided there is some well-defined formal definition of what is meant by a bit. However, computer engineers can find examples of bits that are indeterminate, and it is for this reason that sum check bits accompany every computer word. These check bits provide additional information so that bits that are ambiguous can be detected and made distinct.

9.2 The Paradigm Leap

The *Tractatus* is a magnificent piece of work and is an effective description of how programming languages should be linked to a computer through 'sense' (as with meaning) assignment. There is no problem with the engineering necessity of this approach to 'sense and meaning'. On a broader scale, it sidesteps many of the paradoxes of the linguistic philosophy of the day. However, it has *one fatal flaw* when applied to the human use of language. Wittgenstein eventually exposed this flaw. He noted that *it is not possible to unambiguously describe everything within the propositional paradigm.* He found that the normal use of language is riddled with example concepts that cannot be bounded by logical statements that depend upon a pure notion of referential objects. So I now turn to Wittgenstein's second great work where he explores the issues this raises (Wittgenstein 1953).

Wittgenstein illustrates this problem of defining concepts, using a propositional framework, in his Philosophical Investigations. We will refer to paragraphs in this work as **PI** n where n is an integer. In his illustration, he attempts to define a 'game' (**PI** 69–**PI** 71). He makes clear that such an unambiguous definition cannot be achieved. If you try to create such a definition then you will always fail both to exclude all examples that are not games and to include all examples that are.

It is through such considerations that Wittgenstein proposed a new linguistic philosophy that was based upon what I will call 'inferential semantics'. David Gooding (University of Bath, private communication 2004) notes that:

- The view epitomised by Wittgenstein's Philosophical Investigations is that meaning, grammar and even syntactic rules emerge from the collective practices (the situated, changing, meaningful use of language) of communities of users.

It is because of this observation by Wittgenstein that we make the distinction between **rational and irrational sets** (see Chap. 8–A Rational Set).

> An *irrational set* is where no finite set of rules can be constructed that can include unambiguously any member of that set and, at the same time, unambiguously exclude any non-member of that set.

By way of illustration, consider the set of chairs and a possible specification (Fig. 9.3). Here we have a typical chair (1), a high chair (2), a bar stool (3), a shooting stick (4) and a shooting stick that is also an umbrella (5) and finally a chair that is a maze that cannot even be sat upon. Each of these stages eliminates a rule in the original specification of a chair. It is always possible to find some exception to a finite set of rules that attempts to identify a member of the set 'chair'. Even if every exception were added to a membership list this would break down by simply discovering a context in which at least one member would cease to be identified as a member through the use of the rules. The more additions made of extreme cases to the set, the more opportunities there will be for finding situations that exclude accepted members of the set.

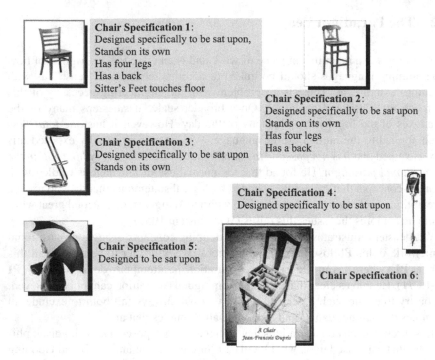

Fig. 9.3 An attempt at identifying a chair

9.3   Examples of Irrational Sets

We are thus in a position where most things are not potentially unambiguously describable. The following examples are drawn from the press where the limitations of rules and the indeterminacy of irrational sets have some devastating effects.

9.3.1   The Problem of Rules

9.3.1.1   Offensive Words

From a report by David Hewson, Sunday Times, April 4 2004.

> Can't an intelligent filter analyse a page beforehand and make a machine judgement on its suitability? There are stacks of those around, too, and pretty worthless they are. Peacefire (www.peacefire.org), a web group opposed to online censorship, carried out an interesting experiment recently. It created dummy pages supposedly run by small sites; each carrying examples of anti-gay hate speech. Posing as individuals, the organisation complained about these pages to the big content-filtering programs, including SurfWatch, NetNanny and CyberPatrol.

Sure enough, the filtering companies responded by blocking the offenders. Then Peacefire revealed the true sources of the quotations—all were taken verbatim from the websites of conservative organisations, including the Family Research Council, Focus on the Family and Concerned Women for America. Would the content-filtering companies now block these big and influential lobby groups? Not yet, which means you can read the self-same daft words on their sites, along with plenty of other material, but not on the bait pages that Peacefire erected to test the system.

9.3.1.2 Safety

From a report by Jeremy Clarkson, Sunday Times, April 11 2004.

The essence of the quotation was that the Health and Safety Executive (HSR) has attempted to provide legal control over all behaviour at work to such an extent that it is impossible to actually do his job. The nickname for the HSE is the Programme Prevention Department.

9.3.2 The Problem of Irrational Sets

9.3.2.1 Guilt

Report on the film 'Capturing the Friedmans' by Cosmo Landsman, Sunday Times, April 11 2004.

He found this film riveting because every time new evidence was present he kept on changing his mind about who was guilty until by the end of the film he was still unsure. The fascination about the film was concerned with the nature of memory and the way facts can be so fluid. It was a perplexing and poignant film.

9.3.2.2 Murder

Report on the execution of Paul Hill at Starke, Florida, CBSNEWS.com, September 4 2003

The execution of Paul Hill for the murder of a doctor who performed abortions and his bodyguard left U.S. abortion providers anxious – and wary that the former minister may become a martyr to the anti-abortion cause and spur others to act violently.
Paul Hill's final statement . . . if you believe abortion is a lethal force, you should oppose the force and do what you can to stop it
Paul Hill should be honoured today, the abortionists should be executed. Said Drew Holman
We think that unborn children should be protected and it should be law. Said Sheila Hopkins, a spokeswoman for the Florida Catholic Conference. We definitely reject his statement that it was justifiable homicide.

Attempts at providing a rational description of irrational sets has stimulated extensions to the 'crisp' set by assigning a 'value' to a membership. Examples are fuzzy and probabilistic membership assignments. However, fuzzy sets are rational in that members are assigned a membership number that is explicit and essentially ordinal. Such assignments can be expressed by a finite set of rules. Similarly, a probabilistic assignment of a member is also rational where a rule is in the form of a ratio of integers that specifies its membership. So there is difficulty transforming an irrational to a rational set by simply assigning some kind of membership function.

Even though there are irrational sets we still have rational sets, and so denotation remains one mechanism for relating meaning to a name. For irrational sets there is an additional and more important mechanism for meaning assignment based upon human usage and context. It is this latter mechanism that provides the link between the program and the world it is designed to represent and is the other half of the dual semantics.

9.3.3   Some Predictions from this Thesis

So we have computer programs with a semantics based upon computer bits but we create programs that cannot rationally be assigned meaning to the very problem domain for which they have been written. Programs must remain in the domain of rational sets if they are to be implemented on a machine. However, we do have the freedom to use the program's accidental properties, such as variable names and the addition of annotation, without affecting the program's meaning with respect to the computer. We can choose the names we use and select the computer organisation from the possibilities bounded by the essential (minimal expression of a) program.

During the 1960s variables in programs were severely limited to about 4–8 characters or integers. This limitation could make programs obscure to even experienced programmers. The advance of more flexible naming and the addition of annotation made programs very much more readable. The early endeavours, such as COBOL, attempted to make the program expressions reflect an English sentence so that non-programmers, such as clerks, could understand it. This did help, sometimes but it could also be very confusing. The problem was that the real programming features, such as column position, became lost in the English 'descriptions'.

A proposition, and hence a program, can adopt many equivalent forms. It is the job of a compiler to make a transformation of a program in order that it is acceptable for a particular computer to run it. For any computer there are an infinite but bounded number of possible structural forms for a given program. The possibilities are bounded by the limitations of the compiler and the intended final form of the program (the essential program). Apart from these limitations the choice of form chosen is in the hands of the programmer. This means that:

- Reverse engineering is impossible unless domain information is used. This is because there is no rational link between a real world domain and the program. The world is always open to novel interpretations that depend upon purpose.
- Design methods will generally only limit what is possible to implement unless they are 'complete'. A 'complete' method is one that constrains the possible designs to that of the limits of the machine being programmed.

- Machine mismatches can be detected through tautology. This is already done with such ideas as a parity bit; a mechanism for assuring the correctness of a computer word by indicating that there should be either an even or odd number of bits.
- Programs on 'quantum' computers are bounded by operations that do not depend upon knowing an interpretation. A 'quantum' computer is one that is based on the idea of a 'qbit' or quantum bit. This works at the atomic level where 'superposition' is possible. Superposition means existing simultaneously in more than one state (two in this case). A qbit has two simultaneous states and so every operation is performed on all possible states simultaneously. This, in effect, allows massive operational parallelism. Small-scale experiments have shown it can work in principle. The problem, in practice, is the maintenance of the very special environment in which it can happen.
- Formal 'objects' (e.g. Windows in Object Oriented) will be stable but informal 'objects' (e.g. persons, chairs or games) will never be fully captured or be stable because they are irrational sets (see example above).
- It will not be possible to completely represent certain human functionality such as natural language understanding on any machine that is not adaptable.
- Increasing a training set for machine-learning algorithms will eventually cause degradation in its recognition performance if the set includes irrational distinctions. This is because there will arise increasing number of contradictions as further training examples are given.

9.4 Inferential Semantics

From an engineering point of view the only information that can be experienced by an individual is the result of the interaction of the individual's sense organs with the world. This is not a passive view, since these organs are also controlled by an inference engine; namely the human mind. It is only through inference and the senses that we experience the world and relate to other people. So, like the computer, we might be able to trace the sense of our understanding of the world through the tracing of internal constructs to our senses. However, this would not be of any great help to other people since it is unlikely that we are identical in the same way as two computers that are constructed according to a defined engineering diagram are identical. If we were to be different by as little as one bit we could not ever be sure that a 'program' would mean the same if 'run' in different heads or that it would even 'run' at all. So tracing and knowing the 'program' (or our internal constructions) is not very useful. This puts some doubt on the value of tracing circuits in the human brain as a means of understanding how 'it works'.

What could work, from a purely pragmatic point of view, is if individuals could construct models of the world, and of other people, that were sufficient to meet the needs of surviving in the world and with others. This model does not have to be exact, just sufficient. However, to do this we have to extend our semantic model to have another definition of meaning; a definition that does not depend upon the direct referencing of objects. For Wittgenstein, in the Philosophical Investigations, he extends the idea of the meaning of a word to include its use in language (PI 43).

> PI 43 For a *large* class of cases – though not for all – in which we employ the word "meaning" it can be defined thus: the meaning of a word is its use in the language. And the *meaning* of a name is sometimes explained by pointing to its *bearer*.

We can interpret this extended definition of meaning to imply a process of inference. During conversation, both listened to and participated in, a process is going on where a model of the meaning of words is being constructed through inference. This is a group activity and one designed to construct something common in the way language and the world may be perceived; a way that allows communication to occur. However, these models are only understood by their effectiveness, their ability to make predictions and their coherence within a group-dynamic situation. They can never have been 'seen' directly since they only exist within an individual.

This lack of boundaries for concepts is the *family resemblance* effect detected by Wittgenstein, such that 'games' form a family, and he illustrates this by further examples in the PI (PI 67). It is this effect that fuzzy sets, probability and belief networks, were intended to overcome (see also PI 71) without losing the power of referential assignment. In 2003, a research team in Mexico, in conjunction with Salford University, started to explore the use of family resemblance with a learning system in order to approach human performance in categorization (Vadera et al. 2003). However, despite this insight, they remain firmly fixed in assessing their results within the classical paradigm and consequently they did not really move our boundaries of understanding any further.

The tension caused by the dual semantics that pivots on the essential (defining) and accidental (non-essential) meaning of the signs used in programs has been recognised, as can be seen by the continued search for new languages, program structuring and systems design methods (e.g. Java, conceptual modelling and object oriented programming). The central problem of the human context has also been addressed through the pursuit of natural language understanding, naïve physics (the physics as described for every day purposes), case-based reasoning (reasoning using examples) and adaptive interfaces. There is a belief that given sufficient power or moving beyond the Turing machine would somehow solve the problem. This has not been demonstrated with such efforts such as many-fold increases in computer power or parallel mechanisms including neural nets. None of the approaches tried so far have really succeeded. Many of the pursuits have been constrained by the formal bounds represented by the Tractatus, and of those people who have tried to break away with novel approaches none of them have bridged the gap identified here.

9.5   The Real Challenge

An alternative to Wittgenstein's family resemblance is Lakoff's (Lakoff 1986; Lakoff and Johnson 1980) use of prototypes (paradigms) and metaphor instead of reference. With either route we have a more acceptable approach to human relationships in

Fig. 9.4 Showing where change can occur to solve the dual semantic problem

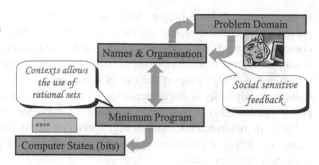

that there will always be a need for human judgment because what is acceptable behaviour or performance is a time sensitive and socially dependent notion. The requirement to encapsulate a wide range and ever changing perceptions of a problem domain will be the need for a continuous link with human activity. Such perceptions cannot be predicted and hence planed for in advance. Thus many of the current principles of design will have to be shelved, and two distinct design paths must be forged that involve the two independent elements of a program: the formal rational and the informal irrational (Fig. 9.4).

The challenge is this: can we construct computing based upon:

* family resemblance rather than sets,
* paradigms rather than concepts,
* metaphor rather than deduction?

Can we devise systems that have judgment rather than decisions? One possibility is that we might be able to write dynamic, socially sensitive interfacing-compilers that can match any program to any user (see Fig. 9.4).

Such a compiler would be in 'conversation' with its user, other users and machines via (say) the Internet, absorbing human cultures and language so that its generated semantic and semiotic mappings made a program usable by a person. This might provide a more natural communication between people and machines; it may identify what is really meant by common sense.

9.6 A Science of Mechanisms

The original idea behind the grand challenge in 2005 (see Chap. 8) was to provide a series of challenges that would be represented by non-classical computing. It was a hope that such explorations would produce computational engines that somehow would avoid some of the limitations found in the current crop of computers. It was noted during the meeting that many of these difficulties would either identify:

the existence of irrational sets

or

the mismatch between the computer and the problem domain.

It was suggested that a bigger challenge would be to develop a Science of Mechanisms. This science would evolve a way of arranging mechanisms into family organisations and in particular identify such mechanisms by their organisational, features; features that are relevant to being able to counter the above issues of mismatch and will also support the use of irrational sets. A result would be a way of reducing complexity of implementation by construction mechanisms that match the problem. Flexibility to change (as required for irrational sets) would be provided by a change in mechanism definition. Mechanism definition would also include the soft variants in terms of program organisation and the possibility of combining distinct physical implementations.

References

Lakoff G (1986) Women, fire, and dangerous things. University of Chicago Press, Chicago

Lakoff G, Johnson M (1980) Metaphors we live. University of Chicago Press, Chicago

Vadera S, Rodriquez A, Succar E (2003) Family resemblance, Bayesian networks and exemplars. AISB Quarterly No. 114, p 1, 11s

Wittgenstein L (1921) Tractatus Logico-Philosophicus (English edition 1961). Routledge and Kegan Paul, London

Wittgenstein L (1953) Philosophical investigations. Blackwell, Oxford

Chapter 10
Knowledge for Design

"It is to be noted that when any part of this paper appears dull there is a design in it"

Richard Steel (1672–1729)

10.1 Knowledge-Based Systems

Having dealt early with the issues of intelligence and the dual semantics of computer programs in Chap. 9, we must now address the issue of how to design a knowledge-based system.

A Knowledge-based system was coined to distinguish a database system from one that captured expertise or 'knowledge'. Such systems are a product of Artificial Intelligence research. They have taken on many roles as people come to terms with the idea of manipulating knowledge. In the first instance, a knowledge-based system was considered by many people to be a direct replacement of an expert. The "Turing test" was often evoked as a paradigm for a knowledge-based or expert system. This paradigm is where given the limited means of communication with a computer it should not be possible to tell the difference between the knowledge-based system and an expert (hence the term expert system). The original designers of such systems had high expectations that have never really been fulfilled.

The Turing test, as I have suggested in Chap. 1, has always been a misconceived approach to a specification of the objectives of Artificial Intelligence, since it has the appearance of a clear definition in that it uses equivalence, but this notion of equivalence does not include the most important element. This element is the exact manner in which a user of a knowledge-based system would attempt to make the distinction between a person and a program to determine the criteria to be satisfied that a person and a program are in practice equivalent. It is within this set of actions or this specification of the criteria that the real difficulties lay.

The analogue of knowledge was often considered (although only half seriously by the practitioners) as a sort of substance that was extractable (mined) from experts. The extraction process (knowledge acquisition) is accomplished by interviews with the expert where every utterance, action and gesture (if possible) is recorded on audio and/or videotape. The script is then analyzed (the 'ore' refined) by a knowledge engineer, sometimes with the help of a computer 'induction' program. The induction

© Springer International Publishing Switzerland 2014
T. Addis, *Natural and Artificial Reasoning,* Advanced Information
and Knowledge Processing, DOI 10.1007/978-3-319-11286-2_10

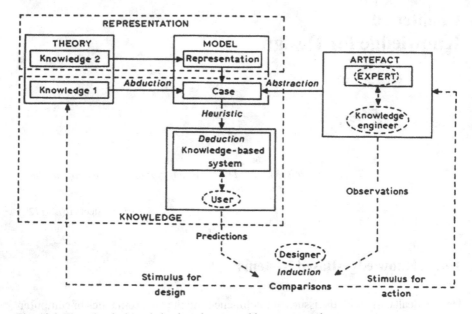

Fig. 10.1 The role of a knowledge-based system with respect to a theory

program will identify (with respect to the tasks to be performed by the expert) the information-carrying statements or actions and reject redundant statements or actions (Chap. 4).

The result of knowledge acquisition would be a model of the expert in the form of a representation that was at least indirectly convertible to a computer implementation. The target representation will depend upon the knowledge-based system used. Many systems are variants of a 'production rule' system that presumes the existence of a deductive inference unit that can work under the guidance of some simple heuristics to infer an expert's actions from the model. The model of the expert is given in the form of 'if... then... ' rules. This is a rule of the form "Rule 34: If the patient has a high temperature and (Rule 56 or Rule 57 are true) then the patient has flu". Many of these expert system models may be fine-tuned with the aid of weightings (sometimes called certainty factors or probabilities) that are assigned to each of the rules (see Chap. 6).

These models can never be complete since the systems that use them rarely have the capability to interact directly with the environment and even those that do will be deprived of many of the refinements of the human senses. The models have to rely on a human agent (the user) who must be able to interpret the meaning of the words generated by the model. These words instruct the user in an exploration of and the actions to be performed in the task domain (See Chap. 9). Thus, a less ambitious view of a knowledge-based system is as an aid or intellectual assistant to a skilled user (Addis 1985). The exact position of a knowledge-based system in the scheme of activities is shown in Fig. 10.1.

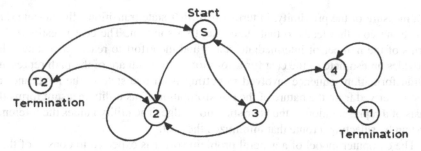

Fig. 10.2 States and transformations in a problem space

The model is referred to as the knowledge of the 'Expert'. The model is derived from the knowledge acquisition results provided by the 'knowledge engineer' and these results are interpreted by the designer in terms of the 'Theory' (Fig. 10.1; 'Knowledge 1'). The process of deriving the model from the 'Theory' depends upon 'Abduction' and 'Abstraction' (formerly called type 2 and type 1 abduction respectively—Addis 1987). The model is a 'Case' (an element of the extension) of the theory of knowledge given in terms of some representation scheme ('Knowledge 2'). The model is driven by deductive inference and controlled by heuristics (Abduction type 3) towards a chosen goal. Induction uses the results of the model and observations to either, confirm (justify) the model or to stimulate further action and design.

Knowledge-based systems provide possible intellectual assistance through the animation and automation of representations (vehicles of thought). In order to build better aids to thought we need a better grasp of what is involved in the human use of representations (so we can automate aspects of that use). The account, as is normally assumed in AI, is based upon problem solving as portrayed by Newell and Simon (1956). This theory (of knowledge) is a derivative of a human problem-solving model, an example (a case) of which was first implemented as the Logic Theory Machine (LTM). The LTM was later extended to a General Problem Solver (GPS). This theory was proposed in order to describe the general behavior of people reporting on their thought processes as they were solving problems (Newell and Simon 1973).

In essence, the theory states that problem solving is a process of exploring a "problem space" for a solution. A problem space can be considered as a directed graph (see Fig. 10.2). The nodes of the graph represent the different possible states of a problem. There is usually a single start state that indicates the initial situation and a set of termination states that indicate the desired result. The arrows that go from node to node represent the actions that are available to an agent in that state, and these actions transform the problem from one state to the next. Problem solving is the discovery of a path from the start state (S) to one of the termination states (T1, T2). The solution is the sequence of transformations (arcs) that make up the path.

The theory has its foundations in utility theory (Luce and Raiffa 1957). Utility theory is a means through which choices can be assessed (their utility) and decisions can be made. The utility of a state in Newell and Simon's version of decision theory is a measure of the proximity, in terms of further state transitions, that a state (and hence the cost that leads to that state) has to a solution. The cost is estimated in terms of the number of intermediate states and the effort to reach each state. This provides an estimate of the cost for a solution path. Each arc of the path represents a transformation sequence involved in getting from one state to the next, and the cost is derived from the nature of the transformation. This utility measure forms the basis of a representation of the heuristic knowledge. The utility guides the inference system by selecting a route that minimizes the cost.

The computer model of a general problem solver is expected to consist of three elements that are related to different kinds of case knowledge:

- a data representation that describes a set of problem states and has the potential to describe all the problem states (the abstraction of the problem),
- a set of data updates that describes how a given state can be transformed to a new state (the deductive system),
- a set of heuristics that provides guidance to a search algorithm through the problem space (the heuristic knowledge).

These elements may be represented in a wide variety of forms depending upon the knowledge representation scheme used (e.g. clauses, rules). Many AI programs will have these three elements made explicit in their design even though they may have been designed through a different theoretical framework (e.g. object oriented programming, semantic nets, frames, case systems, etc.). Most of the alternative current AI theories (of knowledge) are concerned primarily with representation.

The appeal of Newell and Simon's theory is that the states of the problem can be represented as propositions. These propositions are formal representations of natural sentences that are written thus:

All (x) Elephant (x) - > Colour (Grey, x)
[All elephants are grey]
Exists (y) Name (Dumbo, y) and Elephant (y)
[There is an elephant called Dumbo]

and the transformation from one state to the next is the application of deductive inference to selected propositions. The deductive inference step is an extension of Modus Ponens called Resolution. The only requirement is that the propositions must be normalized into clauses, a process that can be done automatically. This process is appealing because it demonstrates "human thinking" as proposed by logicians. Further, it defines the start of an important research program into modeling human cognition that has deep foundations in Mathematics and the formal traditions of Science. The program can draw upon a long history of development that includes work from many of the best thinkers of the last two millennia. This research program has been pursued vigorously by many centers in the UK such as Imperial College (London) and Edinburgh University.

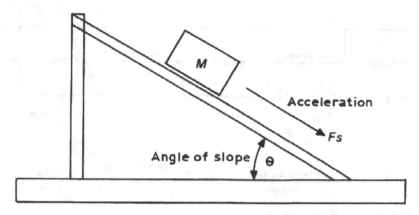

Fig. 10.3 A spatial representation of a slide

10.2   The Role of a Model

Newell and Simon's problem-space is defined by means of linguistic (propositional) representations and the manipulation of linguistic representations to solve problems. This has stimulated the development of animated and automated sentence manipulators (the logic research program). However, scientific and engineering thinking uses other vehicles to model that should not be regarded as reducible to just sets of sentences.

As an illustration of what is outside the philosophy of the logic research program, consider the process of designing a simple slide as shown in Fig. 10.3. Such a slide may form part of the transportation system for a product in a factory. This product will have specific dimensions, weight and composition. After the drawing of a sketch that shows the spatial relationship of the components of the slide, it is required to determine the acceleration of the product down the slide so that the velocity may be calculated at its point of reception.

Reference is now made to the theory of Dynamics. In a wider context, a theory in this paper does not necessarily mean a formal theory. Any set of statements that forms some coherent description of the world that can be used to "render facts likely" (Peirce 1934) will be considered a theory. A theory, for example, is a set of propositions that reduces the uncertainty in the world for an agent. Some aspects of the theory of Dynamics (Newtonian Mechanics) may be presented as such a series of statements thus:

T1. Every Body travels in a straight line unless a force acts upon it.

T2. Momentum is the product of mass and velocity.

T3. Force is the rate of change of momentum.

T4. For every action, there is an equal and opposite reaction.

T5. Gravity is an acceleration caused by the mutual attraction of mass.

T6. Weight is a force due to gravity.

T7. Forces (and hence velocities) will add as vectors.

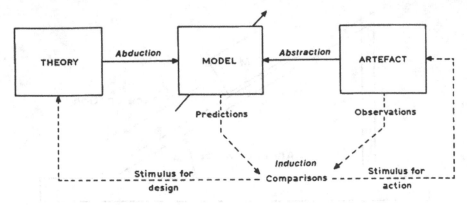

Fig. 10.4 A cycle in the design process

From this theory a more formal dynamic model may be constructed using mathematics. In this case a first attempt will appear as:

M1. A Body of mass M on a slide.

M2. The slide is at angle θ with respect to the horizontal.

M3. The weight of the Body is $W = M*G$ where G is the acceleration due to gravity.

M4. The force down the slide $Fs = W*Sin\,(\theta)$.

The slide is constructed and it is found that the actual acceleration is much less than that predicted. After checking the calculations, reference is then made back to the Theory (see Fig. 10.4). The Theory restricts the set of possible explanations for this discrepancy and guides the designer to create a better model. In this case, the theory limits the set of possible proposals to the existence of another force acting on the Body. This force then 'explains' the discrepancy between the model and the observations; this force is called 'friction'.

The notion of friction does not come directly from the theory but is an interpretation of both experience (i.e. there is a recognizable feeling of resistance when moving the Body on the slide which becomes greater with increased pressure between the surfaces) and the Theory (i.e. only forces can influence the motion of a Body). The process that generates the insight (that these disparate experiences and concepts should be amalgamated into a simple causal element identified as friction) is called 'abductive' inference. An important component of abduction is the element of contact by an agent with the world. The Model is modified thus:

M4'. The force down the slide

$$Fs' = W*[Sin(q)\,K*Cos(q)]$$

where K is the coefficient of friction for the materials in contact.

The coefficient of friction K is a concept that has evolved from the need to adjust the model to fit the observations (see Fig. 10.4). This indicates that the notion of friction does not and cannot emerge from only the manipulation of the sentences that make up the theory.

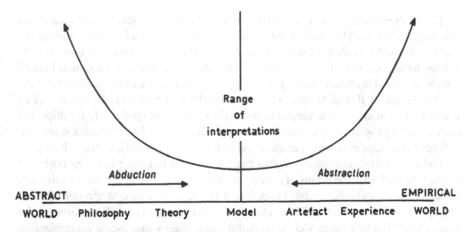

Fig. 10.5 The Model as a point of contact between theory and Artefact

A precise relationship between a theory and a model cannot be easily defined as they both represent a range of possible interpretations and share many of the same properties (cf. Aris 1978). There is a continuum of theories or models ranging from the non-specific (most general) to the identification of unique cases. The relationship between a theory and a model is that a model will be associated with a more specific situation (a case) than a theory. The complete range of models derivable from a theory will be called the 'extension' of the theory. The theory from which a model is derived is called its 'intension'.

Figure 10.5 illustrates the model as the end-product of several stages of abduction. The model emerges from the potentially infinite set of possibilities that may be presumed to exist within the abstract world of the human imagination. However, the model is also the end-product of several stages of abstraction of the potential distinctions in the empirical world. The model captures only a subset of the possible features of an artifact. In the above case, it does not show the color, texture, smell or structure of the materials; it's a coherent subset, which serves our purpose. A model and a theory both together encapsulate an understanding of the world that is the result of purpose and experience. A model and its associated theory will be called 'declarative knowledge' if the model relates to at least one feasible artifact (i.e. can be constructed). What is feasible and the methods used to make such a judgment, such as the comparison of predictions with observations, are referred to as 'inductive inference' or just 'induction'.

In the case of the slide, the mathematical model will describe the active forces of interest provided the right combination of calculations is applied. The knowledge of how to perform a particular chosen calculation correctly is 'deductive inference' or just 'deduction'. Mathematical calculations are deductive in the sense that they are 'valid' operations and truth preserving. The understanding of how to perform the three forms of inference; abduction, deduction and induction will be called 'inferential knowledge'.

The mathematician, given the purpose of the model, will select the right combination of calculations. This understanding of how to use the model to make appropriate predictions will be called 'heuristic knowledge'. Heuristic knowledge may be considered to be the result of another form of inference since it requires a similar kind of insight observed in abduction; the perception of the significance of certain particulars.

The design of this slide (the artifact) currently uses two models: the model of forces represented in mathematical terms, and the model of spatial relationships that uses a scaled projection of the slide on to two dimensions. The two models are two different abstractions from experience and two different abductions from theory.

The two models are related in that there is a clear mapping between points of contact. In this case, the points of contact are the angle of the slope and the direction of the forces acting on the Body[1]. Other design tasks, such as the construction of VLSI chips, will use nine or ten different models to represent different abstractions of the same object. Each of the models is related to some theory that uses a generalization of the characteristics to be controlled and formed in the design. A theory is only useful if it provides this control. The control is incorporated in the constraints (lawful behavior) and in the procedures for deriving the consequences of any design decision within the domain of the theory. Hence, the laws of electronics (e.g. Ohm's Law) provide a means through which particular circuits (electronic models) may have predictable performance.

Related to each model type are one or more preferred representations and a means of deducing measurable features of the artifact. Before the invention of Cartesian Projection as a method of depicting a normalized view of objects, the only means of representing spatial relationships was through sketches. Sketches (or perspective drafts or drawings) do not allow the possibility of extracting measurements or making detailed predictions of the distance between any two points on the object. Sketches do show certain ordinal relationships such as next, above, below, inside and meshing. However, the Cartesian projections, with the aid of a ruler and in some cases a little geometry, will provide not only this ordinal information but will also give a prediction of the distance between any two points.

Figure 10.6 shows details of the elements involved for one of the models in designing the slide. The theory involves both the representation scheme (mathematics) and the generalization of a particular aspect of the world (dynamics). The theory is made explicit by the model in the form of equations (case). Both the theory and the artifact influence the model. A mathematician interrogates the model using calculations. This person is usually the same person as the designer and who may use a calculator or lookup tables. The engineer must be able to interface with the artifact (the construct) through measurements (e.g. the angle of slope and the acceleration) in order to provide observations that can be compared with the predictions of the designer; the artifact must engage the model. The mathematician, engineer and designer indicate the skills (tacit knowledge) required to progress a simple design.

---

[1] The triangle of forces is not shown.

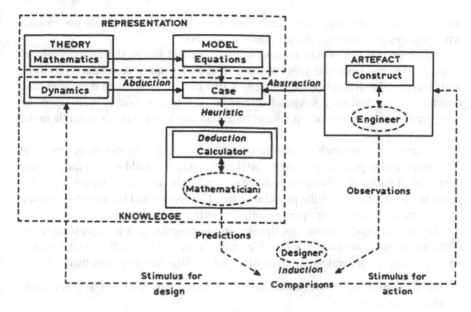

Fig. 10.6 The representation of knowledge and the skills for design

Although the model is the main component to be altered in the design process, the effectiveness of both the theory and the artifact are continually under review. If the models cannot be made adequate to reflect the artifacts, the theory will be modified, and an artifact will be reconsidered in the light of predicted performance and the achievement of the purpose. Progress can only be made if there exist both the beginnings of a theory and the inklings of an artifact from which a case model can be created. However, to modify a theory would seem to require the existence of a meta-theory, which has the same relationship to the theory as that which the theory has to the model. Model, theory and meta-theory will be referred to as different "levels" of knowledge. A theory is abduced from a meta-theory and supported through induction from experience with its models.

10.3 The Limits of Logic

The logic research program, after some initial success, seems to have reached a point where progress has slowed. There are several reasons for this, both technical and fundamental.

The "technical" reasons are to do with the excessive expansion of the problem space when faced with only a small increase in problem scale. This effect is known as the combinatorial explosion. The attainment of better heuristic knowledge and methods of assessing the state utility is a major objective in this research program. However, there is currently no general theory that explains heuristics nor describes how such knowledge may arise. Each case must be dealt with on its own merits where the designer supplies the heuristic component.

Techniques for the system to automatically extend the model as the problem space is explored have had some success in reducing the search space for some problems (e.g. Truth Maintenance Systems). However, in many cases these elaborate techniques have had only marginal effects. In the end, it usually falls upon the designer of the system to incorporate as much domain knowledge as possible in the heuristic component.

An alternative approach to the search space problem is to use more powerful computers, and in particular to use parallel processing. It would seem natural to use parallel exploration of a divergent problem space, but the amount of improvement depends upon the structure of the problem space. The control and intercommunication of the parallel processes for optimum effect is still a research topic.

The "fundamental" reasons for the slowing of progress call into question many of the assumptions on which logic and formal systems are based. It is clear from the description of the general structure of Artificial Intelligence programs that:

1. The concept of truth never enters into the issue of design except as a marker to show valid deduction,
2. There are several elements that must still be provided by the designer, the knowledge engineer and the user.

The elements comprising 2 are:

- The heuristic knowledge and purpose for which the solution is required (the 'heuristic' component).
- The range of interpretations of the symbols and structure in the model (the 'abductive' component).
- The association of the distinctions in the world with the primitives for each case (the 'abstractive' component).
- The creation of a model from a theory and its subsequent modification in the light of experience (the 'abductive' and 'inductive' component).

These are similar or associated reasons to those reasons why Wittgenstein explored an alternative view to his Tractatus and why Peirce concerned himself with semiotics and abductive inference. Part of the problem can be illustrated by a re-drawing of Fig. 10.3 as shown in Fig. 10.7.

Figure 10.7 suggests that the boundaries of first order and second order logic are restricted to the abstract world and limited to the relationships between theory and its models. Thus, the range of interpretations is not open-ended. However, there may be an infinite set of interpretations within each range. The vertical axis in Figs. 10.5 and 10.7 is an ordinal measure of transfinite numbers. The mapping of theory to model is a second order issue since the theory is used to generate new predicates. In the slide example, the new predicate Friction (x, f) was implied where x is a body and f the frictional force.

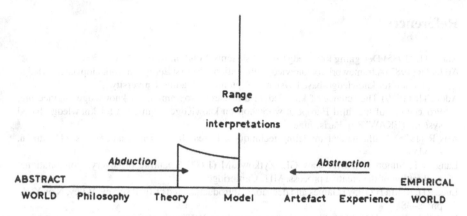

Fig. 10.7 The boundaries of first and second order logic

The mechanism through which this generation of predicates occurs is not fully understood; second order logic is incomplete. It is for this reason that the counterargument that logicians might raise concerning the generalization of logic to include any number of stages of abstraction cannot be fully justified. The complete formal step between levels of knowledge has not yet been achieved.

There are two-level 'abductive' programs that incorporate both theory and model based on something like a simple second-order logic (e.g. Langley et al. 1987). Nevertheless, the engagement of the model with the world still requires human action except in some very primitive cases (e.g. thermostats and other control mechanisms).

The argument for continuing the logic research program is strong and it is not the purpose of this chapter to suggest otherwise. What is being proposed is that alongside this research program should be a parallel research program. This program should include the human agent and a program that attempts to provide a richer structure to the knowledge description; a structure that can cope with a formal description of heuristics, interpretation, abduction and induction, a structure that may even be able to define intelligence unambiguously.

The benefit is not a proposal to develop automated models—that's already commonplace—but to provide automated aids to the process of moving between artifact, model and theory. The relationship between artifact and model, and model and theory is one of generalization and the major limitation of the logic research program is that by confining its attention to linguistic representations it cannot adequately encompass the full process by which humans move between the particular and the general. It is not merely the incompleteness (in the logician's sense) of second-order logic, which stands in the way; it is the incompleteness, in the ordinary sense, of the representations use by logician's. Here is where there is room to run a research program alongside the logic program (Addis 1989).

References

Addis TR (1985) Designing knowledge-based systems. London: Kogan Page

Addis TR (1987) A framework for knowledge elicitation. The first European workshop on knowledge acquisition for knowledge-based systems, September, Reading University

Addis TR (1989) The science of knowledge: a research programme for knowledge engineering. Proceedings of the third European workshop on knowledge acquisition for knowledge-based systems (EKAW' 89), Paris, June

Aris R (1978) Mathematical modeling techniques. Research notes in mathematics 24. Pitman, London

Langley P, Simon HA, Bradshaw GL, Zytkow JM (1987) Scientific discovery: computational exploration of the creative process. MIT, Cambridge

Luce RD, Raiffa H (1957) Games and decisions: introduction and critical survey. Wiley, New York, pp 12–38

Newell A, Simon HA (1956) The logic theory machine. IRE Trans Inf Theory

Newell A, Simon HA (1973) Human problem solving. Prentice-Hall, Englewood Cliffs

Peirce CS (1934) Scientific method. In: Burks AW (ed) Collected papers of C.S. Peirce, vol. VII. University Press, Cambridge

Chapter 11
Measures of Intelligence

He gave man speech, and speech created thought, which is the measure of the universe.

P. B. Shelley,
(1820, Prometheus Unbound)

11.1 IQ as a Measure of Intelligence

We will now describe a program, devised and constructed by Dr. Mohamad S. Zakaria (See Zakaria 1994). This program uses the models of only the three forms of inference, 'abduction', 'deduction' and 'induction' as described in Chap. 4. Abstraction will be done manually and is therefore pre-defined. The roles of the three forms of inference in creating and validating a hypothesis will be tested using a simple IQ test. This test requires the inferring of a hypothesis that is the generator of a sequence of numbers. The origin of these hypotheses was taken from Eysenck's numerical sequence IQ tests (Eysenck 1974a, b). The IQ test sequences and the extensions of the sequences generated by applying the inferred hypothesis are used as a testing ground for the implementation.

First, I will attempt to explain the rationale of using IQ as a measure of intelligence. Using the IQ tests to measure intelligence has always been controversial, largely because there is a great deal of disagreement between experts about the nature of intelligence. We have already looked at the inadequacy of both Turing's and Simon and Newell's definition in Chaps. 1 and 5.

Eysenck notes that 'there is no satisfactory criterion that exists to measure intelligence'. He adds that if there really were a satisfactory criterion, then intelligence tests, in their current form, would probably be superfluous. However, we might be prepared to agree that people of high intelligence are more likely to succeed at intellectual tasks involving solving problems by applying existing principles to new facts, the discovery or invention of relations between existing facts, learning the new interconnected facts and principles, and other similar activities.

Training in schools and universities attempts to introduce students to areas of knowledge requiring the use of such abilities. The success of the student is measured by examinations. In part at least, these examinations are to measure individual student's intellectual abilities. As the late Professor Edwin G. Boring pointed out, intelligence, by definition, is what intelligence tests measure (Jensen 1969).

© Springer International Publishing Switzerland 2014
T. Addis, *Natural and Artificial Reasoning,* Advanced Information
and Knowledge Processing, DOI 10.1007/978-3-319-11286-2_11

Intelligence tests deal with discovering relationships and educing correlates by noting similarities and differences among given facts. They are the measurement of general intelligence, known as the 'g' factor in psychology. They assess our pattern of abilities to discover the relevant qualities and relationships between objects or ideas that are before us and to evoke other relevant ideas. No psychologists have ever claimed that these tests can also measure other qualities such as character and artistic talent. Controversial they may be, but most competent judges agree that they provide a better measure of intelligence than any other at our disposal.

The validity of intelligence tests is also shown by the fact that their results are highly correlated with other activities in which intelligence plays a dominant part. For example, Eysenck noted the correlation between the results of intelligence tests with the success of students at university (Eysenck 1974b, p. 20). Students who obtain a first-class degree have usually scored ten IQ points higher upon first entering university than did students obtaining lower-class degrees; successful students have usually scored some 15 points higher than students who failed to obtain a degree at all. The close relationship found between IQ and the success at university is remarkable. For the very same reason, intelligence tests have been profitably employed and widely used by psychologists. They have also been used, for example, by school medical officers in the diagnosis of mental deficiency (e.g. the Terman and Merrill 1936, 1960, New Stanford Revision of the Binet-Simon Scale was once the most popular in Britain), by specialized training centers (such as pilot school), and by top universities (Oxford and Cambridge) as a mean to assess their potential students.

Argument about the nature of intelligence has been going on since 1920s. Eysenck pointed out in 1974 that "it is fair to say that it may even be that in the next twenty years we will know a little more about the nature of intelligence than we do at present". He continued "until then we shall have to contend with our ability to measure it with a certain degree of accuracy, and with such data as can be collected by means of intelligence tests" (Eysenck 1974b, p. 38). It is now 40 years later, and very little progress has been made.

There is another reason the IQ test is being used. Throughout modern history, professional psychologists devised intelligence tests. They depended on a pre-conceived norm of a mental function, and were standardized so that their results would fall within the normal or Gaussian curve of distribution. The standardization of an intelligence test involves the expert use of statistical techniques. It also involves much time and labor, because in order to establish norms, the tests were applied to a representative sample of those for whom it is intended—a sample in which all the relevant differences in the whole group are represented in their proper proportions—and the distribution of scores for every age group were determined.

This standardization is very important in that it provides a scale to measure intelligence. In this respect, measurement of intelligence resembles measurement of height—or, indeed, anything else. Knowing the height of a 16-year-old boy, we know whether he is tall, short or average by comparing him with the average height of boys of 16. Similarly, if we know the score the boy obtains in an intelligence test, we can determine his brightness or dullness by comparing it with its appropriate norm. The tests and the scale were rigorously tuned to reflect human intelligence throughout the history of their construction in Europe and the USA.

IQ tests are used to measure human intelligence rather than machine intelligence. This is of paramount importance since rather than constructing a machine with intelligence capability, I am attempting to describe a model that was devised by Zakaria (1994) of the human decision-making process within a problem IQ domain. Since no predefined framework for this decision-making process existed in this domain at the time the model was constructed, its form was based upon IQ tests. The comforting component about this very practical approach is that these tests reflect human intelligence derived from empirical evidence. A definition of intelligence may be disagreed with but performance cannot be denied.

For this purpose, a subset of intelligence tests was selected, to measure the success of this model. The range of tests seeks to assess intelligence in a direct and reliable manner. These tests contain a number of miscellaneous problems, since it is only in this way that the test can yield a measure of that general ability (the g factor) which is intelligence. However, these problems aimed for the fundamental objective: the demand for relational and constructive thinking which involves the discovery of relationships and the induction of correlates. From the set of 18 different tests (each with between 35 and 40 problems), only those that deal only with numerical sequence extrapolation were selected, since they served the purpose and objective of testing the model proposed.

11.2 Sequence Extrapolation as a Model

Given a sequence of numbers, the system is organized to find a simple rule from which such a sequence might have been generated. The creation and validation of hypotheses are performed by interacting and co-operating retroductive, deductive and inductive inferences.

Note that retroduction is closely related to 'abduction' as described in Chap. 2 (see Fig. 2.9). Retroduction selects a concept drawn from a set of concepts and constructs (abduces) a specific hypothesis to 'explain' the observed facts. In this case the observed facts are a sequence of numbers. Abstraction is not needed here since a computer easily recognizes numbers and the basic transform functions for numbers.

In its simplest form, the process is similar to the simple 'generate and test' procedure (see Chap. 2, Fig. 2.9). However, the process is more complex than this simple cycle in that the results at each stage influence the way in which each element in the cycle behaves. There is a "tension" among the three inferences and this "tension" provides feedback data from one inference to another in order to improve the quality and credibility of a potential hypothesis. Figure 11.1 illustrates this tension.

Note that Fig. 2.9 in Chap. 2 and Fig. 4.4 in Chap. 4 there is an extra inference of 'abstraction'. Abstraction infers the relevant features that form the appropriate hypotheses. In Chaps. 2 and 4, I considered 'abstraction' as a fourth inference. However, I will not consider it here because, first, this is not usual in the literature and second, I am dealing with only numbers and the sequences that use the notion of

Fig. 11.1 The interaction
between the different types of
inferences

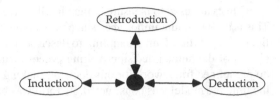

numbers. The abstraction element for inference is thus already done. The mechanism
described here is simplified by excluding any direct and dynamic modification of
one inference type by another. The processes of inference will remain fixed for this
implementation.

The black solid circle in Fig. 11.1 is a controller that manages the flow of information (thick arrow) between the three inferential mechanisms. A tension is created
when the three inferential mechanisms cooperate to formulate a viable hypothesis.
Communication between the mechanisms involves a cycle of retroduction, deduction and induction as well as the feeding-back of information, which will ensure that
a hypothesis is applicable within the three mechanisms. In a normal mixed IQ test
that involves other sequences than numbers, the process of 'abstraction' becomes an
important component of this tension (c.f. Chap. 2).

For a given set of facts (e.g. a sequence of numbers), it is the role of *retroduction*
to create a reasonable hypothesis for those facts (e.g. that particular sequence). *Deduction* exercises the hypothesis and returns a prediction of a new fact (e.g. the next
number in the series). The validation of the retroduced hypothesis is the function of
induction that ensures that the hypothesis is suitable for the purpose (e.g. the prediction is correct, the calculation was not too complex, it fits all or most of the facts and
the form of the hypothesis is simple).

The process of creating and validating a hypothesis is governed by:

- a set of hypothesis generators called concepts,
- a set of criteria, and
- two stages of learning that orders the formation of these concepts and criteria.

The learning process and the final selection of a hypothesis from the set are dependent
upon the validation of the hypothesis against a criterion. The criterion is selected from
a set of criteria (see Table 11.1) each of which relate to a hypothesis or concept. The
validation process (i.e. induction) is the test for specified features of the generated
hypothesis against a pre-set criterion (see Table 11.1).

11.3   Learning in Retroduction and Induction

However, the process of inferring a hypothesis depends not only upon the cycle of
retroduction, deduction and induction but also upon two stages of learning. There is a
primitive learning scheme in both the retroductive and the inductive module. Learning
in retroduction is a process of using the features of the abstraction to choose a concept

Table 11.1 Criteria for induction

Criteria	Meaning
CR1	The size of the hypothesis representation should not exceed a certain threshold value
CR2	All parameters used in the formulation of a hypothesis should be in integer form
CR3	The length of coefficients is set 1
CR4	All parameters are rational numbers
CR5	All coefficients are less than or equal to 10 and greater than or equal to -10

from which to generate a hypothesis (see Table 12.1 in Chap. 12). The process of hypothesis generation can be expensive and therefore a good initial choice of hypotheses will improve the potential success. However, this choice is in some sense making a pre-judgment and is in competition with induction. Learning in induction is the selection of a criterion from a set of criteria that relates to each concept. It is interesting to see that both the learning processes are complementary to each other to achieve symmetry. The learning in induction (the validation of a concept) is the inverse of learning in retroduction (the generation or selection of a concept).

There are two kinds of learning used in retroduction. The first kind of learning is a simple training set to establish a norm from which insight may be gained. This enables the system to orientate towards generally humanly accepted hypotheses as opposed to workable but humanly unacceptable hypotheses. The second kind of learning uses the facts given (e.g. the number sequence) in order to do a running test of confidence between competing hypotheses. We test both mechanism of learning over the same set of data in order to compare the relative changes in performance.

11.4 The Basic Concepts

This model employs five basic quantitative concepts to act as hypothesis generators. The concepts are shown in Table 11.2.

The five concepts can be recognized by the way they are formed.

11.4.1 INTER

This is a relationship between an element S_i in the sequence S and with those preceding it.

$$S_i = A_i * S^{fi}_{i-1} + k_i$$

For a particular sequence the start value, A(i), f(i) and k(i) need to be determined in order to fit this function.

Table 11.2 A list of concepts C that relate to hypotheses H

Rank. concept probability, D	Description	Example series
1. INTER 48 %, 0.09	A quantitative relation between elements in a sequence	4 3 5 17 83 497 3479 $4*2-5, 3*3-4, 5*4-3$
2. PERIODIC 42 %, 0.15	An oscillation in differential coefficient shift of a sequence	24 21 15 21 18 24 18 15 9 15 12 18 12 9 So first level of differential gives: $-3, -6, +6, -3, +6, -6$, rpt
3. POLY 7 %, 1.38	A polynomial function that fits into a given sequence.	0 1 4 9 16 25 36 49 64 Square of 0 to n
4. PRIME 2 %, 4.76	A prime function that fits into a given sequence	75 147 363 507 867 1083 1587 $3*$ Square (prime)
5. FACTORIAL 1 %, 5.85	A factorial function that fits into a given sequence	1 1 2 6 24 120 720 Fact(n)

Table 11.3 The generation of an INTER sequence using equation S_i

i	A_i i + 1	f_i 1	k_i i - 6	S
0				**4**
1	2	1	-5	$2.4^1 - 5 = 3$
2	3	1	-4	$3.3^1 - 4 = 5$
3	4	1	-3	$4.5^1 - 3 = 17$
4	5	1	-2	$5.17^1 - 2 = 83$
5	6	1	-1	$6.83^1 - 1 = 497$
6	7	1	0	$7.497^1 - 0 = 3479$
7	8	1	1	$8.3479^1 + 1 = 27833$
8	9	1	2	$9.27833^1 + 2 = 250499$

Example:

An example INTER sequence with:

$$\text{Start value} = 4, A(i) = i + 1, f(i) = 1 \text{ and } k(i) = i - 6$$

is

$$4, 3, 5, 17, 83, 497, 3479, 27833, 250499,$$

and is generated as shown in Table 11.3.

Table 11.4 Initial sequence cycle

Position	0	1	2	3	4	5	6	7	8	9	10	11
Number	24	21	15	21	18	24	18	15	21	27	|12	18

Table 11.5 Sequence cycle

Position	10	11	0	1	2	3	4	5	6	7	8	9
Number	12	18	24	21	15	21	18	24	18	15	21	27

11.4.2   PERIODIC

This is an oscillation in the differential coefficient shift of a sequence where POS_{min} is the position of the smallest number in the sequence and LCD_i is the Least Common Divisor. The function 'mod' is taken in the programming sense of being the remainder after integer division.

$$\text{Sub-harmonic function} = \sum ((i - POS_{min}) \bmod LCD_i)$$

Example:

Here we highlight the start of the cycle with the symbol 'l'. The complete cycle and the initial positions is shown in Table 11.4

$$(24, 21, 15, 21, 18, 24, 18, 15, 21, 27, |12, 18, \mathbf{24, 21, 15, 21, 18})$$

The start is found by looking for the minimum value (i.e. 12). The numbers after the pair (12, 18), in bold italic, match the numbers in italic at the beginning of the sequence. So, this sub-sequence starting at 12 represents the initial part of the complete cycle. So doing 'a right shift circular seven times' on the numbers (an old style computer operation applied to bits in a computer word) we have:

$$|\mathbf{12, 18,} \; 24, 21, 15, 21, 18) \; (24, 21, 15, 21, 18, \mathbf{24, 18, 15, 21,} 27,$$

So the sub sequence in italic *24, 21, 15, 21, 18* is the same as the italic *24, 21, 15, 21, 18 at* the start of the sequence. One of these sub-sequences can be deleted to give the minimum cyclic component of the total sequence as in Table 11.5

Taking the original given sequence starting with 24, 18, the cyclic component starts at position 10 (numbering from 0). The length of the cycle is 12. This has the least common divisors (LCD) of (3, 4). Using the Sub-harmonic function above we can express another formula for this periodic sequence as a function of the index i as (Table 11.6):

$$Pf(i) = S_{Min} + K * \sum ((i - POS_{min}) \bmod LCD_i)$$

$S_{Min} = 12$ -> minimum value in sequence

$POS_{min} = 10$ -> position/index of minimum value

Table 11.6 Application of Pf(i) for sequence example in Table 11.5

Index	Calculation	Result
10	$12 + 3.[((10 - 10) [mod3 + mod 4])]$, **$12 + 3.[0.mod 3 + 0.mod4]$**	12
11	$12 + 3.[((11 - 10)[mod3 + mod4])]$, $12 + 3.[1.mod3 + 1.mod4]$, **$12 + 3.[1 + 1]$**	18
12	$12 + 3.[((12 - 10)[mod3 + mod4])]$, $12 + 3.[2.mod3 + 2.mod4]$, **$12 + 3.[2 + 2]$**	24
13	$12 + 3.[((13-10)[mod3 + mod4])]$, $12 + 3.[3.mod3 + 3.mod4]$, **$12 + 3.[0 + 3]$**	21

Table 11.7 Periodic function at second level of differentiation

Differential (depth) (exponent)	Sequence	Variance
0	6 12 21 31 43 58 74 92 113 135 159	2668.85
1	6 9 10 12 15 16 18 21 22 24	36.23
2	3 1 2 3 1 2 3 1 2	0.75
3	-2 1 1 -2 1 1 -2 1 1	2.41

$K = 3 - >$ coefficient is required since all numbers must be divisible by 3. This will generate the correct values from POS_{min}

So far the PERIODIC concept is at the surface but it could occur at the first or second levels of differentiation. This is determined by selecting the row with the minimum variance. For example Table 11.7:

In Table 11.7 we see that the minimum variance is at level 2.

It is also possible to extend the periodic sequence to (say) the third differential of the series but no examples in IQ tests were ever found that conformed to that level of complexity.

11.4.3   POLY

This function fits a polynomial function to a given sequence. The general formula for such a function is:

$$F(x) = ax^n + bx^{n-1} + cx^{n-2} + \ldots.. + dx^2 + ex^1 + f$$

The process for fitting this polynomial function to a sequence is normally called regression analysis.

Table 11.8 First stage of sequence differentiation to that of a constant number

Differential (depth) (exponent)	Sequence
0	6 11 18 27 38 51 66 83 102 123
1	5 7 9 11 13 15 17 19 21
2	2 2 2 2 2 2 2 2

Example:

$$(6\ 11\ 18\ 27\ 38\ 51\ 66\ 83\ 102\ 123)$$

This sequence was originally generated by the function:

$$F(x) = x^2 + 2x^1 + 3$$
$$d/dx\ F(x) = 2x^1 + 2$$
$$d^2/dx\ F(x) = 2$$

Step 1. Differentiate the sequence until a constant difference is achieved (Table 11.8):
Step 2. The final differential (depth) gives the first exponent.
In this case it is x^2.
Step 3. The coefficient for the first exponent is obtained by taking the ratio of the final number, in this case 2, with the factorial of the exponent (also 2).

$$2/(1 * 2) = 1$$

so the first term will be x^2.
Step 4. For each element in the sequence its values will be:

$$1\ 4\ 9\ 16\ 25\ 36\ 49\ 64\ 81\ 100$$

Step 4. These values are subtracted from each element in the sequence. This is because:

$$(x^2 + 2x^1 + 3) - x^2 = 2x^1 + 3$$

$$(6-1)\ (11-4)\ (18-9)\ (27-16)\ (38-25)\ (51-36)\ (66-49)\ (83-64)$$
$$(102-81)\ (123-100)$$

$$= 5\ 7\ 9\ 11\ 13\ 15\ 17\ 19\ 21\ 23$$

So this is the sequence for $(2x^1 + 3)$
Step 6. The procedure is repeated for this next set of numbers (Table 11.9).

Table 11.9 Second differentiation stage to a constant	Differential (depth) (exponent)	Sequence
	0	5 7 9 11 13 15 17 19 21
	1	2 2 2 2 2 2 2 2

This gives exponent $= 1$ and coefficient $= 2$ for the second term.

$$(2/1) = 2$$

Step 7. Generating the next set of numbers using 2x we have:

$$2\ 4\ 6\ 8\ 10\ 12\ 14\ 16\ 18$$

Step 8. Subtracting 2x from these new first set of numbers.
   This because the sequence is $(2x + 3) - 2x = 3$

$$(5 - 2)\ (7 - 4)\ (9 - 6)\ (11 - 8)\ (13 - 10)\ (15 - 12)\ (17 - 14)\ (19 - 16)\ (21 - 18)$$

$$= 3\ 3\ 3\ 3\ 3\ 3\ 3\ 3\ 3$$

Step 9. This gives the final term 3 at depth 0 so we have:

$$F(x) = x^2 + 2x^1 + 3x^0$$

which may be rewritten in a more normal form as

$$F(x) = x^2 + 2x + 3$$

And is the original generating function abstracted from the sequence.

11.4.4   PRIME

This function generates sequences using the prime number sequence as its source. The sequence generated can take on the general form as fir INTER:

$$S_i = A_i * \textbf{Prime}^{fi}_i + k_i$$

The basic sequences are generated from the Prime number sequence:

$$2\ 3\ 5\ 7\ 11\ 13\ 17\ 19\ 23\ 29 \ldots \ldots$$

A simple example is the square of the prime numbers:

$$4\ 9\ 25\ 49\ 121\ 168\ 287\ 361\ 529\ 841$$

So you could have twice prime squared plus a constant. Such a complex form as this is unlikely in normal intelligence tests.

11.4.5   FACTORIAL

This is similar to PRIME except the generating sequence is now factorial. Factorial is shown by the symbol '!'. The factorial of 0 is represented as 0! defined as having the value of 1. 1! is also1. 2! is $1 * 2 = 2$, and $3! = 2! * 3$. So in general we can say:

$$\mathbf{n!} = (n - 1)! * n$$

where n is any integer. So the first ten, starting at 0!, factorials are:

$$1\ 1\ 2\ 6\ 24\ 120\ 720\ 5040\ 40320\ 362880$$

so the sequence of the squares of factorial would appear as:

$$1\ 1\ 4\ 36\ 576\ 14400\ 518400$$

Like PRIME it can have, in principle, a coefficient, exponent and offset that can also be functions.

The next Chap. 12 will use these functions to identify for a given numerical sequence the most likely concepts to apply.

References

Eysenck HJ (1974a) Check your own IQ. Penguin Books, London
Eysenck HJ (1974b) Know your own IQ. Penguin Books, London
Jensen AR (1969) How much can we boost IQ and scholastic achievement? Harv Educ Rev 39:8
Terman LM, Merrill MA (1936) Measuring intelligence. Houghton Mifflin, Boston
Terman LM, Merrill MA (1960) Stanford-Binet intelligence scale: manual for the third revision form L- M. Houghton Mifflin, Boston
Zakaria MS (1994) A model of machine intelligence based on the pragmatic approach. PhD Thesis, Computer Science Department, Unversity of Reading, March

Chapter 12
Implementing Intelligence

Routine, in an intelligent man, is a sign of ambition.

W. H. Auden,
(1958, 'The life of That-There Poet')

12.1 Features of Intelligence

I have specified in Chap. 11 the different concepts as defined by Zakaria (1994) in his thesis which characterize sequence types. However, this does not help in identifying what concept should be tried when given an IQ test sequence. For this it is required to identify features of sequences and associate them with the range of generating concepts. The problem is that the features assigned can apply to more than one concept. This issue can be readdressed as a form of pattern recognition in which the pattern of features will identify the most likely concept to apply to a particular sequence.

The problem of inferring a concept from a sequence of numbers is very similar to identifying a hypothesis from experimental observations, as described in Chap. 6. Here we found that the running confidence test is an important choice in a learning mechanism in that it can limit the amount of computation. When the degree of confidence in a particular hypothesis reaches a certain low level then the computation on that hypotheses will stop. The remaining hypotheses are further examined until there is a winner; then this hypothesis is put forward. This avoids having to perform deduction on all potential hypotheses. In addition it is this mechanism that provides part of the tension between the three inference mechanisms through an exchange of information on how well the competing hypotheses fit their respective criterion.

The abstraction of features from the facts gives rise to the formation of a hypothesis generated from one of the several predefined concepts. The abstracted features are a computationally simple test made on the data that will give some indication of the underlying series generator. A simple Bayesian decision-making system is then used to select the concept to be deployed in the hypotheses generator (see Chap. 6). The selection is either made under a simple pre-learning stage or learning as combined in a running window system. The learning that leads to a final choice of a concept depends not only upon the features that go towards the generation of the hypotheses but also upon a different set of features that show the general characteristics of, in

© Springer International Publishing Switzerland 2014
T. Addis, *Natural and Artificial Reasoning,* Advanced Information
and Knowledge Processing, DOI 10.1007/978-3-319-11286-2_12

Table 12.1 The four features (Features type 1) associated with a number sequence

Feature	Meaning, Example
F1	The sequence is either monotonically increasing or decreasing, 1 2 3 4 5 6 7
F2	All the numbers in the sequence have the same parity, 2 4 6 8
F3	The parity of the numbers in the sequence alternate, 1 2 3 4 5 6 7
F4	The size of each number in the sequence is either monotonically increasing or decreasing, 1 10 100 1000 10000

this case, a numerical sequence. The concepts are the target classes of a Bayesian learning mechanism for which this specific set of features provides information. The four features of a sequence are shown in Table 12.1 below.

Information about the prediction of a hypothesis is deduced and provides feedback to the retroduction process to refine and improve the hypothesis if there is a need for it. This result also serves as a framework for inductive testing. The consequence of induction causes further retroduction. The interaction of the three types of inference suggests why, while it is possible to generate a large number of hypotheses for given observable facts, people tend to generate and accept the first valid hypothesis that satisfies their preconceived criteria (Wason and Johnson-Laird 1968).

12.2   Implementation of Intelligence

The role of the controller, as shown in Fig. 12.1, is to monitor the progress of the creation, the prediction and the validation of hypotheses. It also keeps track of whether a hypothesis was successfully generated and validated during each cycle.

The ovals describe the main mechanism, the clear boxes indicate ordered lists of concepts, etc., and the shaded boxes give the information and its structure to be processed by the main mechanism. The 'thick' arrows pick out the main processing cycle.

The controller governs the process that assesses the relative confidence for the hypothesis generated by each concept. In one set of tests extending the original simple Bayesian learning into a 'running' Bayesian learning system generates the confidence. The controller feeds a portion of the number sequence to the retroduction by taking a sample of the extended sequence. This is achieved by partitioning the sequence into "windows" and each "window" will be subjected to retroduction at each cycle. Figure 12.2 shows two methods (A and B) of using a running window. A window (w_x) is a 'running' sample of a sequence. If X_1 to X_m is a sequence, then "windows" for X (size n) are generated as:

Fig. 12.1 The overall system

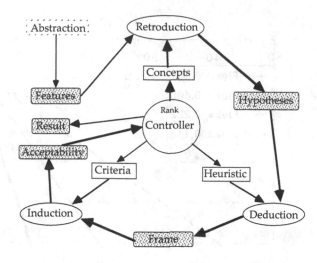

Fig. 12.2 Running probabilities 'with' (a Direct learning) and 'without' (b Window learning) event memory

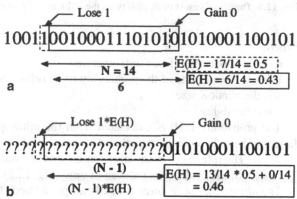

$$\{ \ (X_0, X_1, X_2, ..., X_n)$$
$$(X_1, X_2\ X_3, ..., X_{n+1}),$$
$$(X_2, X_3, X_4, ..., X_{n+2})$$
$$...$$
$$(X_{n-m}, X_{n-m+1}, ..., X_m)\}$$

A running probability matrix (see b in Fig. 12.2) is used to trace the occurrences of successful hypothesis. A function to update the running probability matrix is given by Addis (1985, p. 260) and is also used for belief adjustment as described in Chap. 11. So we have:

$$nP(H)_t = (n-1)\ P(H)_{t-1} + \alpha$$

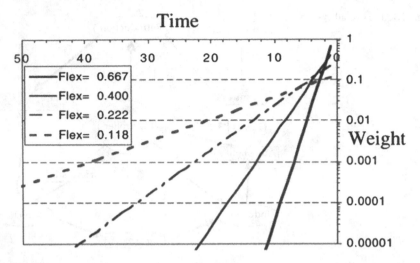

Fig. 12.3 The effectiveness of flexibility on the influence of past events on current belief

Where

$\alpha = 1$ if H occurs at time t or 0 otherwise

$P(H)_t$ is the estimate of the probability of an occurrence of H at time t

n is the window size

$1/n$ is flexibility

The probability P(H) is calculated from the initial probability. The success or failure of a prediction by a hypothesis for each window is used to dynamically rank concepts. The influence on any decision is derived from the accumulated evidence. The effect of the evidence is reduced in time (Fig. 12.3)

The *abstraction* of features is fixed and predefined. The two sets of features are orientated towards either determining the concept that might best fits the facts—the set called Features type 1 (see Table 12.1) or in providing the concepts data (e.g. the number sequence) to generate a specific hypothesis suitable for prediction—the set called Features type 2 (see Table 11.2 and in Chap. 11, Table 12.2). The position of the two sets of features in the system is shown in Fig. 12.4

It is the *first abstraction (Features type 1)*, which is *the initial abstract set of features* we discussed earlier. The purpose of this abstraction is to identify a list of features F1 to F4 (Table 12.2) from a window, w_x, provided by the controller. The drawn feature list is used to rank concepts from which a hypothesis will be generated to account for the sub-sequence in the current window w_x.

The *second abstraction (Features 2)*, the drawing of the number sequence to serve as the concept data, is done manually. The number sequence together with the ranked concepts (see Table 12.2) will be used by the retroductive mechanism to generate a suitable hypothesis for the sequence. The probability of this hypothesis having Feature 2 will then be updated to reflect past experience of a successful matching between hypothesis and features.

Table 12.2 Probability density table for features type 1

Concept (Probablity)	F1	F2	F3	F4
Inter (0.48)	0.35	0.41	0.37	0.00
Periodic (0.42)	0.30	0.27	0.30	0.00
Poly (0.07)	0.29	0.24	0.33	0.00
Prime (0.02)	0.03	0.03	0.00	0.00
Factorial (0.01)	0.04	0.05	0.00	1.00

Fig. 12.4 Learning concepts using features

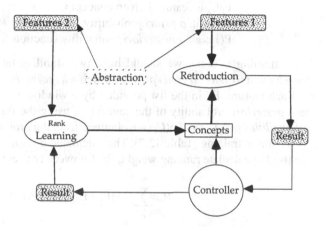

The initial probabilities of each hypothesis are either fixed to make each equally probable or are calculated from a training set by using a trainer. The trainer keeps past classifications of hypotheses and its features with its probability value in *two tables*. These are:

- A *probability density-table* to keep track of the history of occurrences of a hypothesis with the features of a sequence that produce such hypothesis,
- A *running probability table* to keep records of occurrences of each hypothesis.

Bayes rule provides the underlying mechanism for our classification. Both tables have to be 'trained' using a training set to establish their probability values. The effect of training is to accumulate experience and use them to "recognize" variations to be used for our classification of hypotheses. Training data was provided from standard IQ tests set by Eysenck (1974a, b). This data gives sequences from where actual hypotheses and features were extracted and used as input for the training session. Using these training patterns, we update the two probability density-table using the rule

$$P(C_i|F_j) = \frac{p(F_j|C_i)\,p(C_i)}{p(F_j)}$$

where

$$p(F_j) = \sum_{i=1}^{n} p(F_j|C_i)\,P(C_i)$$

C_i is concept i
F_j is feature j
$C_i|F_j$ is concept i given feature j
$F_j|C_i$ is feature j given concept i
$p()$ is an *a priori* probability function
$P()$ is an *a posteriori* probability function

Once training is done, we should have two stabilize tables to be used to guide retroduction to *select a concept* from which a *hypothesis* can be constructed.

Each feature, F_j, in the list provided by a window w_x will be used to calculate an *a posteriori* probability of the concept,c_i, using the Bayesian rule. The *a priori probabilities* $p(F_j|C_i)$ and $p(C_i)$ are obtained from the probability density-table given by the initial training (Table 12.2). The calculated *a posteriori probabilities*, P(C|F), are used to calculate ranking weight, R_i, for every concept C_i using

$$R_i = \sum_{j=1}^{|F\,L|} \log P(\,FL_j\big|C_j)\log P(C_i)$$

where FL is the feature-list and |FL| is the cardinality of the list, i.e. how many features are in the list.

This ranking function R_i is actually a variation of Shannon's entropy (Information Theory). The concepts are ranked according to their relative entropy. The concept C_i with the highest relative entropy value with respect to the range of features FL_j will be the most likely candidate to produce a correct hypothesis. The reason for this is that the features that contain the most information about the link between an observed sequence and the associated concept, are those that change the most with a change of concept. If it fails, the next highest ranking will be used.

12.2.1   The Deductive Process

The deductive process begins with an abduced hypothesis and prepares it for inductive testing. The deductive process draws consequences from the abduced function (i.e. prediction, size of representation, etc.) in preparation for the inductive testing. All this information is packaged and passed on as a frame. A frame is a set of predefined information requests that provide the information to fill the fields in a pre-set empty form.

12.2.2 The Inductive Process

The inductive process is the qualitative assessment of the abduced hypothesis set against pre-defined criteria (Chap. 11, Table 11.1). These criteria are primarily concerned with determining whether the hypothesis is simple enough to warrant acceptance. The set of criteria employed for this validation are the obvious features such as size of representation (it must be within a certain threshold value), parameters should be rational, the level of differential depth should not exceed a certain limit, etc. The criteria selection for assessing the abduced hypothesis is governed by the inverse of learning employed in retroduction. We employed a probability density table (as in retroduction) to keep track of the history of selection of criteria for each hypothesis and a criteria probability table to keep records of occurrences of criteria. The rule for updating the probability density table is similar to $P(C_i|F_j)$ above:

$$P(Cr_i|H_j) = \frac{p(H_j|Cr_i) \, P(Cr_i)}{P(H_j)}$$

where

$$p(H_j) = \sum_{i=1}^{n} p(Cr_j|H_i) \, P(H_i)$$

The calculated *a posteriori* probabilities of each criteria in the density table, $P(Cr|H)$, are used to calculate the determinant of the criteria $D(Cr_i)$ for the abduced hypothesis using:

$$D(Cr_i) = \sum_{j=1}^{n} \log P(Cr_i|H_j) \log P(H_j)$$

All non-zero $D(Cr_i)$ are taken to be the criteria to be assessed. If an abduced hypothesis matches all these criteria, it is an acceptable hypothesis. Otherwise, the retroductive process takes control and creates a new hypothesis as a function of the next concept in the ranking.

12.3 Feedback Assessment

Before the actually inductive assessment is carried out, there is a feedback assessment carried out. Feedback assessment looks for "irregularities" in the abduced hypothesis. These "irregularities" are used to refined a hypothesis to fit important criteria of acceptability. For example, given a function:

$$f(x) = x^4 - 16x^3 + 96x^2 - 256x + 256$$

from a sequence (256 81 16 1 0 1 16 81 256. . . .), the deductive process will detect that the retroduced function consists of fairly large numbers. The criteria indicate that the sequence should not be generated from a function starting from an index 0 or 1. Two features of the hypothesis (i.e. coefficients and the largest exponent) give a clue that the sequence may be generated from a function starting with index 4 or − 4. The alternating sign (+ and −) suggest that the most likely index is − 4. This information is returned to the retroduction so it can be used in refining the hypothesis.

If no such refinement is necessary, criteria assessment will be carried out.

If the factual information is exhausted before a suitable hypothesis reaches a stage of confidence or has achieved a satisfactory pass of the criteria, a second stage of hypothesis generation is begun. Under these conditions, it is assumed that the facts are generated (can be explained) by more than one hypothesis. There is a set of strategies based on symmetry that attempts to examine sub-sequences. The controller breaks the main sequence apart into sub-sequences (e.g. taking alternate values as two independent sequences) where each subsequence will be subjected to the same rigorous process of creation and validation.

12.4   Experiments and Discussion

We carried out two sets of experiments to test the model (see Fig. 12.5 and also Chap. 2, Fig. 2.10). The purpose in the first set of the two experiments is to test intelligence using Direct Learning (DL1, DL2). The 'D' indicates that all the information in a series is used, thus every given number in a test sequence is considered. This is similar to 'A' Fig. 12.2 except that every example is given from the beginning. The '1' will indicate that no previous learning is done on other training sets whereas the '2' shows previous learning on example series have been done before the final test sequence is given.

The alternative learning method is to use Window Learning (WL1, WL2), or running probability, as described in Chap. 11 and shown as 'b' in Fig. 12.5. In order to see clearly the behavior of the running probabilities, all hypotheses were processed at all stages through a numeric sequence. Thus the model would attempt to work out each next number in the given test sequence using each potential concept shown in Chap. 11, Table 11.2. The best one of the competing beliefs is chosen to formulate and present as an answer.

In the first experiment 1 of the first set DL, the probability of the likelihood of each concept was set initially to 0.2 (all of five potential concepts shown in Fig. 11.2 have an equal chance of being selected). In the second experiment '2' of this first set DL, the model was initially trained by using 85 sequences obtained from Eysenck (1974a, b) as the training set. The role of this initial training is to bias each concept towards the expected normal distribution implied by Eysenck's collection of test sequences.

In the second experiment, the running conditional probabilities WL1 and WL2 were calculated for each initial condition and the results obtained are shown in the graphs (see 'b' in Fig. 12.2)

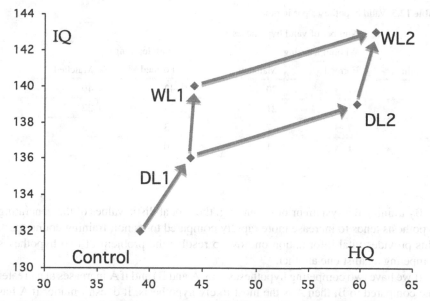

Fig. 12.5 The results of running the model with all the information in a given series DL1 and 2 as shown in a or limited to a window WL1 and 2 as shown in b Fig. 12.2

The running probability (i.e. y-axis) is the weighted average of **four** examples of a test sequence using a window size of **seven**. The selection of window size seven was made after running the model for various window sizes. We found that for our examples, seven was the optimal number for any significant differences to be detected in the values of the running probability. However, we must stress that seven is not an ideal number for all sizes of window. Different samples may need to be smaller or bigger in order for a change in the values of running probabilities to be significant. Note here that Eysenck only used an average of four numbers in his sequences for IQ tests.

The behavior of the system is shown by the graphs. This graphs indicate a similar trend for both experiments. The generating hypothesis shows an increase in its probabilistic values over time while others tend to collapse or be unstable. There are instances where two hypotheses are competing against each other where both their conditional probability values are on the increase. This phenomenon suggests that both hypotheses are actually two different manifestation of the same thing. For example, some polynomial functions can be represented as a periodic functions and vice-versa.

The results showed that the running conditional probability has the potential for limiting the exploration for a hypothesis. As we continue to assess a sequence, the probability value of some concepts increases while others decreases. A consistent decrease in probability value indicate that a particular concept should be abandoned from further consideration.

Table 12.3 Valid hypotheses per iteration

	Number of valid hypotheses			
	Without learning		With learning	
Iteration	Formed	Matched	Formed	Matched
1	41	20	42	40
2	21	21	24	22
3	7	7	3	3
4	1	1	0	0
5	0	0	1	1

By training the system prior to running, the probabilistic values of the generating hypothesis tends to increase more rapidly compared to its non-training counterpart. This provides vital information on how to resolve the problem of two hypotheses competing against one another.

If we have two competing hypotheses (say A and B) and if A increases at a greater rate compared to B, then A is the most likely hypothesis. It doesn't matter if A has a lower probabilistic value since its rate of change will cause it to close its gap on B and eventually will surpass B at some point.

However, it is important to note that since both A and B are competing against one another, they are really two representations or manifestations of the same thing. The behavior provided by the trained system merely pinpoints the generating hypothesis based on experience and the criteria for validation.

Another result is that the generating hypothesis tends to be more stable than related hypotheses. For example, the trained system where the intended hypothesis is a factorial, we noticed that the behavior of the factorial hypothesis is stable. However, there are two other hypotheses where their behavior fluctuates. This would suggest that the inappropriate hypotheses are either unstable or their confidence level decrease over time.

The second set of experiments shows the difference between a system with no learning and one with learning. The table below gives the results of running the system for 85 samples. The first experiment performs a running assessment calculated on each sequence and the running probability obtained together with the probability values in the density-table used to rank concepts. In both cases, the system managed to generate hypotheses for 70 out of the 85 samples (Table 12.3).

We ran two experiments on each sample. In the first, we did not employ any training and learning at all. A predefined ranking of concepts was used and the system merely traversed the list to build a hypothesis. The iteration is the number of times it has to traverse the list before a hypothesis was successfully found. The result shows that it manages to build hypothesis from the first concept in the list for 41 samples, 21 samples have their hypotheses constructed from the second concept, etc. However, the result also shows a disappointing 20 out of 41 hypotheses actually matched with the intended (generating) hypothesis.

Table 12.4 Used reason types and their formal limitations

Intelligence function	Characteristic
Abstraction	Closed, predefined features, two levels
Retroduction	Closed, predefined concepts, infinite and uncountable
Deduction	Closed, predefined heuristic
Induction	Closed, predefined single criteria

By employing learning and training to create a ranking of hypotheses (a ranking list), we can see a high percentage of successfully formed hypotheses that matched the intended hypotheses. This goes to show that learning and training can improve the intelligence by providing better or more appropriate hypotheses. Learning does not increase the ability to solve harder problems and hence the IQ value of the system remains the same.

In both cases, the system managed to find hypotheses for 70 of the samples. The other 15 samples cannot be fitted into any of the concepts employed.

12.5 Conclusion

What kind of intelligence are we implementing in our sequence recognition? We categorized that intelligence in the manner described in Sect. 2 as follows (Table 12.4):

12.5.1 Intelligence Quality Specification

Since all intelligence functions in this model are closed and predefined, the potential for a sensible response to a generation of a new domain and new concept is zero. This is an example of a 'closed' inferential system. There is no new insights (concepts) created here. What actually occurs is that hypotheses are built as a function of a quantitative concept selected from a list of predefined concepts. Once a concept is selected, its generator will derive all of its parameters. Induction will then evaluate the viability of that hypothesis against a predefined criteria.

It is important to note that the employment of multiple concepts only improves the range of intelligence; it does not improve the quality of intelligence. The more concepts being employed, the more choices we can have to build our hypotheses. The choice of concepts to build a hypothesis is based on Bayesian statistics. No doubt there are other techniques that may be used for the classification of concepts. However, the best technique should be based on sound statistical techniques. Bayesian is well known for being the most comprehensive and widely used technique. The attraction of Bayesian technique can be seen from its simplistic rule:

If we have no current observations to draw upon, then we must make all of our judgments from previous experience. If we have both previous experience and current perceptions based upon observational data, our judgment must be based on both.

The human decision making model that was devised based on IQ tests looks very promising. IQ tests present, not all, but some facts, and there are many possible solutions to the problem presented. We are required to make the best and most practical judgment. We first start by looking at the features of the facts. By extracting the features of the facts given, we should be able to pinpoint to the right class of hypothesis as our best judgment based on previous experience. The problem remains of extracting only the right set of features, since they help us tune into the right hypothesis.

Having put forward the right hypothesis to account for the facts given, we proceed to assess the hypothesis against a purpose. Since the criteria for IQ is simplicity, the nature of the hypothesis should help us to select the 'correct' criteria of simplicity that will then be evaluated to determine the acceptability of a given hypothesis.

Since IQ tests reflect how human judgments are made given limited facts, then the framework of feature-extraction and criteria-selection technique that closely resemble pattern recognition techniques is a good candidate for human intelligence. I make no claim that this approach *is* the model of human intelligence. However, in the absence of a standard technique of human decision-making process, this approach using the solving of IQ tests seems to give acceptable results.

One of the attractions of the taxonomic approach is the symmetrical nature of the model produced. The reverse process of ranking and selecting concepts for retroduction is employed in the selection of criteria for induction to create an equilibrium. Each of these may employ learning as described in Chap. 11.

Hypotheses are used to make predictions and in our case, to predict the next number of a given sequence. We ran our model against 85 samples taken from Eysenck (1974a, b). He also provided a graph to determine IQ value. Interpreting the results in terms of such scoring system, our system has an IQ ranging between 132 and 143 points depending on learning technique engaged.

References

Addis TR (1985) Designing knowledge-based systems. Originally Kogan Page, now Chapman & Hall, Published October. Hardback: ISBN 0 85038 859 7. Soft back: ISBN 1 85091 251 3

Eysenck HJ (1974a) Check your own I.Q. Penguin Books, London

Eysenck HJ (1974b) Know your own I.Q. Penguin Books, London

Wason PC, Johnson-Laird PN (1968) Thinking and reasoning, penguin modern psychology UPS 11. Penguin Book, New York

Zakaria MS (1994) A model of machine intelligence based on the pragmatic approach. PhD Thesis, Computer science department, University of Reading March

Chapter 13
Figuratively Speaking

> *A man's life of any worth is a continual allegory—and very few eyes can see the mystery of his life—a life like the scriptures—figurative.*
>
> J. Keats letter to G. and G. Keats,
> (14th February–3rd May 1819)

13.1 The Problem with Reference

Dr. David Billinge, a Computer Science lecturer at Portsmouth University, gives regular pre-concert lectures at the local Guildhall. His interest in music and language raised the question of how the communication of the emotional content of music can be justified using referential semantics. This was particularly puzzling because emotions do not have any externally shared reference points. This apparent lack of external references for emotion raises the interesting primary question, "How can the semantics of emotion ever be established?"

I will describe in this chapter, drawn from David Billinge's work, our initial hypothesis into the potential consistency of a response to music by two or more people and explain why we view these responses as private and knowable only by the respondent. Despite this, people do discuss music and so David and I adopted a position that people communicate using 'tropic' or figurative language. But why would a figurative language help?

We developed a model of the discourse based upon our initial hypothesis as well as a simple diagrammatic language that people can use to talk about music and its emotional content. A functional model evolved from these diagrams, and a working model in a schematic programming language was constructed. With this model we can show that some kind of communication is possible, in principle, with private referencing. One conclusion is that such private referencing could be an underlying mechanism for other creative acts.

The basic question we are exploring here is, '*Is it possible for people to have a mutually consistent response to the world given only internal and private references?*' This chapter describes the conceptual and computer model we constructed that shows that communication is possible with such a virtual referencing semantics.

The above question arose from our work in trying to analyse the nature of people's descriptions of musical effect. The original purpose of this analysis was to find a set

© Springer International Publishing Switzerland 2014
T. Addis, *Natural and Artificial Reasoning,* Advanced Information
and Knowledge Processing, DOI 10.1007/978-3-319-11286-2_13

of emotionally descriptive keywords that could be used in order to build an artistic decision support system. Such a system would enable a concert planner to construct a musical program that would provide a defined and structured emotional content. For this we needed to find out how people talked about music. In particular we were interested in the experienced and enthusiastic concertgoers. We discovered from the observation of the language people used while they discussed music under controlled conditions that there seemed to be no consistent way in which words were employed to describe music. It was only when we considered metaphor that we could make sense of what we had observed. In particular, we noted that speakers used metaphor creatively and it was because of this that an inconsistency was observed. The question then arose as to why people found it necessary to use metaphor. We concluded that it was because the descriptions were about personal feelings. Since feelings are private, the accepted external referential mechanism of language cannot take effect.

People routinely have such conversations not only about art but also about many other subjective views of the world and yet they still believe they are communicating successfully to others. David and I saw the act of communicating musical experience as a microcosm of this much larger issue. The issue of how people manage to converse when so often they appear, from a referential point of view, not to be saying what they mean.

It is essential to point out what we are *not* researching. We are not trying to show what music means, (if indeed that is a real problem at all), and we do not believe that people need to agree on artistic descriptions as they would need to agree on descriptions of, say, poisonous mushrooms in the forest. Meyer (1956, 1967, 1973), Cooke (1959) and many others gave extensive consideration to these issues (see Billinge 2001 for a full account). What we are trying to show is how people can communicate figuratively, and for that we do need to establish that some common understanding of a language exists.

13.2   Tropic Communication

It is the view of some linguists that our natural language does not function as a computer language with defined terms and unambiguous reference (Lakoff and Johnson 1980). Our language is overwhelmingly figurative; it is 'tropic' communication. A trope is a figure of speech such as metaphor; a type of analogy, metonymy (meaning by association) or synecdoche (meaning by relating to a sub- or super-set). If this is the case, and if we also wish to build machines that work within the same paradigm as people so that emotion can be communicated, then such tropic communication must be understood. However, the process behind such communication seems to depend upon the construction of descriptions from purely internal reference points; namely primary emotions or emotional-archetypical situations. How such a system can work is puzzling, but one way of understanding and exploring the process is to build a computer model.

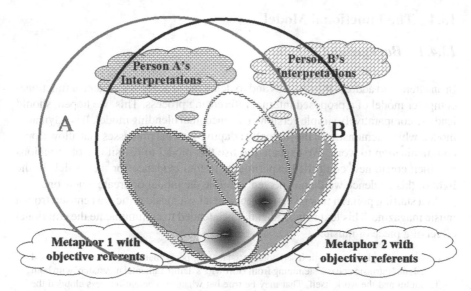

Fig. 13.1 Venn diagram of the emotional landscapes for actors *A* and *B* and the effect of two metaphors

13.3 The Conceptual Model

A model that has many of the properties we are looking for and that seems to support the creative construction of metaphorical descriptions of musical effect is 'conceptual blending'. Conceptual blending (Fauconnier and Turner 2002) suggests a way in which different situations (such as given by mixed or simultaneous metaphors) can be brought together to form new perceptions of the world. As with metaphor such perceptions can then be used to infer consequences and thus possible action.

In order to ensure that conceptual blending fulfils the role of describing tropic communication we need to review our initial observations (Billinge 2001; Billinge and Addis 2001, 2002), drawn from the field of musical literature and critical reviews.

The Venn diagram summarises these results (see Fig. 13.1). It is also an indication of the process as we saw it at the time but in a way that leaves too much to the imagination. The diagram is essentially static and does not show all the necessary dynamics of creating descriptions through hidden and private references. What we needed to show was that the internal referencing was a possible basis for communication and that it could be stable. We had to determine the strategies needed for it to work and to show the underlying assumptions required. Only then could we consider designing some kind of experiment that would support or reject our initial proposal that internal referencing could be possible as a basis for communication. Such communication could then be used as means of retrieval of music effects from a database of music. This database would then form the basis of a music-programming aide; an expert system for artistic program designers.

13.4   The Functional Model

13.4.1   Background

In an attempt to address these issues and to detail the process, we created a functional computer model of a proposed internal referencing process. This, we hoped, should lead to a comparatively simple version of a conceptual blending model. It is a dynamic model, which demonstrates the mutually adaptive internal processes that allow tropic communication to work. We expected to use this model to revisit our observations and then create new controlled experiments to find evidence for the model. In the light of this evidence we then expected to refine the model or create a new one.

As a starting point in this investigation, a text by a music critic was chosen from a music magazine. This text is typical and it is intended to communicate the emotional effect of a piece of music.[1]

> (X's) refreshingly iconoclastic insert notes insist that this performance of the Brahms' Second reveals an 'intrinsic unease' stemming from Horowitz's 'temperamental mismatch' with both Toscanini and the work itself. That may be true but whatever contentiousness clouded the recording session, the heat of the occasion forged it into an interpretative virtue. The result is one of the most arresting recordings of this warhorse ever made. Granted, it's controversial. This is not the place to seek out the succulence of Brahms's harmonies (passages that are poignant in other hands sound nervously expectant here) or the sweetness of his melodies (calls for dolce and espressivo are rebuffed even in the third movement). Rather, Horowitz and Toscanini deploy every available tool to scratch out any signs of tenderness from this normally bighearted score: barbed attacks, gaunt tone, angular phrasing, contestatory treatment of accompaniments, urgent tempos, highly strung rhythms (dotted figures have a special edge). The climaxes erupt with an unaccustomed violence; and while the finale is notable for its leggiero, it's the lethal lightness of a well-aimed stiletto. It is, in other words, far from easy listening. But despite a few moments of scramble, the performance has such ferocious commitment that it's hard to resist. If the stately account of the Tchaikovsky sounds less heterodox, that's largely because, in my view, the work is more overtly dramatic to begin with. Still, even here, the music is pushed to extremes. Every single bar crackles with tension and Horowitz and Toscanini forgo the music's lyricism in order to wring every possible thrill from the score. It is, without doubt, a cruel sacrifice; but once again, the reading is so electrifying that you're compelled to go along with it.[2]

On the surface this is a set of undefined, maybe poetic, words. This is especially problematic if seen, as we did in our initial experiments, as a source for a discrete lexicon. However if we inspect the text for metaphors a different view emerges. The metaphors may also be considered the medium for transmission of the musical experience.

The author of the example critical comment sets the stage with a statement of the stance he takes and intends to convey.

---

[1] A more detailed account of this work was presented by the authors at the ECAI'02 conference in Lyons, France in August 2002. See Billinge and Addis (2002).

[2] From International Record Review, Vol 3 Issue 5 August 2002: ISSN 1468–5027 p.27.

X's refreshingly iconoclastic insert notes insist that this performance of the Brahms' Second reveals an 'intrinsic unease' stemming from Horowitz's 'emperamental mismatch' with both Toscanini and the work itself.

The way he reinforces this message is to write in terms of conflict, violence and tension whilst using harmoniousness as a foil. It would be inappropriate to go into this in overmuch detail so a few examples must suffice. The text is full of conflict metaphors:

Iconoclastic insert notes ... contentiousness clouded the recording session ... one of the most arresting recordings of this ... it's controversial ... calls for dolce and espressivo are rebuffed ... deploy every available tool to scratch out any signs of tenderness ... barbed attacks ... gaunt tone ... contestatory treatment of accompaniments ... lethal lightness of a well-aimed stiletto ... you're compelled to go along ...

And at the other end of the emotional scale it has a significant number of metaphors of harmony and pleasure:

the succulence of Brahms's harmonies (passages that are poignant in other hands) ... the sweetness of his melodies ... signs of tenderness from this normally bighearted score ... the music's lyricism ...

These examples are typical of the written genre and indeed of the spoken discourse. Modelling this must involve simplification thus we chose to work in terms of messages being conveyed between exclusive private worlds where the only common factor is the source of the experience and its comparators.

13.5   The Initial Model

We wanted to show how the reactions of an Actor B to a piece of music, as perceived by Actor A, might be quantified to enable processing into an internal model of B held by A. Such a process will involve a form of *negotiation* and *learning* that requires the use of tropic communication by both Actors. It should be noted that the weightings we apply are not seen as 'real' mental artefacts that exist within the human brain (although they might). Any measures we use are simply convenient representations of emotional intensity within the computational model.

We start by describing how the processes are modelled.

Figure 13.2 will illustrate the situation. This diagram shows an external world in the central rectangle that consists of six metaphors for artistic objects, in this case musical performances (events) of pieces (objects) called Triangle Music, Circle Music etc.

In this world Actors A and B listen to Triangle Music and then A modifies its[3] internal interpretation of Actor B's description from its own perception of the music.

---

[3] The English term 'his', as is the traditional syntactic convention, could have been used here where it is considered gender neutral. However I have used 'it' since an actor in this context is a programmed artifact.

Fig. 13.2 Tropic communication using internal views

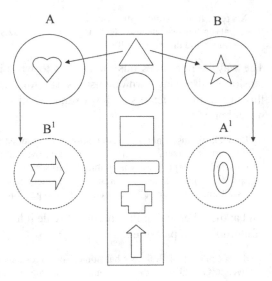

It is postulated that Actor A's and Actor B's internal emotional reactions to this external stimulus differ. The different shapes within the hard circle associated with each actor are intended to represent this difference. We use a simple model that will illustrate how discussion will lead inevitably to the kind of differences of opinion commonly experienced by those discussing art works. We assume B provides a figurative description in which its (B's) differing perception of the effect of Triangle Music is conveyed to Actor A. This will, in turn, adjust A's model of B's perception.

The process is now traced in more detail. As noted, the series of shapes in the central oblong represent different pieces of music experienced by both A and B. They can therefore describe their respective reactions to the first of these, Triangle Music, by comparing the effect of Triangle Music with the effect of Circle Music, Square Music, and so on. This use of comparative reference is what we take to be characteristic of figurative discourse. A's initial emotional reaction to Triangle Music is represented by a heart shape, B's by a star. This implies that both Actors have their own individual responses. In conversation B describes to A how it feels about Triangle Music. As a result of this explanation, A begins to build an internal representation of what it believes to be B's emotional reaction: this is shown in Fig. 13.2 by the soft circle B^1. A can never know exactly what reaction has taken place in B's mind because we cannot describe our emotional states directly, only indirectly via the use of what we have described as "Tropic Communication", the use of metaphor, simile and other tropes; a figurative language. The inevitable result of this tropic description is that A's picture of what is in B's mind is inaccurate, thus B^1 is shown containing a polygon only loosely similar to the star B is "actually" describing. The only means B can use to describe its reaction to Triangle Music is by making statements like "It was more dramatic than Circle Music", or, "It was much less lively than Cross Music", and so on. We note that 'dramatic' and 'lively' are emotional dimensions that are understood internally by each actor.

In parallel with these inputs, A has to interpret B's comments via its own emotional reaction, which is a 'heart' reaction shown in Fig. 13.2. Further, when B draws a comparison with Circle Music as above, A's interpretation of the comparison not only has to modify from the basis of a 'heart' effect, it also has to be modified using A's and not B's, reaction to Circle Music. So when B says, "Triangle Music was more dramatic than Circle Music", A's internal model B^1 is modified by a statement which could be stated like this.

> B thinks that the dramatic impact of Triangle Music is more than the dramatic impact of Circle Music so I must alter B^1 to reflect how I perceive the dramatic nature of Circle Music to make it more dramatic than my perception of Triangle Music.

A has no means whatever of directly observing what B thinks about anything. It has to make a creative leap from state B^1 to, perhaps, state B^2, B^3, and so on, until B has finished drawing comparisons with all the available music know to them both. What this model is intended to convey is not only the inaccuracy that must inevitably follow from A trying to picture something it can never see, i.e. an image inside B's mind, but also show that there is a convergence of the internal models that results from the accumulation of comparisons.

We aim to show how the feedback triggers adjustments of A's emotional reaction weightings and leads to its reassessing its categorisation of the basic emotional states conveyed by its experience of the artistic event. With these states changed, Actor A is obliged to rework its internal descriptions and adjust internal references so that they are acceptable both to himself and to Actor B. This also suggests that without some common external reference (the event) no change of their internal models can take place. It also implies that the order of the description B is giving to A will be important since every step in the description is relative to the adjusted made in the previous steps.

13.6   The Abstracted Initial Model

The extended nature of the above description was reason enough for us to view the further modelling of this interaction by, so far as we are able, refining it down to the bare essentials. Figure 13.3 is still a diagrammatic representation but it provided for us a means of resolving the various objects into numeric measures and program labels.

In Fig. 13.3 the different music pieces are represented as P to S, the Actors as A and B and the heavy arrow shows the potential for an indefinite number of additional Actors C, D, E and so on. The lines represent one of many simplified single-emotional reactions to Music P, Q, R and S. We call these lines 'dimensions' and they are associated with each external object. For example the extent to which the music P makes Actor A happy (say) is shown by the position of the bisecting vertical line at '*', the horizontal line representing the continuum between totally-without-happiness on

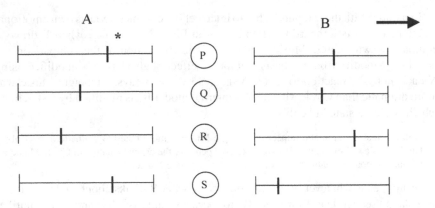

Fig. 13.3 Further abstracted model of tropic communication

the left and fully-happy to the right. Thus Music P makes A strongly happy, Music Q makes A moderately happy and so on through R and S.

Actor B's happiness quotient is similarly shown and we can see it is different for Music R but quite similar for Music P. Thus when B tells A that Music P makes him feel happier than does Music S, Actor A will interpret that declaration against its (A's) internal model of the happiness quotients it has attributed to Music P and Music S. Since A finds P to be less-happy music than S it might well respond to B by expressing surprised disagreement. B, who cannot be aware of A's internal ratings, will come back with a further comparison with which it hopes to clarify the extent of Music P's happiness in its estimation. It might respond, "OK, but surely you find R happier than P." It can be seen that this will not bring agreement since A's internal model still will not be able to support that belief, but it will enhance A's understanding of B's vision of the world as it modifies its model of B's vision in repose to the discussion.

The use of continua to represent strength of emotion, and statements of sequence to represent the tropic communications which are all that may pass between A and B, allowed us to construct a functional model which would simulate the course of an internal model change.

Adding the potential for an Actors C, D, E and so on, allows us to extend the model to simulate another factor, the process by which A may choose with whom it wants most to talk. If A converses with B and C, it will eventually find that one or the other of the actors will tend towards a better agreement with its own assessments. In future exchanges A may choose to take the views of C more seriously because they agreed better with its own perceptions last time they talked. To account for this we adopt the notion of belief (see Chap. 7 and Addis and Gooding 1999) as a weighting of C's (and others) views in A's estimation. Tropic communication such as this takes place in a social situation and it is our personal experience that such changes in social bonding do, in fact, take place with people.

13.7 The Basic Functional Model

The current model shows how actors negotiate an agreed internal emotional framework that neither of them can observe directly. This serves in turn as a model of how they also agree on choices of metaphor and other tropes, as well as creating a figurative description that both accept as an adequate representation of their feelings. We further show how the current model reflects these differing effects as numerical weightings, and discuss the types of experiment that we can carry out to refine the model.

I will now use a numeric identification instead of the alphabet to distinguish the model from the above discussion. The starting point for Actors 1, 2 and 3 is they have no musical experience, having attended no concerts. So we show them as having no knowledge of what we describe above (Fig. 13.2) as Triangle Music, Circle Music, Square Music, and so on. They have no means of communication about the effect of these virtual compositions because they have no reference points. They cannot describe reactions in terms of **'more'** or **'less' happiness** (for example) because they have no happiness-concept concerning this music to begin with. The dimension of experience chosen could be anything, love, hate, anger, happiness, like etc. We choose the latter just by way of an example.

We show this state of affairs by rating an actor's belief in the effect on others within the chosen realm of a piece of music. Since belief must never exceed unity, the maximum value of 1 is distributed evenly over a 7-part scale thus:

$$[0.143 \,|0.143|\, 0.143 \,|0.143|\, 0.143 \,|0.143|\, 0.143]$$

The choice of a 7-part scale will need an explanation because we refer to these dimensions as continuous. We have adopted the notion of belief from Addis and Gooding where it applies only to scientific hypotheses. A hypothesis is a discrete object drawn from a set of competing hypotheses. In this case a value is treated as an object drawn from an ordered set of distinct values. Because a centre value is important, any odd number will suffice. 3 or 5 were rejected as too limited and 9, 11, 13 and beyond as unnecessarily complex for demonstration purposes. 7 can be seen as a usable compromise. We use 0 to represent no (happiness) and 6 to represent absolute (happiness). Only the actor itself knows this measure and for now we will not pursue questions such as "how does it know?"

After experience of a single object our actors can only make absolute statements like "Triangle Music makes me feel (happy) or (nothing)", so communication between actors 1, 2 and 3 is limited to (happiness current), and (happiness absent). Internally the object will have triggered a degree of (happiness) but it cannot be expressed. In our model we will represent this personal experience as a belief of 1 for one of the seven positions on the continuum because "it knows what it likes".

If we communicate with actor 4, who has never attended any concert, then Actor 1, for example, could tell Actor 4 that the music was of no consequence, or report that "it should have the experience". This level of effect is akin to Pierce's 'firstness' where there is no possibility of further description other than first hand experience. Actors 1,

Fig. 13.4 Actor 2's and 3's views of other's view of object 1

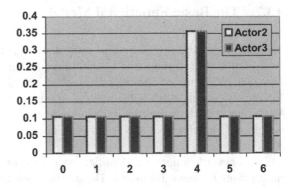

Fig. 13.5 Actor 2's and 3's views of other's view of object 2

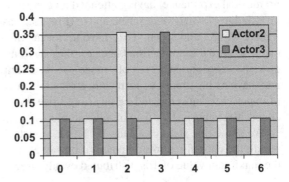

2 and 3 have experienced something they can graduate internally but cannot express, but Actor 4 lacks the experience that even allows identification of the dimension.

The actors are now exposed to the second object, Circle Music. A similar process of adaption takes place. Owing to the fact that Actors 1, 2 and 3 have one item of prior experience they can now compare that emotional effect with the effect of object two on an identified dimension. This gives them a better and a subtler means of communication in that they can convey internal comparisons.

To represent the experience of attending a concert (event 1) we instruct our model through queries. Note that all interactions are called "queries" in the schematic functional programming language 'Clarity' from which the modal was constructed. (*See Drawing Programs, Tom & Jan Addis, pub Springer 2010. Also see Addis and Townsend-Addis 1995, 1998, 2001, 2002. A free version of 'Clarity' is available at* 'www.clarity-support.co.uk' *including the belief system and other example programs.*)

QUERY > actor_only_concerts (no_query) #1
True
Each actor, knowing its own response to the objects, then modifies its initial neutral assessment of others' views. The function 'show_views' displays all actors' perception of other actors for all objects. For clarity we have graphed the results. Since this is the view of Actor 1 concerning the others we have also dropped its view for simplicity (Fig. 13.4, 13.5)
QUERY > show_views #1
True

Fig. 13.6 Clarity function for consulting and changing view

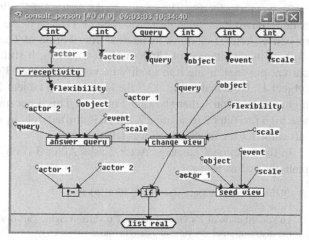

Fig. 13.7 Object 1 modified by object 2 for actor 2

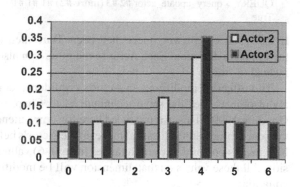

All Actors initially assume, without any other knowledge, that all other Actors will have the same view as themselves. The distribution of effects has now changed from the base distribution of 0.143 and all the actors have an increased rating at one point of the scale to a new value of 0.357. Since all of the seven positions on the scale still have to total to unity, the remaining items dropped back to 0.107.

We now illustrate a single communicative exchange between actors 2 and 3 using the function 'consult_person' shown in Fig. 13.6. Note that the *parameters* 'actor 1' and 'actor 2' in Fig. 13.6 are the first and the second actors. In this example these parameters are filled with value 'actors 2' and 'actors 3' respectively.

Figure 13.6 shows two processes: 'answer_query' and 'change_views'. In this example Actor 2 asks Actor 3 "Is Object 2 of **higher** value than Object 1?" In this case the response is "**No**". This then triggers 'change_view' for Actor 2, which is graphed in Fig. 13.7. The change can be seen in relationship to Actor 3's view that remains unchanged since it has no information yet about actors 2's opinion.

To be more specific, when Actor 2 asks Actor 3 if Circle music (object 2) is liked better (**more**) than Triangle music (object 1), it gets the answer "No" (**False**). In response, Actor 2 modifies its internal distribution of Triangle music (object 1) by shifting its distribution of Circle music (object 2). It shifts it to be higher than the current position, using it to modify its vision of Actor 3's view of Triangle music (object 1). Note that in Fig. 13.7 the happiness in Object 1 (Triangle music) is now higher, in position 3, than shown in Fig. 13.3. This is because Object 2 (Circle music) was high for Actor 2 in position 2, which is shifted right by one position. The extreme left value for the modification was taken as zero.

In the functional language Actor 2 asks Actor 3 if object 2 is more (happiness) than object 1 as follows:

QUERY > answer_query (**more** #2) **#3** #1 #1 #1
False
The distribution of 2's view of object 2 is shifted right. This distribution is used to modify
the distribution of 2's view of Triangle music (object 1).
QUERY > query_update_actor **#2 #3** (**more** #2) #1 #1 #1
True

If the result of 'answer_query' had been **True** then the shift would have been in the opposite direction. Each Actor to the other can also ask queries using '**same as**' instead of '**more**'.

The effect of modifying an Actor's confidence concerning the views of others about objects uses the same technique as in Chap. 6 and 11 (also see Addis and Gooding 1999). This is reproduced here for convenience. The confidence of each of the seven dimension values that make up the Actor's belief profile is H_h. A hypothesis here means one of the seven (h ranges from 0–6) values on (say) a happiness dimension. All these values on that dimension will be modified according to the following equation:

$$E_n(H_h) = \frac{(M-1).E_{n-1}(H_h) + E_{n-1}(H_h/R)}{M}$$

M ranges from 1 to infinity. The larger M, the smaller the effect any evidence has on the change in confidence. We can thus define concept receptivity as follows. This ranges from 0 to 1 for each agent as:

$$receptivity = 1/M$$

This reflects the influence of any consultation upon the consulting Actor.

$$\sum_h E_n(H_h) = 1$$

The value of $E_{n-1}(H_h/R)$ in the $E_n(H_h)$ equation will be 1 for the selected value and 0 otherwise. In this way the selected belief value will increase and the others will reduce to compensate accordingly.

The value **0.25** was selected for receptivity. This choice needs some explanation. To some extent it is arbitrary insofar as anything between 0 and 1 might be chosen.

If a value close to zero is chosen then no change could effectively take place; if 1 were chosen there could only ever be an exchange of one viewpoint for another and no negotiation of belief would be possible. We opted for **0.25** as the 'experience' unit because if a new 'experience' arrives to compete for the Actor's attention it has only to discard **0.25** of its current happiness. If we continue in a figurative vein by suggesting that each new experience be mixed with those added before, we have a situation for the gaining of experience-knowledge as follows. Actor X gains (say) four experiences, red experience, blue experience, orange experience and purple experience. These experiences together modify X's view such that it only has to discard **0.25** of the overall stock of experience to make way for the new experience. Enough of all the previous experiences remain to count as useful learning. This is an engineering type of decision rather than one that has any scientific or strictly logical basis.

The number of discrete values along each dimension considered by an Actor can vary. The confidence in a particular value is affected not only by experience and queries but also by the number of values along a dimension available for consideration. In our case we have only to consider seven along a single dimension. In order to allow for a changing number of values we used the same idea that was originally proposed by Addis and Gooding (1999) for belief (also see Chap. 6). Here we introduced a dynamic threshold, the indifference value 'I'. In this case the value 'I' defines those happiness values larger than which are to be actively considered as happy. 'I' represents the general normal happiness (contentment) of an individual actor instead of a group confidence as in the belief model.

To calculate the indifference value 'I' a function is needed that will change smoothly between limiting values. It should be easily calculable from any number of different values along any particular dimension, in this case happiness. A quantity that varies in time in this way is the inverse of entropy. Entropy is an expected measure of the log of a range of values. This can be used as a general measure of an Actor's general happiness while listening to the music at time n. In the following equation 'a' and subscript 'a' is used to denote a particular Actor. This 'Entropy(Agent$_a$),' is called the general happiness measure for an actor 'a' in the Model Entropy, where the term model denotes the set of values that makes up the Actor's view of a piece of music. Model Entropy is given by:

$$\text{Entropy}_n(\text{Agent}_a) = -\sum_{\text{Ha}} E_n(H_a) * \text{Log}_2(E_n(H_a))$$

From this equation we can obtain an inverse of the entropy which gives an expected value for $E_n(H_a)$. This will be denoted by $I_n(H_a)$. $I_n(H_a)$ will be called an Indifference Threshold for the actor 'a' at event 'n':

$$\text{Indifference Threshold}(a, n) = \log_2^{-1}(\text{Entropy}_n(\text{Agent}_a))$$
$$= I_n(H_a)$$

The expression $E_n(H_a)$ is the expected probability of a dimension (happiness) value for actor 'a' at conversation moment 'n'. The measure of a value $E_n(H_a)$ above $I_n(H_a)$

Fig. 13.8 The top level of the
functional model

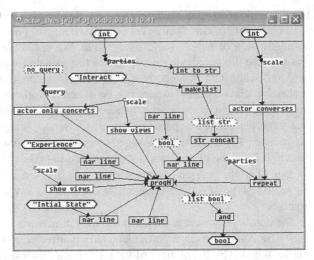

is considered to be significant, that is to say, the actor is said to be 'happy' or whatever
the emotional dimension is being measured.

13.8   A Commented Run of the Model

Figure 13.8 is the top level of the model in the Clarity schema. The sequence of
the program events goes clockwise from the output < list bool > of function 'progN'
shown in the schema. So first a new line with function 'nar_line', then the text "Intital
State" followed by a new line is printed. Next the function 'show_views' is called
with a parameter marked as 'scale'. The value of 'scale' is the last parameter of the
main function 'actor_lives' and so on (see Addis and Addis 2010).

Our initial trial of the model was run so that every actor was initialised as to be
indifferent to objects 1 and 2, where I = 0.143, about all values as follows:

Initial State

Actor 1
1[0.143 0.143 0.143 0.143 0.143 0.143 0.143] I = 0.143
2[0.143 0.143 0.143 0.143 0.143 0.143 0.143] I = 0.143
Actor 2
1[0.143 0.143 0.143 0.143 0.143 0.143 0.143] I = 0.143
2[0.143 0.143 0.143 0.143 0.143 0.143 0.143] I = 0.143
Actor 2
1[0.143 0.143 0.143 0.143 0.143 0.143 0.143] I = 0.143
2[0.143 0.143 0.143 0.143 0.143 0.143 0.143] I = 0.143

Each actor then has a single experience of two objects 1 and 2 (e.g. all attend a
concert with two pieces of music) and this modifies their neutral view with this
certain experience thus:

13.9   The Single Experience

Actor 1
1[0.107 0.107 0.107 0.357 0.107 0.107 0.107] I = 0.165
2[0.357 0.107 0.107 0.107 0.107 0.107 0.107] I = 0.165
Actor 2
1[0.107 0.107 0.107 0.107 0.357 0.107 0.107] I = 0.165
2[0.107 0.107 0.357 0.107 0.107 0.107 0.107] I = 0.165
Actor 3
1[0.107 0.107 0.107 0.107 0.357 0.107 0.107] I = 0.165
2[0.107 0.107 0.107 0.357 0.107 0.107 0.107] I = 0.165

Without this experience, no changes or modifications are possible. So we, in effect seeded this experience in order to give the actors different evaluations of what they heard. The values that have a belief greater than the indifference threshold are highlighted.

Eight cycles of consultation take place where each Actor asks all other actors a sequence of questions concerning their own experiences. The questions are formalized as (**more** n) or (**same** n) where 'n' is the music reference (1 or 2). The replies are used to modify each Actor's own distribution of beliefs on some view of the group's opinions:

13.10   Consult

(**more** 1)
Actor 1
1[0.107 0.107 0.107 **0.357** 0.107 0.107 0.107] I 0.0.165
2[**0.253** 0.113 **0.235** 0.113 0.113 0.113 *0.060*] I] 0.158
Actor 2
1[0.107 0.107 0.107 0.107 **0.357** 0.107 0.107] I 0.0.165
2[0.113 0.113 **0.253 0.235** 0.113 0.113 *0.060*] I] 0.158
Actor 3
1[0.107 0.107 0.107 0.107 **0.357** 0.107 0.107] I 0.0.165
2[0.113 0.113 0.113 **0.376** 0.113 0.113 *0.060*] I] 0.171
(**more** 2)
Actor 1
1[*0.060* **0.178** 0.113 **0.310** 0.113 0.113 0.113] I 0.0.161
2[**0.253** 0.113 **0.235** 0.113 0.113 0.113 *0.060*] I] 0.158
Actor 2
1[*0.060* 0.113 0.113 **0.178 0.310** 0.113 0.113] I 0.0.161
2[0.113 0.113 **0.253 0.235** 0.113 0.113 *0.060*] I] 0.158
Actor 3
1[*0.060* 0.113 0.113 0.113 **0.376** 0.113 0.113] I 0.0.171
2[0.113 0.113 0.113 **0.376** 0.113 0.113 *0.060*] I] 0.171
(**same** 1)
Actor 1
1[*0.060* **0.178** 0.113 **0.310** 0.113 0.113 0.113] I 0.0.161
2[**0.211** *0.123* **0.197** *0.114* 0.128 0.128 *0.099*] I] 0.148

Actor 2
1[*0.060* 0.113 0.113 **0.178 0.310** 0.113 0.113] I 0.0.161
2[0.132 0.128 **0.207 0.192** 0.114 0.128 *0.099*] I] 0.148
Actor 3
1[*0.060* 0.113 0.113 0.113 **0.376** 0.113 0.113] I 0.0.171
2[0.132 0.128 0.128 **0.276** *0.109* 0.128 *0.099*] I] 0.152
(same 2)
Actor 1
1[*0.091* 0.164 0.122 **0.239** 0.127 *0.127* 0.129] I 0.0.149
2[**0.211** 0.123 **0.197** 0.114 0.128 0.128 *0.099*] I] 0.148
Actor 2
1[*0.097* 0.127 0.121 0.159 **0.239** 0.127 0.129] I 0.0.149
2[0.132 0.128 0.207 0.192 0.114 0.128 0.099] I 0.0.148
Actor 3
1[0.097 0.127 0.127 0.116 **0.276** 0.127 0.129] I 0.0.152
2[0.132 0.128 0.128 **0.276** 0.109 0.128 *0.099*] I] 0.152
In the final modification after seven more cycles we have:
Actor 1
1[*0.089* 0.167 0.131 **0.198** 0.136 0.138 0.142] I 0.0.146
2[**0.180** 0.132 0.191 0.126 0.138 0.139 *0.094*] I] 0.146
Actor 2
1[0.093 0.139 0.133 0.160 **0.198** 0.136 0.142] I = 0.146
2[0.145 0.137 0.172 **0.186** 0.126 0.139 *0.094*] I] 0.146
Actor 3
1[*0.093* 0.138 0.138 0.127 **0.227** 0.135 0.142] I 0.0.148
2[0.145 0.138 0.135 **0.227** 0.121 0.139 *0.094*] I] 0.148

Given the limited experience of each Actor this shows that there is the possibility of convergent internal standards. The limitation is that the upper bounds of the evaluation of the objects cannot be shifted until new and 'better' objects have been experienced. Actor 1 has inferred correctly the relative position of object 2 with respect to object 1 and Actor 2 has adopted an evaluation of object 2 that is approaching a consensus.

13.11   Future Development

This initial experiment with this model was only intended to establish the possibility of inferred internal referencing. Experiments that are more extensive will need to be done to show what might be the limitations and stability of such internal and inferred references. More Actors experiencing a wider range of objects over an extended set of events is required. Investigations into the way in which the internal referencing might change are needed as well as the seeing if there is the possibility of distinct sub-groups of Actors appearing due to drift. Such drift would be expected as soon as the Actors become independent of the forced consultation sequence used here. The model could be extended along the lines of Gooding and Addis (1999—also see Chap. 7). We would intend to use the development of this model to revisit our observations and we would expect this to lead to the construction of new experiments.

13.12 Conclusions

We have shown within the limitations of this model that internal referencing can have some external meaning. This relies firmly on the common humanity of the individual actors, in that they have to share a common cognitive structure. This study also suggests that without some common external reference with which this cognitive structure may interact no communication can take place.

Moreover the results suggest that more experience and interaction would produce internal models that are more congruent. Despite this potential for convergence, there could remain important differences between individuals. It is these differences that could be the source of creative acts, since perceived novelty occurs because the observer lacks the internal logical structures to construct the observed act. This implies that creativity is a result of individual differences remaining despite social interaction. Because we do share a common cognitive structure it should not be surprising that some people will develop common internal views at the same time. This would result in new insights occurring independently and simultaneously within a particular culture. This should not suggest that people need isolation to be creative, quite the reverse; people need to be in communication in order for novelty to be recognised and accepted.

References

Addis T, Addis J (2010) Drawing programs: the theory and practice of schematic functional programming. Springer, London. ISBN 978-1-84882-617-5

Addis TR, Gooding DC (1999) Learning as collective belief-revision: simulating reasoning about disparate phenomena. AISB Symposium, 6–9 April. University of Edinburgh, London, pp 19–28. ISBN 1 902956 04 4

Addis TR, Townsend Addis JJ (1995) Diagrams for design: a schema interpreter for knowledge systems. Proceedings of the 15th annual conference of the British computer specialists group on expert systems (ES95), pp 231–247

Addis TR, Townsend Addis JJ (1998) A functional schematic interpreter: an environment for model design. Int J Syst Res Inf Sci 7:263–299. ISSN 0882-3014

Addis TR, Townsend Addis JJ (2001) Avoiding knotty structures in design: schematic functional programming. Int J Vis Lang Comput 12:689–715. ISSN 1045 926X

Addis TR, Townsend Addis JJ (2002) An introduction to clarity: a schematic functional language for managing the design of complex systems. Int J Hum Comput Stud 56(4):331–422. ISSN 1071 5819

Billinge D (2001) An analysis of the communicability of musical predication, PhD thesis. University of Portsmouth, Portsmouth

Billinge D, Addis TR (2001) Some fundamental limits of automated artistic decision making. Symposium on AI and creativity in arts and science, AISB'01. The 2001 convention of the society for the study of artificial intelligence and the simulation of behaviour, 21st–24th March. University of York, London

Billinge D, Addis TR (2002) Modelling the role of metaphor in artistic description. ECAI, 15th European conference on artificial intelligence, Lyon, France, Workshop 17. Creative systems: approaches to creativity in AI and cognitive science, pp 55–58

Cooke D (1959) The language of music. Oxford University Press, Oxford

Fauconnier G, Turner M (2002) The way we think: conceptual blending and the mind's hidden complexities. Basic Books, New York

Gooding DC, Addis TR (1999) A simulation of model-based reasoning about disparate phenomena. In: Magnani L, Nersessian N, Thagard P (eds) Model based reasoning in scientific discovery. Kluwer, London, pp 103–123. ISBN 0-306-46292-3

Lakoff G, Johnson M (1980) Metaphors we live by. University of Chicago Press, Chicago

Meyer LB (1956) Emotion and meaning in music. The University of Chicago Press, Chicago

Meyer LB (1967) Music, the arts and ideas. University of California Press, California

Meyer LB (1973) Exploring music. University of California Press, California

Chapter 14
Seeking Allies

> *There is no such thing as absolute certainty, but there is*
> *assurance sufficient for the purpose of human life.*
>
> John Stuart Mill,
> (On Liberty, 1859)

14.1 Exchanging Information

In this chapter I will describe in some detail a formal computer model of inferential discourse based on the belief system (see Chaps. 6 and 7). The key issue is that a logical model in a computer, based on rational sets, can usefully model a human situation grounded on irrational sets (see Chap. 9). The background of this work is explained elsewhere, as is the issue of rational and irrational sets (Billinge and Addis 2004; Stepney et al. 2004). The model is based on the Belief System (Addis and Gooding 1999—Chap. 7) and it provides a mechanism for choosing queries based on a range of belief. We explain how it provides a way to update the belief based on query results, thus modelling others' experience by inference. We also demonstrate that for the same internal experience, different models can be built for different actors.

The problem of what information is exchanged between people talking about music arose when we started to investigate the possibility of providing a computer aid to help music planners devise acceptable music programmes (see Chap. 13 and Billinge 2000; Billinge and Addis 2003). In order to create such a computer aid we needed to formalise the way people perceived music and communicated their perceptions to each other. Studies of people attempting to pass this information on seemed to fail completely and further, no correlates were discovered between the words used and the music features (e.g. minor chords relating to sadness). This was totally unexpected. It seemed that talking about music had no effective role and yet people do talk and there is a complete industry devoted to communicating about the subjective perception of music. Our observations did not make sense and this required us to reconsider our methods.

The essence of the original approach was to take the simple surface observations of communication, such as words, taken under controlled experimental conditions, and then apply statistical and linguistic analyses based on simple denotational semantics. Since these analyses failed to produce a result we then considered a deeper approach

© Springer International Publishing Switzerland 2014
T. Addis, *Natural and Artificial Reasoning,* Advanced Information
and Knowledge Processing, DOI 10.1007/978-3-319-11286-2_14

in which we posited a mechanism of inferential semantics. The mechanism was proposed on the observation that communication of music was rich with metaphor as a descriptive aid, metaphors that can be drawn from more explicit and positive domains such as war or nature. Meaning was thus inferred from relationships evoked by these metaphors that can then be applied to describing unobserved and less concrete ideas such as music perception. The problem with metaphors is that they are a culturally based and a dynamic trope (a figure of speech that changes in context or time). It is because of this that language falls firmly into the area of irrational sets with the consequent difficulties. A technical solution invokes the process of tracking meaning through a belief system (Chap. 12, Addis et al. 2004; Billinge and Addis 2004; Stepney et al. 2004).

I described in Chap. 12 how an inferential semantics that uses metaphor might work. Such a process required two distinct mechanisms. The *first* was a belief system originally created to show how scientists decide what experiments to perform or with whom to communicate in order to find out which of several possible hypotheses about the world is workable. Workable here means making the world more predictable (Chaps. 5 and 6). The *second* mechanism was the internal modelling of other people's beliefs derived from conversation (Chap. 12). This latter process was bypassed in the original belief system by assuming that the model would be the same as the actual perceptions (Chap. 7). These actual perceptions were made accessible within the computer model by allowing the computer actors (agents) to have partial information of another's perceptions. How this might be accomplished with people was not considered until the second mechanism of modelling people's beliefs was designed. These processes were emulated as computer programs to show how they might work in practice. For such complex processes involving many different scenarios, it was only through running such computer models that these processes could be tested for coherence.

Constructing a computer program as though it were a theory is not enough. Theories also have to be tested against the world, and the effectiveness of a theory can only be assessed in its ability to make successful predictions. Any theory that makes the world predictable is useful, and a better theory will improve on this by making more secure or detailed predictions. A theory can also provide a framework in which to design experiments and recognise significant features. Even a completely inadequate theory can play this latter role, and without designed experiments and puzzling observations, a new theory cannot be coherently created. To this end we produced a computer model of music communication not to say 'This is how it is with people' but to say 'This makes the world a less surprising place' (Peirce, in Weiner 1966).

14.2   The Experiment

The experiment is described in detail elsewhere (Billinge and Addis 2003, 2004). A summary of the process is that four people (A1–A4) were asked to listen to four pieces of classical (but little known) music. Each piece of music lasted about 10–15 min. Each person was asked to keep abbreviated notes on what they heard and to rate the music on a single linear scale ranging from 1 to 10 in units of 1. Evaluation of two pieces of music could be the same. They were then asked to form a committee to discuss the music with the purpose of recommending that one of the pieces should be included in a concert programme. The discussion was recorded. For completion the committees were asked to arrive at a group opinion and rank all four pieces of music on a scale 1–10.

The final part of the experiment, and as it turned out the most significant, was to ask the individual participants to rank their fellow committee members in terms of whose judgement they would take the most notice of when deciding to go to a concert. This will be referred to as 'ally choice'.

The design of the experiment was primarily to explore the use of metaphor during the discussion. The actual recordings taken during these discussions have yet to be fully analysed. However, Dr. David Billinge and I were primarily interested in the relationship between the music and ranking. We were also interested in how the discussions might influence opinion, hence the individual-before and the group-after rankings of ally choice. The test of the effectiveness of a person's internal models of others was to be assessed from the individual ranking of a chosen advisor.

The delay in analysing the discussions was taken because we wished to view these data in the light of a computer model of inferential semantics. There are arguments to suggest that this is bad practice, since we are prejudicing our observations with the computer model. Such prejudice will cause us to observe only that which will support the model and thus our observations will be tainted and in doubt. We reject such an argument because the history of science supports the need for an initial theory (Kuhn 1985), provided such a theory can be tested and has the possibility of being rejected (Popper 1959). Theories are particularly helpful in observing complex situations, such as group discussions, because they do limit what should be observed. The real test of a theory has been discussed above, but a theory also plays a further important role by providing a basis for puzzlement and modification. If you don't have a theory then you cannot be puzzled by what you observe. We therefore, required a satisfactory model of discourse that could do the job of limiting what we observed (at least initially) in the conversation.

14.3   The Computer Model

The process that models the inferential semantics is driven by the belief system (Chap. 7, Addis and Gooding 1999, 2008). The belief system, in this case, models each user as a single undefined dimension of values for each piece of music involved in a discussion. The values on the dimension are discrete and ordered. Each value is considered an independent hypothesis that has a level of belief associated with it. The actions open to the belief system, in order to update these associated beliefs, is limited as to a fixed set of queries that may be addressed to another person. 'Person' in this case is a part of the computer program that is normally referred to as 'Agent', but in this chapter we will use the more appropriate and original term 'Actor' (Hewitt 1979).

The range of queries given provides a basis for the process of question and inference required to update the model.

We (David Billinge and myself) use the initial decisions made by the participants during their evaluation of the music heard in experimental sessions to initiate the model. We then compare the predicted order of ally choice made by each agent in the model as assessed from the agent's perception of others, as drawn from a simulated conversation, with the actual outcomes of the sessions. We plan to modify the model to show from recorded conversations of the participants in our experimental sessions how the patterns of questioning compare with that generated by the model. The model has n actors and m aesthetic objects. The m objects in our experiments are pieces of classical orchestral music to which our actor/participants have a response. Actors have a response-scale for each piece of music representing their own subjective impression. Further, an actor has a separate scale of belief for the response to each piece of music for each other actor as derived from the conversation. In the model the actors can ask questions in turn and can only ask one question per turn. Only the actor asking the question can update its scales of belief from another actor's response.

We made three assumptions: *first,* that each actor accepts that other actors initially have the same perceptions of the heard music and thus the same ratings; *second,* that each modelling actor tends to ask the other actor about the music of which it, the questioner, has the most uncertain belief scale (e.g. highest entropy—see Chap. 6); and *finally* that the modeller can have no doubt of its own experience. In this way an actor tracks the subjective experience of others; an experience that may change over time. We also assumed that, as supported by our observation of the experimental work with people, an actor will choose as an ally the fellow actor who is closest in m scale distance. The significance of this result is that it should show that a subjective[1] experience can be inferred through conversations and we also suggested that this might actually be the major purpose of peoples' discussions.

Finally we describe how we expect to adapt the model to fit in with observations to take into account other factors that decide group decisions. Our model should thus become more able to predict conversational behaviour and final group decisions from knowing individuals' perceptions within this scenario.

14.4   Analysis of the Experimental Results

Seven experiments were carried out with four people and one with only three people. Where ally-ranking information is important only the seven fully populated experiments are considered here.

The basic ordinal and numerical data from these experiments includes:

- Each subject's personal scale for each piece of music.
- The order in which the music was played.

---

[1] An evaluation, of a potentially shareable event, that is accessible only by a single actor and related to that actor's observation and assessment of that event.

- The evaluation order for the pieces of music agreed by the group after discussion.
- The order of preference for another actor as mentor or ally.

To enable us to make ordinal comparisons without the problems of individual scale choice we used a relative z-score. This is employed differently from the normal use of a z-score since we consider each individual subject as though they had their own personal distribution. Thus each subject's personal scale is normalised according to the following equation.

$$z - \text{score (i)} = (x_i - \mu_i)/\sigma_i$$

where i is a particular actor, x_i is a value given by that subject for a piece of music, μ_i is the mean of the subject's values and σ_i is the standard deviation of the values adjusted for a small sample (Moroney 1963, p. 137) such that $\sigma_i = \sigma/\sqrt{n}$ where n is 4 in this case.

In this way all the scores are normalised such that all their scores are:

- distributed about a common mean of zero
- the spread of their evaluations is made equal.

Thus the only significant information is the ordering. However, since all scales are now normalised the relative ordering (nearer or further from other pieces of music) information can also be compared. Each subject is represented as a single point in a four-dimensional music space where each dimension represents one of the pieces of music they are judging.

Having eliminated personal scaling differences we can see if there are any similarities in choice combinations. We now look to see how independent the four music dimensions are. We are asking the question, *"Does knowing a person's first choice make it possible to predict their second choice?"*

However, from the correlation analysis of pairing pieces of music, no significant correlation is found (Fig. 14.1). This indicates that there is no pattern of common approval between items; i.e. approval of Stravinsky does not imply approval of, say, Stenhammar. (See example in Fig. 14.1).

The result was also corroborated using the raw (non z-score normalized) analysis and using optimised principle component analysis (Billinge and Addis 2004). This result confirms that we can treat music space as a set of independent dimensions so that distance calculations in this space conform to normal n-dimensional geometry.

The raw un-normalised values were also used to see if there was any correlation between the group scaling and the average of all the individuals' scales. We found that these were positively correlated (see Fig. 14.2). This result suggests that participation within the discussions has some influence on the individual with a statistical significance $r = 0.7584$. For 22 experiments, as looked up in statistical tables, an r-value of 0.6524 is better than 0.001 probability that a correlation exists, i.e. there is a 0.1 % chance of this happening accidentally. For the 24 experiments we did this would be even better, i.e. less likely to occur by chance.

By contrast, and as we have noted in previous findings (Billinge and Addis 2004) no information about music experience or content is exchanged during these group

Fig. 14.1 Correlation
between two pieces of music

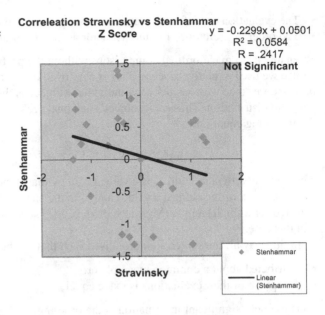

Fig. 14.2 Group scale vs. all
individual average

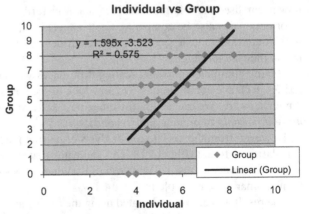

conversations. It is clearly possible for such information to be exchanged as suggested
in Chap. 13. This is a puzzle, so we pose a further question: "*If musical experience is
not being exchanged then what influences the group decision?*" We speculate that the
group discussion is actually performing a different task than exchanging information
about a music experience. Since it is not concerned with any group experience, could
it be concerned with just the exercise of social dominance?

We observed that the discussion proceeds in all seriousness and that there is an
outcome in the form of ally choice that was not previously acknowledged. The actor's
ally preference order seems to relate to the similarity of the order of the evaluation
of music between them. Plotting the distance between two subjects in a relative
four-dimensional (music) z-space can assess this order similarity.

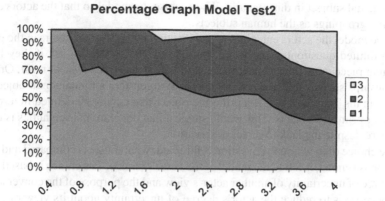

Fig. 14.3 100 % stacked area chart of evaluative distance [*X*-axis] against likelihood of choice [*Y*-axis]

The hypothesis here is that an actor tends to choose others who have a similar view of the music. For the results analysis, the relative z-score distance measure is used to calculate the similarity between each pair of actors. The principle used is that those closest in four-dimensional music space tend to be chosen as the ally. Closeness is derived from the normal application of Pythagoras' theorem applied to a relative 4 dimensional z-score music space. Figure 14.3 shows a cumulative frequency graph giving the proportion of position choice against distance. Those closest (z-score distance of less than 0.8) are 100 % likely to be chosen but at distances approaching a relative z-score of 4 all ally positions are accounted for. Thus at this high inclusive distance all people that can be selected are included.

In Fig. 14.3 the blue area occupying the bottom left quadrant of the graph shows the likelihood of a first ally being selected as the inclusive distance is extended. When the evaluative distance is at its closest, a z-score of 0.4, then the likelihood of first choice is a certainty. As the distance increases the likelihood begins to even out between the first, second (red) and third (yellow) choices because more people are being included. The position of no correlation between closeness and ally choice would give the result that all ally choice positions would be equally likely for all relative z-scores.

14.5 Model Running Results Analysis

Seven experimental runs of our model were done using the start conditions of the seven actual experiments with people.

A model was developed to simulate how one participant can acquire another's internal view of music through conversation and inference using simplified questions without directly asking about their scale. We set the model up by using for each subject the actual initial scores expressed during our experiments. We refer here to the model of a subject as an actor since the software is playing the part of an experimental subject in this scenario. We organise the model so that the actors are in the same groupings as the human subjects.

In the model the actors enter into a conversation with the other actors in the group with a limited questioning repertoire, that is only being able to ask if they like a particular piece more than another piece, and which they liked least or most. Ordinal relationships such as more or less are one of Wittgenstein's fundamental objects as defined in his Tractatus; that is a primitive object that cannot be defined in terms of any other primitive objects. This would suggest that denotational semantics is being used here despite the lack of direct observation.

The choice of to whom the question is directed, what music is compared and what question is framed, is left to the model of the actor's choice. The choice is based upon the degree of uncertainty of another actor's view and the purpose of the conversation. This purpose is to reduce the actor's degree of uncertainty about its view of all the other actors in the group. The mechanism uses game theory as described in Chap. 6 (also Addis and Gooding 1999 and 2008). In the model the other actors don't have access to individual conversations, i.e. they are not listening in; they only know about the answers to their own questions.

Each actor has their own separate sub-model for each of the other actor's internal views and these sub-models are modified according to the answers they receive in response to their questions. Based on these four sub-models (one is the actor's own scale and the other three are scales from its belief model of the other actors), we can calculate the distance measurement for each actor as perceived by any other actor through their sub-model. In comparing the actual mentor choice order with the model distance, we should be able to get similar results to those above (Fig. 14.3) if the actor's belief model does represent other's internal view to some degree.

14.6   Model Data Input and Results Analysis

Seven sets of actual experimental data are used as input. For each set, the model is run 300 times to get the actors' expected belief model result. The Fig. 14.4 shows how Actor 1's view of Actor 2 changes through the conversation.

It can be seen that as the model runs and actor 1 asks questions of actor 2, actor 1 homes in on actor 2's order of evaluation but not exactly how much it 'likes' each piece. The realisation of sequence occurs fairly fast, by less than 30 runs, and thereafter actor 1's belief only strengthens as to sequence and broadens as to the absolute scaling he believes to be the view of actor 2. (See Fig. 14.3 where the bracketed numbers in the key are the actual values for actor 2). Note that actor 1 does not always ask actor 2 at each cycle and in this case only asks actor 2 about ten question before deciding its order. The run of questions (see Fig. 14.4, Music 2 between 50 and 100 runs) is caused, in part, by the relative uncertainty actor 1 has about actor 2 compared with the other actors in the group.

Actor 1's belief model of actor 2 is given in Table 14.1. This includes 4 ranges of belief (series 1–4) for each of the four music objects. The belief concerns the scales

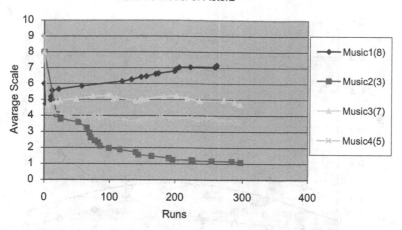

Fig. 14.4 How Actor 1's model of Actor 2's evaluative scale changes over 300 runs

Table 14.1 Actor 1's range of beliefs of actor 2 after 300 runs

x / Music	0	1	2	3	4	5	6	7	8	9	Indifference I(x)	Expected E(x)
				(model)								
Series 1	0.01	0.01	0.02	0.03	0.04	0.07	0.1	0.15	0.23	0.3	0.16	7.18
Series 2	0.5	0.24	0.12	0.06	0.03	0.02	0.01	0.01	0.01	0	0.24	1.09
Series 3	0.04	0.07	0.1	0.12	0.14	0.14	0.13	0.12	0.09	0.1	0.11	4.72
Series 4	0.09	0.13	0.15	0.15	0.14	0.12	0.09	0.06	0.04	0	0.11	3.52

0–9 such that actor 1 has some expectation as to each scale position concerning a piece of music for each actor. The sum of these beliefs for a series adds up to one since the actor must place the music somewhere on the scale. There are three important measures derived from the ranges of belief:

$$1. \quad \text{Indifference}, I(x) = \text{Log}_2^{-1}\left(-\sum_x p_x.\log_2(p_x)\right)$$

Where p_x is the belief of x for a given actor's perception of another actor's view of a piece of music. $I(x)$ represents the value that a belief would need to have if, for the same level of overall uncertainty (entropy), the belief value were to be equal for all hypotheses (scale positions). Under this hypothetical situation all the hypotheses (scale values in this case) would be indifferent to each other. We take this level of indifference to be a threshold above which the hypotheses are considered 'believed' and below which they are not. This threshold is dynamic and tends to become higher as more hypotheses' belief values approach zero.

$$2. \quad \text{Expectation } E(x) = \sum_x p_x.x$$

Distribution of Belief for Actors

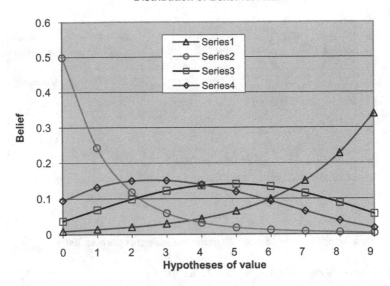

Fig. 14.5 The change of belief of a scale value for actor 2 as perceived by actor 1 after 300 cycles

Expectation E(x) is the expected or average value of the scale over an imaginary time period (n), which in this model is taken to be in the order of four events. It is 'imaginary' because it is in practice calculated in terms of an accumulation of effects such that events occurring further back in time have an exponentially decreasing weight on the current value. The equivalent time period in this case is in the order of four events (see Chap. 7). The consequence of making this time window larger is to reduce the response of the belief value to change, so we have:

$$3. \quad \text{Flexibility } f(p_x) = 1/n$$

Figure 14.5 shows the differences in belief over the range of scales after 300 model cycles. Considering that the beliefs are independent, the smoothness of the curve is comforting. From Table 14.1 we can see that, for Series 1 and 2, the believed values are well defined being 8 or 9 and 0 or 1. For series 3 and 4 the believed values are more spread out, covering a range of five mid range values in both cases. What is plotted in Fig. 14.4 is the expected value rather than the 'believed' values.

Table 14.2 results are subjected to the z-score normalisation process to make them comparable with observed results derived from the experiment. We then get the results shown in Table 14.3:

Then the evaluation distances are calculated by plotting these data sets in four-dimensional space. The distance between each pair of points in 4D space is given indicating how closely allied the other actors are placed in terms of music order in the model.

It should be noted that because each actor has a sub-model of the other actors that is expected to be different. So actor 1's perception of distance from actor 2 is likely

Table 14.2 Actor 1's range of expected values for other actors in the group

Series 1	Series 2	Series 3	Series 4	Actor 1 Model description
6.00	8.00	8.00	9.00	Models himself
7.18	1.09	4.72	3.52	Models actor 2
1.61	4.15	6.02	7.81	Models actor 3
0.86	3.5	5.05	6.96	Models actor 4

Table 14.3 Actor 1's normalised expected values and normalised distances

Series 1	Series 2	Series 3	Series 4	Distance in 4D space	Actor 1 Model description
− 1.61	0.23	0.23	1.15	0.00	Models himself
1.39	− 1.38	0.27	− 0.28	3.69	Models actor 2
− 1.43	− 0.33	0.49	1.27	0.65	Models actor 3
− 1.45	− 0.27	0.43	1.29	0.57	Models actor 4

to be different from actor 2's distance from actor 1. So in comparing the distances derived from the model with the results obtained from the experiments (shown in Table 14.4) we can make some predictions from the relative z-score distance between two subjects' choice of ally. Note that the results in Table 14.4 are 500 runs instead of 300 as shown previously. This accounts for the first line of Table 14.4 being slightly different from the fifth column of Table 14.3.

14.7 Assessing the Results

We can measure the predictive power of the model in terms of the improved information over the null hypothesis. The null hypothesis is where the choice of order is made randomly compared with model differences. The model has simulated a conversational process that allows internal sub-models to be constructed that provides an actor centred view. In Table 14.4 we have scored a successful prediction of order by assigning 1.0 and a partial order as 0.5 only where, due to lack of information, there is 0.5 probability of the answer being correct (rounded to 2 decimal places). All other orderings have been scored 0. So we have:

- Probability of guessing order correctly if random $= 1/3! = 1/6 = 0.17$
- Random Hypothesis Entropy $= -\mathrm{Log}_2(0.17) = 2.56$
- Observed Entropy $= -\mathrm{Log}_2(0.40) = 1.32$

The numeric value of the prediction from the model is the difference of the two hypotheses. This is about 1.2 bits, which means that you roughly double your chance of guessing correctly by running and using the model.

Table 14.4 Results of 500 runs of the model for all the experiments showing relative distance z-scores (left four columns); the right hand four columns are the sequences from the real experimental runs involving people. The complete sequence (1–3) was not always given by these participants

Sequence Similarity	EX.1	A1	A2	A3	A4	A1	A2	A3	A4
1.0									
	A1	0	3.71	**0.66**	0.72	0	3	1	2
0.0									
	A2	3.65	0	3.33	**3.31**	1	0	2	3
1.0									
	A3	0.62	3.44	0	**0.56**	2	3	0	1
1.0									
	A4	1.18	3.26	**0.61**	0	2	3	1	0

Sequence Similarity	EX.3	A1	A2	A3	A4	A1	A2	A3	A4
0.0									
	A1	0	**1.67**	2.16	3.12	0	0	1	0
0.0									
	A2	**1.70**	0	3.28	3.60	1	0	3	2
1.0									
	A3	**2.36**	3.34	0	3.05	1	3	0	2
0.0									
	A4	**2.90**	3.12	3.04	0	3	2	1	0

Sequence Similarity	EX.4	A1	A2	A3	A4	A1	A2	A3	A4
0.5									
	A1	0	**0.756**	3.44	1.88	0	1	0	0
0.5									
	A2	**0.52**	0	3.34	1.84	1	0	0	0
0.0									
	A3	3.47	3.32	0	**2.36**	0	1	0	0
0.0									
	A4	1.73	**1.72**	2.27	0	1	3	2	0

Sequence Similarity	EX.5	A1	A2	A3	A4	A1	A2	A3	A4
1.0									
	A1	0	3.63	1.99	**1.61**	0	3	2	1
0.5									
	A2	3.66	0	**2.56**	3.61	0	0	1	0
0.0									
	A3	**2.21**	2.62	0	3.03	2	1	0	3
1.0									
	A4	**1.29**	3.58	3.01	0	1	3	2	0

Table 14.4 (continued)

Sequence Similarity	EX.6	A1	A2	A3	A4	A1	A2	A3	A4
0.0	A1	0	3.85	3.21	**2.16**	0	1	3	2
1.0	A2	3.84	0	**3.01**	3.37	3	0	1	2
0.0	A3	3.38	**2.85**	0	3.46	3	1	0	2
0.0	A4	**2.11**	3.17	3.44	0	2	3	1	0

Sequence Similarity	EX.7	A1	A2	A3	A4	A1	A2	A3	A4
0.0	A1	0	**2.17**	3.41	3.30	0	2	3	1
0.0	A2	**1.84**	0	2.11	3.97	2	0	1	3
1.0	A3	3.44	**2.02**	0	3.10	3	1	0	2
0.0	A4	**3.33**	3.97	3.63	0	2	3	1	0
9.5/24 = **0.40**									

Using the cumulative binomial probability calculations (Feller 1968) to assess the confidence of these results, we find that the probability of getting eight or more correct sequences is 0.035444 or less than 4 % of the time. For nine or more correct sequences it drops to 0.01176 or slightly greater than 1 % and ten or more it is 0.003339 or a slightly higher than 0.3 %. Since we have predicted 9.5 sequences correctly (using 0.5 where not all information is available) we can be confident in our model to about 1 % that the predictions can happen by chance. This is quite good.

14.8 Ally Choice

The results seem to indicate that the frequency of ally choice order relates to the relative z-score distances calculated. The complete sequences were not always given but where a particular position is given we have included this in Figs. 14.6 and 14.7. We can compare the shape of the cumulative graphs for relative z-score distance for each position (first, second and third) for both the observed and the model. The model is on the left and the observed results on the right:

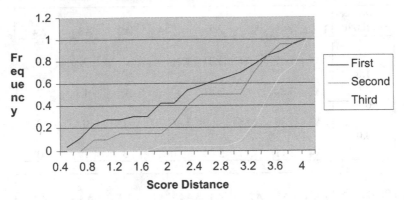

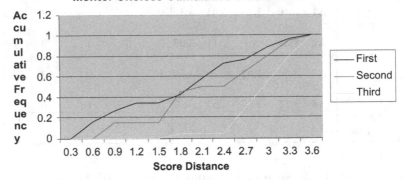

Fig. 14.6 A comparison between observed and model ally choice cumulative probabilities

14.9 Last Words

Our analysis of the experiments with people involving music and our computer model is still to be completed. However, the experiments so far have shown that the ranking choice of music seems to follow no pattern and that for each person each piece of music can be treated like a unique dimension. It may be that because all the pieces of music were 'classical' and therefore of the same type that grouping of choice was masked. The most significant information that has been gathered has been the ally choice. It is possible to surmise that such information has a valuable role in the survival, or at least the wellbeing, of individuals since other people's experiences become valuable surrogates to one's own experiences. This is a kind of metaphor in that the judgement of a close ally is taken to be representative of one's own experience.

The other result that came from the experiments was that the correlation between group results and individual results was significant. However, there is enough variation in the final decision to suggest that there are factors to be considered other than

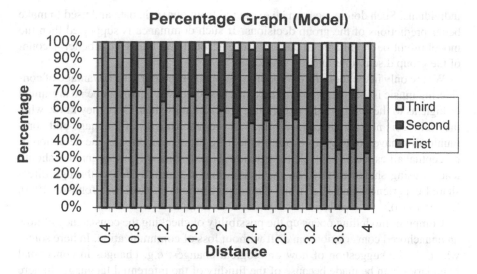

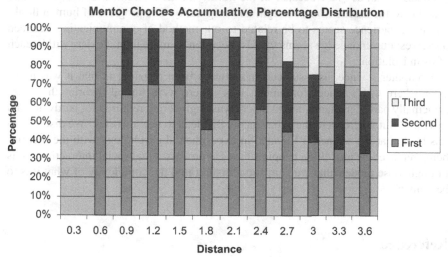

Fig. 14.7 Results of ally choice as structured bar charts: compare Fig. 14.3

just an average weight drawn from everyone's opinion. Similarly, the choice of ally shows sufficient variation from the choice of 'like-mind' to suggest that there are reasons for choice other than selecting a perceptual substitute. For clues to this we will need to look at the details of the group discussion. This, unfortunately, has not been done.

The model has shown similar behaviour to the experimental observations. Details of model discussions would need to be explored to see what causes clustering of interrogation and whether this is reflected in the observed behaviour of people. Further, we can propose that some of the observed variation is the effect of dominance by individuals. Such dominance can be extracted from our scale data and used to make better predictions of the group decisions. If such dominance is supported then the model might be modifiable to take this into account and thus give a better account of the group discussions and ally choice.

We are only in the foothills of modelling human behaviour. The advantage of considering music is that perception of it is purely subjective. There can be no argument or logic as to the nature of the experience for each individual. Only they know what they felt. This neutral stance means that all the mechanisms of language and communication have got to go into communicating these perceptions. The detection of perceptual allies seems valuable for extending ones own experiences and this should lead to using shared metaphors; metaphors that are initially found through direct shared experiences and later from shared perceptions (Lakoff and Johnson 1980; Lakoff 1986).

Computer modelling opens up the possibility of checking the consistency of how an unanchored conversation can drift without loss of communication. In here somewhere, is the suggestion of how ontological changes, e.g. changes in conceptual boundaries, can be made because of the fluidity of the inferential language. In here is a clue to the mechanism of insight and originality. The progress of human thinking and experience seems to be related to our method of communicating between ourselves; our knowledge seems to exist between us more than it exists within each of us in isolation.

Computer science, as a subject, has always been puzzling in that it was never clear where the 'science' component was. There were formal theories that were principally part of mathematics and there was engineering required for hardware and software. But where were the experiments that lead to new theories? We discover in this book that the science is founded in experimental psychology with the theories being replaced by modelling people's thought processes and social interactions. It is through these models that we gain some insight into the complexity of what it is to be human.

References

Addis T, Gooding D (1999) Learning as collective belief-revision: simulating reasoning about disparate phenomena, Proceedings of the AISB'99 Symposium on Scientific Creativity, ISBN 1 902 956044

Addis T, Gooding D (2008) Methods for an abductive system in science Foundations of Science, vol 13, No 1, March 2008

Addis T et al (2004) The abductive loop: Tracking irrational sets (this publication)

Billinge D (2000) An analysis of the communicability of musical predication: a feasibility study for artistic decision support systems. PhD Thesis, University of Portsmouth

Billinge D, Addis T (2003) The functioning of tropic communication: a mechanism for consistent figurative descriptions of artistic effect. AISB'03 symposium on AI and creativity in arts and science, University of Wales at Aberystwyth

Billinge D, Addis T (2004) Music to our ears: a required paradigm shift in computer science European conference on computing and philosophy. University of Pavia, Italy

Feller W (1968) An introduction to probability theory and its applications, 3rd ed, vol 1. Wiley, NY

Gooding DC, Addis TR. (2008) Foundations of Science, vol 13, No 1, March 2008.

Hewitt C (1979) Control structures as patterns of passing messages. Artificial intelligence: an MIT perspective, vol 2. MIT, Cambridge

Kuhn TS (1985) The essential tension: selected studies in scientific tradition and change. University of Chicago Press, London

Lakoff G. (1986) Women, fire, and dangerous things. University of Chicago Press, London

Lakoff G, Johnson M (1980) Metaphors we live by. University of Chicago Press, London

Moroney MJ (1963) Facts from figures. Pelican Books, A236, First published in 1951. Penguin Books, London

Popper K (1959) The logic of scientific discovery 10th Impression 1980, Hutchinson

Stepney S, Braunstein S, Clark J, Tyrrel A, Adamatzky A, Smith R, Addis T, Johnson C, Timmis J, Welch P, Milner R, Partridge D (2004) Journey: non-classical philosophy—socially sensitive computing in journeys non-classical computation: a grand challenge for computing research, 18 May 2004, http://www.cs.york.ac.uk/nature/gc7/newcastle.htm

Weiner PP (1966) Charles S. Peirce: selected writings. Dover, New York

Printed in the United States
By Bookmasters